GLOBAL TRADING ARRANGEMENTS IN TRANSITION

STUDIES IN ECONOMIC TRANSFORMATION AND PUBLIC POLICY

General Editor: Christos C. Paraskevopoulos, *Professor of Economics and Chair, Department of Economics, York University , Canada and President, the Athenian Policy Forum Inc.*

The major objective of the Athenian Policy Forum (a non-profit research organization) is to promote independent objective analysis and stimulate public discussion on issues and problems relating to economic adjustment. This series contributes to this goal by disseminating the results of innovative research on the economic implications of the changing forces of demography, the environment, social and political transformation, technology and trade.

Recent titles in the series include:

Global Trading Arrangements in Transition
Edited by Christos C. Paraskevopoulos

European Union at the Crossroads
A Critical Analysis of Monetary Union and Enlargement
Edited by Christos C. Paraskevopoulos

Global Trading Arrangements in Transition

Edited by

Christos C. Paraskevopoulos

York University, Canada and the Athenian Policy Forum

STUDIES IN ECONOMIC TRANSFORMATION AND PUBLIC POLICY
IN ASSOCIATION WITH THE ATHENIAN POLICY FORUM INC.

Edward Elgar

Cheltenham, UK · Northampton, MA, USA

Published by
Edward Elgar Publishing Limited
8 Lansdown Place
Cheltenham
Glos GL50 2HU
UK

Edward Elgar Publishing, Inc.
6 Market Street
Northampton
Massachusetts 01060
USA

A catalogue record for this book
is available from the British Library

Library of Congress Cataloguing in Publication Data
Global trading arrangements in transition/edited by Christos C. Paraskevopoulos.
— (Studies in economic transformation and public policy)
Papers presented at an international conference organized by York University and the Athens University of Economic and Business in co-sponsorship with the Athenian Policy Forum.
1. International trade—Congresses. 2. International economic integration—Congresses. I. Paraskevopoulos, Christos C.
II. Series.
HF1372.G58 1998
382—dc21 97–47514
CIP

ISBN 1 85898 761 X

Printed and bound in Great Britain by Bookcraft (Bath) Ltd.

TO MY PARENTS
CONSTANTINOS AND MARIA

THE ATHENIAN *Policy Forum Inc.*

We Athenians, in our own persons, take our decisions on policy or submit them to proper discussions: for we do not think that there is an incompatibility between words and deeds; the worst thing is to rush into action before the consequences have been properly debated

Thucydides (460–400 BC)
Pericles' Funeral Oration

Contents

List of figures ix
List of tables xi
List of contributors xiii
Acknowledgements xv
Introduction *Christos C. Paraskevopoulos* xvii

PART I TRADE THEORY, POLICY AND WELFARE

1 Economic and financial integration: implications for nationally-based public policy 3
Christos C. Paraskevopoulos and John N. Smithin
2 Implications of NAFTA on the trade of US economies 11
John S. Kaminaridies, Edward Nissan and Roger Roderick
3 Welfare effects of the completion of the single European market 26
Evangelia Papadaki
4 NAFTA, the EU and agricultural trade 42
Bala Batavia, Nicholas A. Lash and A.G. Malliaris
5 The state of the welfare state in the EU, anno 1992 56
Jozef Pacolet and Katia Versieck
6 Economic integration and regional economic convergence in NAFTA and the EU 69
Elias G. Carayannis, Rajiv Mallick and George K. Zestos

PART II IMPACT OF ECONOMIC INTEGRATION ON INDUSTRIAL ORGANIZATION

7 The role of small and entrepreneurial firms in achieving economic integration during the transition from command to market-based economies 91
Allan Young
8 Trade liberalization in Eastern European countries and the prospects of their integration into the world trading system 101
Jaleel Ahmad and Jing Yang
9 Long-run and short-run effects of economic integration on the inflow of foreign direct investment 112
Petros E. Ioannatos

10 Japanese manufacturing FDIs in Europe: present idiosyncrasies and future prospects 120
Mike Pournarakis, Nikos C. Varsakelis and D. Mardas
11 Tendencies and idiosyncrasies of European trading partners 136
Evrard Claessens and Annemie Cools

PART III LESSONS FROM THE CASE OF MEXICO

12 The growing anti-immigrant debate in the North American region and its impact on Mexico 145
Mónica Verea
13 NAFTA and Mexico: the future of democracy and economic development 160
José Luis Valdés-Ugalde
14 Successful integration and economic distress: the case of Mexico in NAFTA 173
Sima Motamen-Samadian and Etelberto Ortiz Cruz
15 Economic integration, exchange rate and competitiveness: Mexico and the US 188
Pablo Ruiz-Nápoles

Index 211

Figures

2.1 Analysis of variance of exports to Canada: trade and production exposures 19
2.2 Analysis of variance of exports to Mexico: trade and production exposures 20
2.3 Analysis of variance of imports from Canada: trade and production exposures 22
2.4 Analysis of variance of imports from Mexico: trade and production exposures 23
6.1 Real gross domestic product per capita, 15 European Union countries 80
6.2 Total unemployment rates, 15 European Union countries 82
6.3 Real wages in 1990 US dollars (PPP) 84
6.4 Coefficient of variation, real hourly compensation costs of manufacturing workers, 1990 US dollars (PPP) 86
10.1 Foreign direct investment and intra-company trade 128
11.1 Culture, security and economy in time and space 136
11.2 Organization of the cluster analysis 137
15.1 Relative unit labour costs and real exchange rate 196
15.2 Imports and GDP 199
15.3 Exports share and real unit labour costs 201
15.4 Relative wages and relative prices 204
15.5 Productivity indexes 204

Tables

2.1 Exports to Canada and Mexico, 1991 13
2.2 Imports to Canada and Mexico, 1991 16
3.1 Sectoral breakdown of activities 32
3.2 Elasticities of substitution σ_s 32
3.3 Calibrated price spread (Cournot–Nash) 34
3.4 Calibrated ratios of marginal to average costs (Cournot–Nash) 35
3.5 Effects of the 1992 programme, fixed number of firms 37
3.6 Effects of the 1992 programme, variable number of firms 39
3.7 Effects of the 1992 programme, comparisons with other EU countries, variable number of firms 40
6.1 Income per capita, employment rates, wage rates and growth of each by state, 1951–1989 72
6.2 Regional economic convergence in Canada: a cross-classification table 74
6.3 Topology of five top Mexican states by predominant industrial activity 77
8.1 The TS and DS representation: exports and imports of the USSR 107
8.2 The TS and DS representation: exports and imports of Eastern Europe 108
8.3 Statistical output of ADF test for unit root 109
9.1 Estimation results 116
10.1 United States: forms of international transactions, 1986–1993 130
10.2 Forms of international transactions in the Triad: FDI manufacturing sales, exports and distribution by affiliates 131
10A.1 Outflows of foreign direct investment from the five major home countries, 1981–1994 135
11.1 Overview of the four exercises 138
11.2 Basic clusters of the first exercise 139
11.3 Clusters with trade 141
14.1 Rate of growth and net exports, 1982–1994 (sectoral indexes) 176
14.2 Trade structure, exports and imports 177
14.3 Productivity and employment, 1982–1994 (sectoral indexes) 178

14.4 Difference between the nominal value of imports and the real value of imports measured in 1988 real exchange rate 180
14.5 Public finances 181
14.6 Gross national savings, external, public and external, gross rate of investment, ratios to GDP, 1980–1995 182
14.7 Total external debt 184
15.1 Mexico–US unit labour costs 194
15.2 Real exchange rate and relative unit labour costs 195
15.3 Manufacturing trade of Mexico 198
15.4 Manufacturing exports and unit labour costs 200
15.5 Relative wages and relative prices 203
15A.1 Ordinary least squares regression equation (15.1) 209
15A.2 Ordinary least squares regression equation (15.2) 209
15A.3 Ordinary least squares regression equation (15.3) 210

Contributors

Jaleel Ahmad, Concordia University, Canada

Bala Batavia, DePaul University, USA, and Research Fellow, Athenian Policy Forum

Elias G. Carayannis, George Washington University, USA, and Research Fellow, Athenian Policy Forum

Evrard Claessens, University of Antwerp, Belgium, and Research Fellow, Athenian Policy Forum

Annemie Cools, University of Antwerp, Belgium, and Research Fellow, Athenian Policy Forum

Petros E. Ioannatos, GMI Engineering and Management Institute, USA, and Research Fellow, Athenian Policy Forum

John S. Kaminaridies, Arkansas State University, USA, and Research Fellow, Athenian Policy Forum

Nicholas A. Lash, Loyola University of Chicago, USA, and Research Fellow, Athenian Policy Forum

A.G. Malliaris, Loyola University of Chicago, USA, and the Athenian Policy Forum

Rajiv Mallick, Pracon Inc., USA

D. Mardas, Aristotle's University of Thessaloniki, Greece

Sima Motamen-Samadian, University of Westminster, UK

Edward Nissan, University of Southern Mississippi, USA

Etelberto Ortiz Cruz, Universidad Autonomia, Metropolitan–Xochimilco, Mexico

Jozef Pacolet, Catholic University of Leuven, Belgium

Evangelia Papadaki, Université de Montréal, Canada, and Research Fellow, Athenian Policy Forum

Christos C. Paraskevopoulos, York University, Canada, and the Athenian Policy Forum

Mike Pournarakis, Athens University of Economics and Business, Greece, and Research Fellow, Athenian Policy Forum

Roger Roderick, Arkansas State University, USA

Pablo Ruiz-Nápoles, Universdad Nacional Autonoma de Mexico, Mexico, and Research Fellow, Athenian Policy Forum

John N. Smithin, York University, Canada, and the Athenian Policy Forum

José Luis Valdés-Ugalde, Universidad Nacional Autonoma de Mexico, Mexico

Nikos C. Varsakelis, Aristotle's University of Thessaloniki, Greece

Mónica Verea, Universidad Nacional Autonoma de Mexico, Mexico, and Research Fellow, Athenian Policy Forum

Katia Versieck, Catholic University of Leuven, Belgium

Jing Yang, Concordia University, Canada

Allan Young, Syracuse University, USA, and Research Fellow, Athenian Policy Forum

George K. Zestos, Christopher Newport University, USA

Acknowledgements

Most of the contributions to this volume were originally presented at an international conference held in Athens, Greece, in August 1996, organized by York University and the Athens University of Economics and Business, in co-sponsorship with the Athenian Policy Forum. The Athens conference was the third major joint activity of the two universities, under an exchange agreement signed in 1991. The Athenian Policy Forum serves as the research and publications arm of the Exchange Agreement. I would like to thank the two organizing universities, the Athenian Policy Forum, and all participants for their contribution to its success. The Athens University of Economics and Business, as host, should in particular be cited for outstanding organization and publicity.

Special thanks go to Rector Andreas Kintis for embracing the idea of establishing the exchange (an idea conceived on the island of Spetses), and Theodore Georgakopoulos (conference chair) for his involvement and support in making this idea a reality. Livy Visano, Dean, Atkinson College, has provided generous support and encouragement throughout.

In addition, as editor and conference co-chair, I would like to thank the following colleagues who served on the organizing committee or helped in other ways. D. Bourantonis, N. Christodoulakis, G. Eaton, M. Evriviades, G. Karydes, F. Lazar, and T. Moutos. Special thanks are due to W. Northover and J. Smithin for editorial advice, and R. Cook for research assistance.

We appreciate the financial support provided by the following non-academic sponsors: Aspis Bank; Commercial Bank of Greece SA; Eurobank; European Commission; General Bank; General Secretariat for Research and Technology; Hellenic Industrial Development Bank SA; Ministry of Culture; and National Bank of Greece.

We received excellent secretarial support from Eleftheria Apostolidou of the Athens University of Economics and Business who did a superb job, as Conference Secretary, in handling the local logistical arrangements and publicity, and Agnes Fraser (York University) who was equally superb in coordinating the Toronto arrangements.

As General Editor of the series I would like to thank the members of the editorial board for their help in reviewing and approving the manuscripts accepted for publication in this volume. In addition, thanks are due to the anonymous reader at EE Publishing for comments and suggestions which have improved the contributions. Above all I would like to thank the publisher, Edward Elgar, for support and encouragement.

Finally, thanks are due to Jane Croft, Dymphna Evans, Ian Garbutt, Julie Leppard, Francine O'Sullivan and other members of the staff of Edward Elgar Publishing Limited, both at Aldershot and Cheltenham, for their customary high quality work on this volume.

Introduction

Christos C. Paraskevopoulos

This volume is one of the first two under the imprint of the newly established series – 'Studies in Economic Transformation and Public Policy' – published by the Athenian Policy Forum Inc. in collaboration with Edward Elgar Publishing Limited. A companion volume, *European Union at the Crossroads: A Critical Analysis of Monetary Union and Enlargement*, is also forthcoming in the same series.

Most of the contributions in this volume were originally presented at an international conference, held in Athens, Greece, in August 1996, organized by York University and the Athens University of Economics and Business in co-sponsorship with the Athenian Policy Forum (APF). Many of the contributors are either Associate or Research Fellows of the APF.

The Athens (1996) conference on the theme 'Economic Integration in Transition' was the third in a series on the broad theme of economic integration – the largest ever conference on economic integration – and was a follow-up to the earlier conferences held in Athens (1992) and Toronto (1994), respectively.

The aim of the conference – with specialists in attendance from several different countries and four continents – was to evaluate the deepening and widening of the integration process both between the existing trading blocs such as the North American Free Trade Agreement (NAFTA) and the European Union (EU), and elsewhere. The present volume includes a selection of papers that focus on the economic, political and legal aspects of global trading arrangements in the current transitional stage of the integration process.

The chapters in this volume provide a state-of-the-art analysis of key issues facing countries engaged on various levels of integration. A wide range of topics is covered from a diverse perspective. The significant number of contributors from Mexico and Eastern and Central Europe participating in both the conference and this volume provide a unique perspective.

The volume is divided into three parts. Part I contains analyses of the implications of economic integration on welfare and public policy. In Chapter 1, Chris Paraskevopoulos and John Smithin discuss the notion that economic integration threatens the policy independence of the participating countries. A model is presented that shows that short of full monetary union, some scope for independence in public policy is possible.

In Chapter 2, John Kaminaridies, Edward Nissan and Roger Roderick, undertake an analysis of the effects of NAFTA on *regions* within the United States. A statistical analysis of the patterns of regional trade in North America is presented and the possible effects of NAFTA are discussed. In Chapter 3, Evangelia Papadaki focuses on the welfare and industry effects on Greece of Europe 1992 (Maastricht) in terms of a static general equilibrium model. It is predicted that Greece will receive a higher than average benefit from Europe 1992 because of increased competition. Bala Batavia, Nicholas Lash and A.G. Malliaris focus, in Chapter 4, on the Common Agricultural Policy (CAP) and NAFTA and their implications for agricultural trade. The differences between NAFTA and the CAP are examined and it is concluded that the CAP leads to economic inefficiencies; NAFTA, while reducing tariff barriers does not eliminate them. In Chapter 5, Jozef Pacolet and Katia Versieck assess the state of the welfare state in the EU. They provide a critical analysis of the conflict between social policy and economic growth and the econo-political debate between all 15 EU members – on the creation of a 'Social Europe'. They conclude that the present systems of social protection, at the beginning of the 1990s, in the 15-member European Union, are 'robust and viable' and not likely to be affected by further European unification. They found, in fact, that the welfare state in the beginning of the 1990s is 'alive and well' and has not been disturbed appreciably by the discourse in the EMU and internal market. In Chapter 6, Elias Carayannis, Rajiv Mallick and George Zestos explore the issue of convergence in NAFTA and the EU. The results are mixed. In the EU there is no evidence of convergence either in real GDP per capita or in real wages. For the participants in NAFTA there are mixed results. While Canada exhibits evidence of a slow rate of internal convergence, the US and Mexico show convergence only in some areas of their economies.

Part II looks at the effects that economic integration has had on industries in the participating countries. In Chapter 7, Allan Young examines the role of small business and entrepreneurs in adapting a formerly command economy to an open, market-based economy. He argues that while these types of businesses and individuals are likely to ease the transition to an open market economy, the prospects for their success are diminished by several factors, including the lack of an adequate modem banking system. In Chapter 8, Jaleel Ahmad and Jing Yang undertake an econometric analysis to forecast the benefits of several options that face the newly reformed Eastern European economies. It is concluded that the best option for these economies is to seek closer ties with the members of the EU. Petros Ioannatos, in Chapter 9, looks at the effects on foreign direct investment (FDI) on the European Union, using Greece as a case study. An empirical analysis found that while short-term effects are limited, the long-run effects are substantially beneficial. This is followed by Chapter 10, in which Mike Pournarakis, Nikos Varsakelis and D. Mardas examine the evolution of the structure of Japanese foreign direct investment strategy in EU countries through the 1980s and 1990s, as compared to that of the United States. It is found that while initially there was a substantial structural difference between the two strategies, the Japanese strategy has changed to the point that it is now very similar to that of the US. In Chapter 11, Evrard Claessens and Annemie Cools examine European and world-wide regionalism using cluster analysis. Tests are made on the basis of economic, military and cultural ties, and the resultant groupings are presented.

Finally, Part III focuses specifically on the effects on Mexico of the North American Free Trade Agreement. Mónica Verea in Chapter 12, examines immigration (both legal and otherwise) and the attitudes of the United States, and to a lesser degree Canada, to Mexican immigrants. Changes in attitudes of all concerned parties are examined with attention paid to the growing negative perception of immigration in both Canada and the United States. José Luis Valdés-Ugalde argues in Chapter 13 that economic liberalization and democracy are mutually exclusive. It is asserted that by being a signatory to NAFTA, Mexico has eliminated or limited its choice of economic policy and hence has become undemocratic. In Chapter 14, Sima Motamen-Samadian and Etelberto Ortiz Cruz examine the Peso crisis as it relates to Mexico's inclusion in NAFTA. They argue that by not including the effects of NAFTA on financial markets, the Mexican government erred in its assessment of the benefits of joining NAFTA. In Chapter 15, Pablo Ruiz-Nápoles examines the determinants of comparative unit costs. He argues that the traditional comparative advantage approach to analysing trade is inappropriate in an age of increased regionalism. It is asserted that an approach based on absolute advantage is a better predictor of trade patterns. An empirical analysis of trends in relative unit labour costs between Mexico and the United States in presented in support of this hypothesis.

While the arguments presented in this book cannot be considered the last word on global trading arrangements, it is hoped that the discussion here – with particular emphasis on the contentious issues which arise in a process of integrating unequal partners – will help to clarify some of the issues faced when economic partners move towards a closer relationship. The scope and perspectives, however, of the set of studies in this volume are unusual and worthy of a broader audience, and it is hoped that the reader will feel that, collectively, they do represent a valuable further step in the ongoing study of these complex phenomena.

PART I

TRADE THEORY, POLICY AND WELFARE

1 Economic and financial integration: implications for nationally-based public policy

Christos C. Paraskevopoulos and John N. Smithin

1 Introduction

It is a frequently heard argument in contemporary international political economy that the ongoing process of economic integration, both in terms of the growth of the major trading blocs such as the North American Free Trade Agreement (NAFTA) and the European Union (EU), and the overall process of 'globalization', is placing increasingly severe constraints on the conduct of public policy by national governments. At one extreme it is suggested that these constraints are so binding that the traditional nation-state is, in effect, becoming obsolete.

These issues are clearly of major concern, in particular to the 'small open economies' such as Canada. In the domestic political arena, fears are expressed that continuing economic integration implies a cumulative loss of control in such areas as monetary policy, fiscal policy, environmental standards, labour legislation and social policy.

In this chapter, we argue that in assessing this debate it is essential to distinguish between the different elements of the economic integration process, such as trade liberalization, technology transfer and financial integration. We suggest that a relatively greater threat to national sovereignty in public policy-making lies in financial integration rather than in the other categories.

Furthermore, the concept of 'financial integration' is itself somewhat ambiguous. Does this simply mean the liberalization of capital flows, or something more far-reaching, such as, for example, the proposals for monetary union in the EU? The latter type of arrangements would have the most far-reaching implications for national sovereignty in public policy. Conversely, an integration process which stops short of monetary union would continue to allow the exercise of some degree of sovereignty, even in a global economy which was highly integrated in most other respects. To put the point another way, it can be shown that an independent monetary policy is in fact *necessary* if an independent policy is to be pursued in other fields also, such as fiscal policy and social policy.

In what follows, Section 2 distinguishes between alternative models of social protection, drawing on earlier discussions by Paraskevopoulos (1996a, 1996b), and makes the point that it is the ability to choose between alternative models which is allegedly put at risk in the integration process. Section 3 then goes on to make further distinctions between elements of the integration process, in order to isolate their differential impact on the ability of individual jurisdictions to make key public policy decisions. The argument is modelled in a simple algebraic form in Section 4. The final section contains some concluding remarks.

2 Alternative models of social protection

Paraskevopoulos (1996a, 1996b) has distinguished between two alternative models of social protection in the context of the developed or industrialized economies. They are, respectively the 'European' and the 'American' model. Countries on the European model have attempted to defend the standard of living of their populations by placing greater reliance on *equity* considerations, and only to a lesser extent on *market efficiency*. This has required extensive government intervention through rather comprehensive social protection policies and income redistribution schemes. At the other extreme, the American model has placed greater reliance on market efficiency and less on equity. In this environment it is argued that minimum government intervention is actually the best recipe for encouraging growth, innovation and productivity, and hence ultimately to provide a higher effective level of social protection than systems which attempt to do so explicitly.

Needless to say, the geographical designations used to describe the alternative systems should not be taken too literally. For example, in North America the Canadian system of social protection was, until recently, a prime example of what we are calling here the 'European' model. Similarly, in Europe the post-Thatcher UK has obviously moved at least some of the way towards the 'American' model.[1]

Sachs (1996) has made a similar distinction between systems of social protection in the 'transitional' economies which, in the 1990s, have been moving away from their formerly socialist/communist modes of production to more market-orientated systems. In this context he has made a sharp distinction between economies in this category in Eastern Europe and the former Soviet Union (EEFSU),[2] and those in East Asia (China and Vietnam). The former supposedly have extensive systems of social protection (welfare states) inherited from the socialist period, whereas the latter have virtually none. According to Sachs, the East Asian economies thereby have an advantage, in this respect, in the transition process.

In the context of the economic integration debate, the argument is that high levels of social protection add to costs, and hence become increasingly unviable in an era in which the maintenance of international competitiveness is of primary importance. Implicitly, the European model becomes unviable and either the American, or (more likely) the East Asian model, is what remains. More comprehensive levels of protection than this become possible only when they are made 'affordable' by increases in productivity. Certainly, in jurisdictions in which efforts are now being made to dismantle the pre-existing welfare state apparatus, the argument that such systems are no longer affordable is paramount.

In addition, and more controversially, there is also an incentive argument, that high levels of social protection and social security diminish the spur to work effort and innovation. This case is hardly incontrovertible, however, as social cohesion is presumably also an important determinant of morale and hence productivity.

It must be common ground that ultimately the primary determinants of the *absolute* level of social protection which is feasible must be the level of productivity and the stage of development of the economy concerned. In the contemporary debate, however, even relative levels of social protection are also at issue. For example, Sachs (1996) complains that in the late 1980s and early 1990s the EEFSU countries had similar levels of social spending and pension benefits *as a percentage of GDP* to the OECD (Organization for Economic Cooperation and Development) countries, and that this was to the disadvantage of the former. The algebraic model in Section 4 is therefore designed explicitly to provide a simple framework within which to evaluate this type of argument.

3 Economic versus financial integration

Prior to recent developments in Europe, ushered in by the Delors Report of 1989 and the Maastricht Treaty of 1991, it was commonplace to classify the different potential stages of economic integration within a threefold schema. The least integrated system would be a free trade area which would eliminate tariffs between the integrating partners, but not impose a common external tariff, or provide for the free movement of factors (and hence technology transfer) within the area. The next level would be a customs union, which would additionally impose a common external tariff, but still not allow for free factor movements. Finally, a common market would eliminate internal tariffs, establish a common external tariff, and also allow for the free movement of both labour and capital.

The 'new' element added by Delors and Maastricht is, of course, the further concept of a monetary union in which there would be a single currency managed by a union-wide central bank. It is perhaps something of an exaggeration to describe the concept of a currency union as an innovation, as the same term could also be reasonably applied to the situation in existing federal systems such as the US and Canada.[3] However, the recent European debate has served to highlight the significant increase in the degree of integration represented by a monetary union rather than that of a 'single market' or common market.

Another form of financial integration which has received much comment in recent years, and which can usefully be distinguished from the case of monetary union, is the apparent movement in the real world (and on a global scale) towards what was formerly simply the textbook case of 'perfect capital mobility'. The so-called 'globalization of capital markets', meaning the combination of technical change and de-regulation which has greatly increased both the volume and sheer speed of capital transfers around the world, has now made the textbook assumption a seemingly much more reasonable approximation to reality. It is important to note, however, that the definition of perfect capital mobility applies equally to the case where different currencies continue to exist (and in which exchange rates may be free to change), as to cases in which there are either rigidly fixed rates or the extreme of a currency union. This turns out to be crucial in evaluating the potential for the continued existence of different relative national levels of social protection, and other public policy differences, in a world in which there is otherwise a very high degree of economic integration.

4 A simple algebraic model of the integration process

A convenient starting-point is the familiar 'covered interest parity' condition, which states that rates of return across financial centres should be the same when covered by a forward contract. This will hold when there is perfect capital mobility in the sense defined above:

$$i(t) - i^*(t) = (t+1)f(t) - s(t). \qquad (1.1)$$

In this formulation $i(t)$ is the domestic nominal interest rate at (t), $(t+1)f(t)$ is the (log of) the forward exchange rate for $(t+1)$ at (t), and $s(t)$ is the (log of) the nominal spot exchange rate. An asterisk (*) represents a foreign variable.

A much stronger condition is 'uncovered interest parity' implying that rates of return should be equal across financial centres even when *not* covered by a forward contract. This will not hold unless assets denominated in different currencies are perfect substitutes. This, in turn, is unlikely to occur except in the case of either a monetary union, or possibly in an extremely rigid fixed exchange rate regime such as the nineteenth-century gold standard. In the general case therefore:

$$i(t) - i^*(t) \neq E(t)s(t+1) - s(t) \tag{1.2}$$

where $E(t)$ is the expectations operator.

Expressions (1.1) and (1.2) together imply that the forward exchange rate is not, in general, equal to the expected future spot rate. They must differ by a risk premium, $z(t)$:

$$(t+1)f(t) = E(t)s(t+1) + z(t). \tag{1.3}$$

Now recall the standard definition of real interest rates, $r(t)$, and the (log of) the real exchange rate $q(t)$, where $p(t)$ is the log of the nominal price level:

$$r(t) = i(t) - [E(t)p(t+1) - p(t)] \tag{1.4}$$

$$q(t) = s(t) + p^*(t) - p(t). \tag{1.5}$$

Using (1.1), (1.3), (1.4) and its foreign equivalent, and (1.5) we can then obtain the following fundamental expression describing international financial relationships:

$$r(t) - r^*(t) = E(t)q(t+1) - q(t) + z(t). \tag{1.6}$$

In other words, as is well known, real interest rates can only differ between jurisdictions if real exchange rates are expected to change and/or there is a risk premium. In a neoclassical 'steady-state' equilibrium with rational expectations, this would boil down to:

$$r(t) - r^*(t) = z(t). \tag{1.7}$$

There can only be a 'permanent' discrepancy between real interest rates in different jurisdictions if a risk premium is in existence. Note that this could *not* be the case in a currency union or a very rigid fixed exchange rate regime. However, a risk premium may be present whenever there are different currencies and the exchange rate between them could *potentially* change, even if, currently, it is not actually *expected* to change.

We can relate this financial analysis to the issues of economic integration and social protection by employing a simple macroeconomic model adapted from Smithin (1994, 1996) and Mackinnon and Smithin (1993). We further suggest that the ability to provide different relative levels of social protection can be indexed by the ability to levy different payroll tax rates (T and T^*) in different jurisdictions.

Let a simple macroeconomic production function be given by:

$$Y(t) = A(t-1)N(t-1) \tag{1.8}$$

where $Y(t)$ is the output available for sale in (t), $A(t-1)$ is the average product of labour, and $N(t-1)$ is labour input. This formulation clearly has a 'time-to-build' feature, as output currently available for sale was actually produced in the *previous* period. This implies (as, we would argue, is certainly the case realistically) that there must be adequate provision for the cost of financing in any calculation of total costs. An income-based breakdown of GDP is therefore given by:

$$P(t)Y(t) = K(t-1)[1+i(t-1)][1+T(t-1)]W(t-1)N(t-1) \tag{1.9}$$

where $W(t-1)$ is the pre-tax nominal wage rate in $(t-1)$ and $K(t-1)$ is equal to $1+$ the rate of profit (actually realized in (t)). The upper-case letters refer to the levels, rather than the logs of the relevant variables. Now, updating equation (1.9) and its foreign equivalent by one period, taking logs and using (1.8), we obtain:

$$p(t+1) = k(t) + i(t) + T(t) + w(t) - a(t) \tag{1.10}$$

$$p^*(t+1) = k^*(t) + i^*(t) + T^*(t) + w^*(t) - a^*(t). \tag{1.11}$$

Then, finally, using these estimates of future prices and equation (1.4) in (1.7) we can conveniently summarize all the factors which may allow tax rates (and hence relative levels of social protection) to differ between jurisdictions:[4]

$$T^*(t) - T(t) = [a^*(t) - a(t)] - [k(t) - k^*(t)] - \{[w^*(t) - p^*(t)] - [w(t) - p(t)]\} + z(t). \tag{1.12}$$

Presumably, the argument that differences in tax rates, and ultimately differences in systems of social protection, will be eliminated by economic integration, rests on the view that complete factor price equalization will eliminate difference in profit rates and after-tax real wage rates. Similarly that technology transfer will eliminate productivity differences between jurisdictions. In short:

$$k^*(t) - k(t) = [w^*(t) - p^*(t)] - [w(t) - p(t)] = a^*(t) - a(t) = 0. \tag{1.13}$$

Even so, however:

$$T^*(t) - T(t) = z(t). \tag{1.14}$$

We can therefore conclude that unless there is a move to a monetary union, which would eliminate the risk premium (as, for example, in the current EU proposals), there is still some scope for different levels of social protection, even if *economic* integration is absolutely perfect (itself an unlikely scenario) in all other respects.

5 Conclusion

In principle, the ability of different economies to provide different *relative* levels of social protection, from different absolute amounts of GDP, should provide an illustration of J.S. Mill's famous dictum about the separability of the laws of production and distribution. If this were to hold, it should be possible, having produced a given amount of output no matter how large or how small, to distribute it according to whatever the social welfare function happens to be. In a closed system, what would be involved is simply adjustments to other distributive shares, higher levels of social protection requiring lower after-tax real wages or profits.

In the context of the economic integration debate, the standard argument has been that redistribution of this type becomes progressively less realistic as economies become more and more integrated. In this chapter, however, we have shown that some scope for redistribution will remain, as long as the integration process stops short of full monetary union, and exchange rates remain (in principle) free to change. Another way of describing the relationships between equations (1.7) and (1.14) above, is that an independent monetary policy is in fact *necessary* if an independent policy is to be pursued in other fields also, such as fiscal policy and social policy.

It may finally be remarked that, in this respect, proponents of monetary union and the abolition of independent national currencies seem to have their arguments the wrong way round. They tend to argue that the loss of national sovereignty makes eventual currency union, and ultimately regional or world government, an inevitability. In fact, it would be the deliberate abandonment of independent national monetary policies which would make a loss of sovereignty in other areas unavoidable also.

Notes

1. Similar remarks obviously apply to other jurisdictions also, as, for example, in the case of New Zealand on the other side of the globe.
2. Geographically, culturally and historically, many of the nations concerned would more accurately be described as 'Central European' rather than 'Eastern European'. However, we employ Sachs's acronym here for the sake of convenience.
3. Although it should be remarked that even though there are perfect monetary unions in each of the cases mentioned, the respective economic unions are less so, due to continuing interstate and interprovincial trade barriers.
4. Note that in this context: $E(t)p(t+1) = p(t+1)$.

References

Mackinnon, K. and J.N. Smithin (1993), 'An Interest Rate Peg, Inflation and Output', *Journal of Macroeconomics*, **15** (4), Fall, 769–85.

Paraskevopoulos, C.C. (1996a), 'Economic Integration and Social Policy Reform', in C. Paraskevopoulos, R. Grinspun and T. Georgakopoulos (eds), *Economic Integration and Public Policy in the European Union*, Aldershot, UK: Edward Elgar, pp. 135–42.

Paraskevopoulos, C.C. (1996b), 'NAFTA and Social Protection in North America', in C. Paraskevopoulos, R. Grinspun and G. Eaton (eds), *Economic Integration in the Americas*, Aldershot, UK: Edward Elgar, pp. 182–192.

Sachs, J. (1996), 'Reforms in Eastern Europe and the Former Soviet Union in the Light of the East Asian Experiences', National Bureau of Economic Research (NBER) Working Paper, No. 5404.

Smithin, J.N. (1994), *Controversies in Monetary Economics: Ideas, Issues and Policy*, Aldershot: Edward Elgar.

Smithin, J.N. (1996), 'An Alternative Monetary Model of Inflation and Growth', mimeo, York University.

2 Implications of NAFTA on the trade of US economies

John S. Kaminaridies, Edward Nissan and Roger Roderick

1 Introduction

Integration among countries with close geographic proximity has important political and economic dimensions. Constraints on participation in regional arrangements lessen considerably, making potential economic benefits feasible. Integration takes various forms, such as free trade areas and customs unions. The integration thus ranges between reduction in protectionism to a full economic union where policies and perhaps currencies are harmonized.

Frankel et al. (1995), in a comprehensive article, report that because of preferential arrangements, world trade has become more regionalized. The question they ask is whether such arrangements, which deviate from the principle of non-discriminatory trade policies (most favoured nation: MFN), are good or bad. They found that the intra-regional trade is much larger than can be explained by natural determinants such as geographic proximity, common borders or a common language. They also found (p. 92) that although some benefits may result from regionalization, 'the overall conclusion is that the world trading system is currently in danger of entering the zone of excessive regionalization'.

In the aftermath of the Second World War, the United States encouraged free trade throughout the world and was opposed to regionalism. The United States was a key promoter of the General Agreement on Tariffs and Trade (GATT) in the many rounds negotiated since the 1960s. But the rise of regional integration in Europe, Africa and Latin America since the 1960s, and the perception that the Japanese market is closed, found the United States embracing regionalism by way of forming a trading bloc with Canada and Mexico – the North American Free Trade Agreement (NAFTA).

The aim of NAFTA is to integrate the economies of the United States, Canada and Mexico. It holds the promise of a large market access, reduced costs, increased economies of scale and more competition – the elements known to induce economic growth. Common interests in environmental issues and policies are also possible. In the case of the

United States and Mexico, for instance, Richardson (1995) predicts that the demand for skilled workers will go up in both countries.

2 Data and purpose

Hayward and Erickson (1995) investigated the patterns of manufacturing trade flows between the United States and its neighbours Canada and Mexico for the period 1983 to 1991. The data shed some light on the interrelationships of industrial trade of the individual states with Canada and Mexico. Among data provided by Hayward and Erickson (1995) are (i) trade exposure, which is the proportion of a state's total trade accounted for by Canada and Mexico, computed for both exports and imports, and (ii) production exposure, which is trade with Canada and Mexico as a proportion of a state's total manufacturing shipments, computed for both exports and imports. The data are for the 48 contiguous states.

This chapter extends the work of Hayward and Erickson at the regional level. Tables 2.1 and 2.2 show the data for 1991 for total manufactured exports and imports trade, trade exposure and production exposure for both Canada and Mexico. The states are grouped into eight regions as defined by the Bureau of Economic Analysis.[1] The largest regional share of exports to Canada of approximately $29 billion was from the Great Lakes region, which is 42 per cent of the total US exports of approximately $70 billion. The Southeast and the Mideast followed the Great Lakes with respective percentages of 16 and 14. For Mexico, the largest regional share of exports, of approximately $9 billion, was from the Southwest amounting to 35 per cent of the total, followed by the Far West and the Great Lakes with respective percentages of 19 and 16.

The largest regional shares of imports from Canada were by the Great Lakes, Southeast and Mideast with respective trade of approximately $22 billion, $16 billion and $9 billion amounting to percentages totalling 30, 21 and 12. For Mexico, the imports of the four prominent regions were the Great Lakes with approximately $6 billion and the Southeast with approximately $5 billion with respective shares of 26 and 21 per cent, followed by the Mideast and Far West with 15 per cent each for imports of approximately $4 billion.

3 Comparisons by regions

Figures 1.1–1.4 provide summary information by regions for exports and imports trade exposure and production exposure, and show the mean and the standard deviation of each. The figures indicate that both the means and the standard deviations differ greatly among regions. For this reason,

Table 2.1 Exports to Canada and Mexico, 1991

	Canada			Mexico		
Regions	Exports ($ million)	Trade exposure (%)	Production exposure (%)	Exports ($ million)	Trade exposure (%)	Production exposure (%)
New England	4766.9			755.3		
Connecticut	1317.3	17.3	3.4	357.7	4.7	0.9
Maine	374.7	30.6	2.9	19.0	1.5	0.1
Massachusetts	2152.6	21.0	3.2	250.8	2.4	0.4
New Hampshire	357.7	25.1	3.3	56.1	3.9	0.5
Rhode Island	229.0	19.6	2.3	55.9	4.8	0.6
Vermont	335.6	60.2	6.1	15.8	2.8	0.3
Mideast	9641.7			2202.3		
Delaware	631.1	53.8	4.8	117.4	10.0	0.9
Maryland	527.7	17.9	1.7	56.7	1.9	0.2
New Jersey	1533.5	22.8	1.7	399.2	5.9	0.4
New York	3840.1	21.6	2.4	703.8	4.0	0.4
Pennsylvania	3109.3	27.0	2.3	925.2	8.0	0.7
Great Lakes	29092.3			4422.3		
Illinois	4627.7	30.1	30.0	1241.6	8.1	0.8
Indiana	3615.1	39.2	3.6	468.5	5.1	0.5

(continued)

Table 2.1 (continued)

Regions	Canada			Mexico		
	Exports ($ million)	Trade exposure (%)	Production exposure (%)	Exports ($ million)	Trade exposure (%)	Production exposure (%)
Michigan	8 686.4	60.2	6.2	1 504.3	9.1	0.9
Ohio	9 926.4	40.4	4.8	808.3	3.8	0.4
Wisconsin	2 266.7	30.5	2.7	399.6	5.4	0.5
Plains	6 052.4			1 144.6		
Iowa	935.1	24.5	2.1	203.1	5.3	0.5
Kansas	524.4	19.6	1.5	238.3	8.9	0.7
Minnesota	1 158.0	22.5	2.1	219.2	4.3	0.4
Missouri	2 828.8	50.4	4.1	365.8	6.5	0.5
Nebraska	336.0	21.3	1.8	79.8	5.1	0.4
North Dakota	168.6	58.4	5.7	6.7	2.3	0.2
South Dakota	101.5	29.2	2.4	31.7	9.1	0.7
Southeast	11 113.9			3 700.1		
Alabama	809.6	18.5	1.7	281.1	6.4	0.6
Arkansas	714.4	29.0	2.4	238.0	9.7	0.8
Florida	499.2	6.5	0.8	352.8	4.6	0.6
Georgia	1 350.0	20.0	1.6	428.9	6.4	0.5
Kentucky	1 422.9	27.3	2.8	378.0	7.3	0.8

Louisiana	456.8	7.3	0.7	321.7	5.1	0.5
Mississippi	514.8	16.5	1.8	397.8	12.8	1.4
North Carolina	1958.2	19.2	1.7	504.9	4.9	0.4
South Carolina	914.9	17.0	1.9	139.7	2.6	0.3
Tennessee	1583.1	26.8	2.3	463.9	7.9	0.7
Virginia	606.5	10.7	1.0	143.9	2.5	0.2
West Virginia	283.5	19.7	2.1	49.4	3.4	0.4
Southwest	2624.9			9338.3		
Arizona	298.1	8.7	1.3	607.6	17.8	2.7
New Mexico	42.8	6.0	0.8	36.3	5.1	0.7
Oklahoma	612.1	26.7	2.2	137.5	6.0	0.5
Texas	1671.9	7.0	0.8	8556.9	36.1	4.3
Rocky Mountain	1070.0			226.9		
Colorado	467.9	17.2	1.7	127.1	4.7	0.5
Idaho	230.2	10.4	2.5	54.8	2.5	0.6
Montana	58.9	51.3	1.5	3.6	3.1	0.1
Utah	266.6	18.5	2.1	41.3	2.9	0.3
Wyoming	46.4	59.6	1.8	0.1	0.2	0.0
Far West	5737.0			4963.9		
California	3716.5	8.9	1.3	4513.7	10.9	1.6
Nevada	47.4	20.0	1.8	10.8	4.5	0.4
Oregon	681.1	16.0	2.2	60.3	1.4	0.2
Washington	1292.0	4.8	2.1	379.1	1.4	0.6
US Total	70099.1	21.5	2.5	26753.7	8.2	0.9

Table 2.2 Imports to Canada and Mexico, 1991

Regions	Canada			Mexico		
	Exports ($ million)	Trade exposure (%)	Production exposure (%)	Imports ($ million)	Trade exposure (%)	Production exposure (%)
New England	3 607.2			1 379.9		
Connecticut	1 208.7	18.8	3.1	352.6	5.5	0.9
Maine	493.7	19.1	3.9	102.2	3.9	0.8
Massachusetts	1 364.1	11.7	2.0	658.3	5.7	1.0
New Hampshire	243.1	13.4	2.2	89.8	5.0	0.8
Rhode Island	170.1	8.0	1.7	98.0	4.6	1.0
Vermont	127.5	13.5	2.3	79.0	8.4	1.4
Mideast	9 009.5			3 463.6		
Delaware	508.9	27.7	3.9	88.3	4.8	0.7
Maryland	777.9	18.6	2.4	242.3	5.8	0.8
New Jersey	1 664.7	14.5	1.9	592.4	5.1	0.7
New York	2 933.5	11.5	1.9	1 444.4	5.7	0.9
Pennsylvania	3 124.5	16.7	2.3	1 096.2	5.9	0.8
Great Lakes	22 230.4			5 878.5		
Illinois	3 455.2	16.6	2.2	1 187.5	5.7	0.8
Indiana	3 029.9	20.0	3.1	1 006.9	6.6	1.0
Michigan	7 361.3	26.1	4.6	1 480.0	5.3	0.9

Ohio	6 199.5	22.4	3.4	1 610.8	5.8	0.9
Wisconsin	2 194.5	18.9	2.7	593.3	5.1	0.7
Plains	5 887.0			1 624.8		
Iowa	761.2	14.7	1.7	272.4	5.3	0.6
Kansas	929.5	19.0	2.7	221.0	4.5	0.6
Minnesota	1 156.6	16.2	2.1	354.0	5.0	0.7
Missouri	2 646.9	23.2	3.8	631.3	5.5	0.9
Nebraska	266.6	14.9	1.4	103.7	5.8	0.6
North Dakota	65.1	16.7	2.2	18.5	4.7	0.6
South Dakota	61.1	12.1	1.4	23.9	4.8	0.6
Southeast	15 638.3			4 846.9		
Alabama	1 329.3	20.2	2.8	372.8	5.7	0.8
Arkansas	760.1	20.4	2.5	219.2	5.9	0.7
Florida	1 286.2	15.7	2.2	508.4	6.2	0.9
Georgia	2 252.6	19.7	2.6	605.1	5.3	0.7
Kentucky	1 528.5	19.6	3.0	470.3	6.0	0.9
Louisiana	1 326.0	22.6	2.2	225.8	3.8	0.4
Mississippi	784.5	19.8	2.7	244.8	6.2	0.8
North Carolina	2 049.1	13.3	1.8	845.2	5.5	0.7
South Carolina	998.6	15.8	2.1	294.8	4.7	0.6
Tennessee	1 626.1	15.5	2.4	583.0	5.6	0.9
Virginia	1 393.7	19.5	2.3	382.4	5.4	0.6
West Virginia	303.6	20.1	2.3	95.1	6.3	0.7

(continued)

Table 2.2 (continued)

Regions	Canada			Mexico		
	Exports ($ million)	Trade exposure (%)	Production exposure (%)	Imports ($ million)	Trade exposure (%)	Production exposure (%)
Southwest	5750.9			1849.6		
Arizona	690.9	17.4	3.0	277.5	7.0	1.2
New Mexico	126.0	15.4	2.4	53.8	6.6	1.0
Oklahoma	811.7	18.5	2.9	243.0	5.5	0.9
Texas	4122.3	16.9	2.1	1275.3	5.2	0.6
Rocky Mountain	1172.3					
Colorado	438.9	9.5	1.6	410.9	4.9	0.8
Idaho	207.6	20.9	2.2	226.8	5.3	0.6
Montana	120.0	34.4	3.1	52.4	4.6	0.4
Utah	364.3	19.3	2.9	16.2	5.8	0.9
Wyoming	41.5	19.3	1.6	109.1	3.0	0.3
				6.4		
Far West	11223.2			3377.7		
California	7381.5	16.3	2.6	2683.4	5.9	0.9
Nevada	44.0	12.9	1.6	18.4	5.4	0.7
Oregon	1012.8	28.6	3.2	190.8	5.4	0.6
Washington	2784.9	29.9	4.5	485.1	5.2	0.8
US Total	74518.8	18.2	2.5	22831.9	5.4	0.8

analysis of variance, which tests equality of means, was performed for exports and imports for both Canada and Mexico.

For exports to Canada and Mexico (Figures 2.1 and 2.2), the *F*-values were highly significant for trade exposure and production exposure, with *P*-values ranging between 0.001 and 0.014. This indicates that a null hypothesis of equality of means of both variables is rejected, implying that regions on average differ substantially in their exports, some being considerably more active in exports to Canada and Mexico than others.

Trade Exposure

SOURCE	DF	SS	MS	F	P
region	7	3718	531	2.95	0.014
ERROR	40	7195	180		
TOTAL	47	10913			

LEVEL	N	MEAN	STDEV
1	6	28.97	16.00
2	5	28.62	14.45
3	5	40.08	12.22
4	7	32.27	15.59
5	12	18.21	7.36
6	4	12.10	9.80
7	5	31.40	22.36
8	4	12.43	6.85

```
INDIVIDUAL 95 PCT CI'S FOR MEAN
BASED ON POOLED STDEV
-+---------+---------+---------+-----
                 (------*-------)
                (-------*-------)
                           (-------*-------)
                      (------*-----)
            (----*----)
(--------*--------)
                         (-------*-------)
(--------*--------)
-+---------+---------+---------+-----
 0        15        30        45
```

Production Exposure

SOURCE	DF	SS	MS	F	P
region	7	35.54	5.08	4.56	0.001
ERROR	40	44.49	1.11		
TOTAL	47	80.03			

LEVEL	N	MEAN	STDEV
1	6	3.533	1.319
2	5	2.580	1.283
3	5	4.060	1.442
4	7	2.814	1.524
5	12	1.733	0.644
6	4	1.275	0.660
7	5	1.920	0.390
8	4	1.850	0.404

```
---------+---------+---------+-------
                      (-----*----)
              (-----*------)
                         (-----*-----)
                 (-----*----)
        (----*---)
(-------*------)
       (------*-----)
      (------*------)
---------+---------+---------+-------
        1.5       3.0       4.5
```

Note: The eight levels are codes for the eight regions of the United States as defined by the Bureau of Economic Analysis as follows: (1) New England; (2) Mideast; (3) Great Lakes; (4) Plains; (5) Southeast; (6) Southwest; (7) Rocky Mountain; and (8) Far West. N is the number of states in a region (see note 1 for classification).

Figure 2.1 Analysis of variance of exports to Canada: trade and production exposures

Trade Exposure

```
SOURCE     DF      SS       MS         F            P
region      7     526.1     75.2      3.33         0.007
ERROR      40     901.7     22.5
TOTAL      47    1427.8
                                    INDIVIDUAL 95 PCT CI'S FOR MEAN
                                    BASED ON POOLED STDEV
LEVEL       N     MEAN     STDEV    ---+---------+---------+-----------
  1         6     3.350    1.331      (-----*----)
  2         5     5.960    3.194         (------*-----)
  3         5     6.300    2.212          (-----*-----)
  4         7     5.929    2.453          (----*-----)
  5        12     6.133    3.013            (---*---)
  6         4    16.250   14.443                      (------*------)
  7         5     2.680    1.619     (-----*-----)
  8         4     4.550    4.478       (------*-----)
                                    ---+---------+---------+---------+---
                                      0.0       7.0      14.0      21.0
```

Production Exposure

```
SOURCE     DF    SS       MS        F            P
region      7     8.969   1.281     3.86         0.003
ERROR      40    13.268   0.332
TOTAL      47    22.237

LEVEL       N    MEAN     STDEV    ---+---------+---------+---------+---
  1         6    0.4667   0.2733      (-----*-----)
  2         5    0.5200   0.2775      (------*-----)
  3         5    0.6200   0.2168       (------*-----)
  4         7    0.4857   0.1773       (----*-----)
  5        12    0.6000   0.3133         (----*---)
  6         4    2.0500   1.7991                     (-------*------)
  7         5    0.3000   0.2550    (------*-----)
  8         4    0.7000   0.6218        (-------*------)
                                   ---+---------+---------+---------+---
                                     0.00      0.80      1.60      2.40
```

Note: The eight levels are codes for the eight regions of the United States as defined by the Bureau of Economic Analysis as follows: (1) New England; (2) Mideast; (3) Great Lakes; (4) Plains; (5) Southeast; (6) Southwest; (7) Rocky Mountain; and (8) Far West. N is the number of states in a region (see note 1 for classification).

Figure 2.2 Analysis of variance of exports to Mexico: trade and production exposures

By observing the plots of the 95 per cent confidence intervals for exports trade exposure, and exports production exposure for Canada and Mexico (Figures 2.1 and 2.2), it is possible to separate the regions for significant differences in their means. For this purpose, the means are ranked in declining order, remembering that larger values correspond to larger roles in regional exports. For ease of presentation, the regions are denoted by symbols as: New England (NE); Mideast (ME); Great Lakes (GL); Plains

(PL); Southeast (SE); Southwest (SW); Rocky Mountain (RM); and Far West (FW).

The regional lineups for exports to Canada are:

trade exposure: [GL, PL, RM, NE, ME|SE, FW, SW],

and

production exposure: [GL, NE, PL, ME|RM, FW, SE, SW].

The lines separate the regions into two subsets where regions do not differ significantly in their means. From the above arrangements, it is possible to conclude that the regions with the least export activity to Canada are the Southeast, the Southwest and the Far West.

For exports to Mexico, following the above procedures, the lineups are:

trade exposure: [SW|GL, SE, ME, SE, FW, NE, RM],

and

production exposure: [SW|FW, GL, SE, ME, PL, NE, RM].

From the above schematic representations, it is evident that the Southwest region occupies a unique position among the eight regions in exports to Mexico. The least significant regions were consistently New England and Rocky Mountain.

For imports, looking at Figures 2.3 and 2.4, the only significant differences among the regions was for Mexico for production exposure (p-value = 0.007), indicating that at least one region differs significantly from the others in import production exposure. From Figure 2.3, the following is the schematic representation for imports from Canada:

trade exposure: [FW, GL, RM, SE, ME, SW, PL, NE],

and

production exposure: [GL, FW, SW, NE, ME, SE, RM, PL].

The absence of a line separating subsets of regions in the above orderings is consistent with the results in that no significant differences among the regional means were observed.

For imports from Mexico, the following is the schematic regional

Trade Exposure

SOURCE	DF	SS	MS	F	P
REGION	7	245.0	35.0	1.41	0.230
ERROR	40	995.8	24.9		
TOTAL	47	1240.7			

```
                                  INDIVIDUAL 95 PCT CI'S FOR MEAN
                                  BASED ON POOLED STDEV

LEVEL     N    MEAN     STDEV     -+---------+---------+---------+-----
  1       6    14.083   4.264      (-------*-------)
  2       5    17.800   6.133             (--------*--------)
  3       5    20.800   3.624                   (--------*--------)
  4       7    16.686   3.563            (------*-------)
  5      12    18.517   2.737                 (-----*-----)
  6       4    17.050   1.287          (---------*---------)
  7       5    20.680   8.903                   (--------*--------)
  8       4    21.925   8.588                     (---------*---------)
                                  -+---------+---------+---------+-----
                                 10.0      15.0      20.0      25.0
```

Production Exposure

SOURCE	DF	SS	MS	F	P
REGION	7	4.389	0.627	1.15	0.353
ERROR	40	21.815	0.545		
TOTAL	47	26.203			

```
LEVEL     N    MEAN     STDEV     -------+---------+---------+---------
  1       6    2.5333   0.8165        (--------*--------)
  2       5    2.4800   0.8258       (--------*---------)
  3       5    3.2000   0.9028                 (---------*--------)
  4       7    2.1857   0.8513    (-------*-------)
  5      12    2.4083   0.3315         (-----*------)
  6       4    2.6000   0.4243       (----------*----------)
  7       5    2.2800   0.7050    (---------*--------)
  8       4    2.9750   1.2121             (----------*---------)
                                  -------+---------+---------+---------
                                       2.10      2.80      3.50
```

Note: The eight levels are codes for the eight regions of the United States as defined by the Bureau of Economic Analysis as follows: (1) New England; (2) Mideast; (3) Great Lakes; (4) Plains; (5) Southeast; (6) Southwest; (7) Rocky Mountain; and (8) Far West. N is the number of states in a region (see note 1 for classification).

Figure 2.3 Analysis of variance of imports from Canada: trade and production exposures

representation:

trade exposure: [SW, GL, SE, NE, FW, ME, PL, RM],

and

production exposure: [NE, SW, GL, ME, FW|SE, PL, RM].

```
Trade Exposure
SOURCE      DF       SS        MS          F            P
REGION       7     5.608     0.801       1.13         0.362
ERROR       40    28.282     0.707
TOTAL       47    33.890

                                        INDIVIDUAL 95 PCT CI'S FOR MEAN
                                        BASED ON POOLED STDEV
LEVEL        N     MEAN      STDEV      -+---------+---------+---------+-----
  1          6    5.5167    1.5536                (------*------)
  2          5    5.4600    0.4827               (-------*------)
  3          5    5.7000    0.5788                  (-------*-------)
  4          7    5.0857    0.4670            (------*-----)
  5         12    5.5500    0.7154                    (----*---)
  6          4    6.0750    0.8617                     (--------*-------)
  7          5    4.7200    1.0616       (------*-------)
  8          4    5.4750    0.2986             (--------*-------)
                                        -+---------+---------+---------+-----
                                        4.0       5.0       6.0       7.0

Production Exposure
SOURCE      DF       SS        MS          F            P
REGION       7    0.6693    0.0956       3.34         0.007
ERROR       40    1.1455    0.0286
TOTAL       47    1.8148

LEVEL        N     MEAN      STDEV      --------+---------+---------+--------
  1          6    0.9833    0.2229                          (------*------)
  2          5    0.7800    0.0837               (-------*-------)
  3          5    0.8600    0.1140                   (-------*-------)
  4          7    0.6571    0.1134          (------*-----)
  5         12    0.7250    0.1485               (----*----)
  6          4    0.9250    0.2500                     (-------*--------)
  7          5    0.6000    0.2550       (-------*-------)
  8          4    0.7500    0.1291              (-------*--------)
                                        --------+---------+---------+--------
                                              0.60      0.80      1.00
```

Note: The eight levels are codes for the eight regions of the United States as defined by the Bureau of Economic Analysis as follows: (1) New England; (2) Mideast; (3) Great Lakes; (4) Plains; (5) Southeast; (6) Southwest; (7) Rocky Mountain; and (8) Far West. N is the number of states in a region (see note 1 for classification).

Figure 2.4 Analysis of variance of imports from Mexico: trade and production exposures

Therefore, regarding imports from Mexico, based on the above representation, the only significant differences in regional means was for production exposure, as stated earlier.

4 Discussion and concluding remarks

From the end of the Second World War until the late 1970s, the United States, according to Gruber and Welch (1994) followed a foreign trade policy dominated by the spirit of unconditional interpretation of the MFN clause of GATT. The US was the chief proponent of international trade liberalization. By the late 1970s there emerged frustrations and dissatisfactions with GATT implementations which include slowness of some countries to comply; the free-rider problem (some countries benefited to the detriment of others); and the rise of issues not related to GATT such as direct foreign investment, intellectual property, trade in services and innovative tools of protectionism.

According to Kreinin (1995), nations advocating free trade may opt for an international approach or regional approach (economic integration). The regional approach (Waldmann 1986) is a scheme whereby preferential trade agreements are made which encourage deals between two or more countries to open up their markets to each other on better terms than they give to others. Canada and Mexico with populations in 1993 of 29 million and 90 million, respectively (World Bank 1995), are the United States' first and third trading partners. Corresponding exports in 1993 are $100 billion and $42 billion and imports are $110 billion and $40 billion (US Bureau of the Census 1994).

NAFTA is supposed to enhance trade between the United States, Canada and Mexico. A key consideration in assessing the benefits of such a regional integration is the relative magnitudes of trade creation and trade diversion. Trade creation replaces domestic products with cheaper products. Trade diversion substitutes goods produced by the partners for goods produced outside the region. Added to these aspects are benefits resulting from economies of scale, efficiency, higher investment, quicker technological progress and capital accumulation. There is, however, a fear that the US economy will result in a process of deindustrialization because of wage differentials among the partners, especially Mexico.

NAFTA will nevertheless create opportunities for localized regions. There is a geographic bias among northern states and central states towards trade with Canada, and a geographic bias among southwestern and south central states towards trade with Mexico. In particular, the Great Lakes, Plains, Rocky Mountain and New England regions are biased towards trade with Canada, while the Southwest region is biased towards trade with Mexico.

Kubik (1994) has noted that exports to Mexico increased from $12.4 billion in 1986 to $40.6 billion in 1992. Kubik further indicates that although the Southwest and West Coast have benefited the most from the increase in exports, every other region has benefited also. The agricultural states of the Midsouth, for instance, increased their crop sales to Mexico. Overall, some 700 000 US jobs are tied to exports to Mexico with an expected additional increase of 200 000 jobs by 1995.

For trade between the United States and Canada, on the other hand, McCallum (1995) draws a less enthusiastic picture for a dramatic increase in volume of trade. He argues that the effects of NAFTA could be relatively modest as rising trade between the two countries is driven by a reduction in tariff, which is already low and has little room to fall to reach the zero level. There might be other elements which may enhance further trade, such as diminished non-tariff barriers, but these could have minimal effects, at least over the next decade.

Note

1. Regions of the contiguous United States according to the Bureau of Economic Analysis are:

   1. *New England* Maine, New Hampshire, Vermont, Massachusetts, Connecticut, Rhode Island;
   2. *Mideast* New York, Pennsylvania, New Jersey, Delaware, Maryland;
   3. *Great Lakes* Ohio, Michigan, Indiana, Wisconsin, Illinois;
   4. *Plains* Minnesota, Iowa, Missouri, North Dakota, South Dakota, Nebraska, Kansas;
   5. *Southeast* Virginia, West Virginia, North Carolina, South Carolina, Georgia, Florida, Kentucky, Tennessee, Alabama, Mississippi, Arkansas, Louisiana;
   6. *Southwest* Oklahoma, Texas, Arizona, New Mexico;
   7. *Rocky Mountain* Colorado, Wyoming, Montana, Idaho, Utah;
   8. *Far West* Nevada, California, Oregon, Washington.

References

Frankel, J., E. Stein and S. Wei (1995), 'Trading Blocs and the Americas: The Natural, the Unnatural, and the SuperNatural', *Journal of Development Economics*, **47** (1), 61–95.

Gruber, W.C. and O.H. Welch (1994), 'Is NAFTA Economic Integration?', *Federal Reserve Bank of Dallas Economic Review*, 2nd Quarter, 35–51.

Hayward, D.J. and R.A. Erickson (1995), 'The North American Trade of U.S. States: A Comparative Analysis of Industrial Shipments, 1983–91', *International Regional Science Review*, **18** (1), 1–31.

Klein, L.R. and D. Salvatore (1995), 'Welfare Effects of the North American Free Trade Agreement', *Journal of Policy Modeling*, **17** (2), 163–76.

Kreinin, M.E. (1995), *International Economics*, Fort Worth, TX: Harcourt Brace College Publishers.

Kubik, P.J. (1994), 'The North American Free Trade Agreement', in J.L. Clark, P.J. Kubik and L.J. Pratt (eds), *Current Regional Issues*, Fort Worth, TX: Harcourt Brace College Publishers, pp. 19–27.

McCallum, J. (1995), 'National Borders Matter – U.S. Regional Trade Patterns', *American Economic Review*, **85** (3), 615–623.

Richardson, D.J. (1995), 'Income Inequality and Trade: How to Think, What to Conclude', *Journal of Economic Perspectives*, **9** (3), 33–55.

US Bureau of the Census (1994), *Statistical Abstract of the United States: 1994*, Washington, DC: US Government Printing Office.

Waldman, R.J. (1986), *Managed Trade: The New Competition Between Nations*, Cambridge, MA: Ballinger.

Warf, B. and J. Randall (1994), 'The U.S. – Canada Free Trade Agreement: Impacts on U.S. States and Canadian Provinces', *International Regional Science Review*, **17** (1), 99–119.

World Bank (1995), *World Development Report 1995*, Oxford: Oxford University Press.

3 Welfare effects of the completion of the single European market

Evangelia Papadaki

1 Introduction

This chapter aims to evaluate the welfare and industry effects of the completion of the single European market on Greece. Most previous studies on the completion of the internal market (Europe 1992) have singled out a few 'larger' North European members and have aggregated the 'smaller' South European members with the rest of the European members. An exception is the attempt of Gasiorek et al. (1992) to highlight the effects on some 'smaller', 'less-developed' European members by separately identifying Spain/Portugal and Greece/Ireland. Interestingly enough, although in the first set of models the aggregate 'rest-of-the-EU' is essentially non-affected by Europe 1992, in the Gasiorek et al., study it is in these 'smaller' countries that the completion of the internal market has a stronger effect. In view of the concerns over unequal benefits stemming from the European Union for the 'northern' and 'southern' partners, the above results suggest that in order for any conclusion to be valid for this group of countries, a further disaggregation along North–South lines and in particular an identification of a 'smaller' country is necessary. For this reason this study should be of interest not only to those concerned with the Greek economy, but also to those concerned by the effect of the completion of the single market on other 'smaller' – 'less-industrialized' – southern countries.

The methodology I have used is that of Mercenier (1995). It consists of a static multicountry, multisector general equilibrium model with increasing returns to scale, imperfect competition and product differentiation at the firm level. By completion of the single market I shall refer here to the elimination of non-tariff trade barriers (NTBs) within the European Community which is expected to force firms to adopt a single pricing rule within Europe determined on the basis of their EU-average monopoly power. The fundamental mechanism underlying the model is the following. At the eve of integration, NTBs confer on oligopolistic firms the power to price discriminate between national markets. It will in general be the case that firms will charge higher prices in the domestic rather than in foreign markets because of the larger market share they have in the former and the greater price unresponsiveness, which causes the domestic demand to be less elastic to prices. With integration, NTBs are dismantled and consequently price discrimination should cease. As firms are expected to move to a single price strategy, one expects domestic prices to decrease and export prices to rise. If consumer prices decline relative to factor prices, consumers will be better off. In addition, there may be production efficiency gains the magnitude of which will depend to some extent on whether entry/exit of competitors is allowed for. Thus, under the assumption of no entry/exit, efficiency gains could result if existing firms produce greater quantities, at lower unit costs. This effect could be magnified when we allow for free exit/entry. In this case, firms that experience negative profits due to the drop in domestic prices will exit the industry, making it possible for the remaining firms to expand their production and move further down on their average cost curves. This positive outcome from industry restructuring could be offset by the welfare and efficiency cost due to a decrease in the available variety of products. This is because I assume that:

1. consumers have a love for various types of preferences (Dixit and Stiglitz 1977), and
2. production efficiency in all sectors (competitive and non-competitive) increases with the number of intermediate inputs available (Ethier 1982).

The chapter is organized as follows. In Section 2.1 I make a short presentation of NTBs. The description of the theoretical model, the data set and the calibration procedure are found in Sections 2.2 and 2.3, respectively. Industry and welfare results are presented in Section 2.4 for two alternative market structure scenarios: no-entry/exit case (fixed number of firms), and the free entry/exit case (variable number of firms). The general conclusion from all the above results is presented in Section 2.5.

2 Non-tariff barriers in Europe

Although tariffs on intra-EU trade have been almost completely abolished for sometime, non-tariff barriers still exist and the EU 1992 programme is meant to abolish them. These barriers, which appear to be widespread and to be common to all countries, can be grouped as follows

1. customs controls and other administrative formalities (physical barriers);
2. limited access to public procurement;

3. national differences in standards and technical regulations (technical barriers);
4. tax frontiers (fiscal barriers);
5. import quotas and other measures permitted by virtue of Article 115 of the Treaty of Rome.[2]

Barriers (1) and (3) may be classified as cost-increasing barriers. In the first case, customs formalities involve delays and various kinds of administrative procedures which impose a cost on the movement of all goods between member countries. In the second case, national norms and technical standards require producers to manufacture or package goods in forms which are different for other EU markets than those for their own domestic markets. Both these elements produce a wedge between the cost of domestic goods and delivered exports, considerably larger than the transport cost involved.

In addition to increasing costs, all of the above-mentioned trade barriers limit access to the EU market, and in some instances the barrier is prohibitive as is the case with public procurement.

The European Commission prepared a list of 40 industries that were identified as the most sensitive to the abolition of the non-tariff trade barriers and the completion of the internal market. In addition to the level of non-tariff measures, the other criteria that the Commission adopted to identify the sensitive sectors included indicators of market segmentation (price dispersal for identical products sold in the EU), of economies of scale as well as of the degree of intra-EU trade. This list was then adapted to each individual member country, taking into account their specificities. In the case of Greece, the steel, food-processing, textile and leather-goods industries were added to the most sensitive sectors. The sensitive sectors were found to represent 56.7 per cent of value added and 61.5 per cent of employment in the Greek industry. This is much more than in other European countries, which led the European Commission to conjecture that the Greek economy will be particularly affected by the completion of the single European market.

3 The applied general equilibrium model

First are defined the different commodity sets. Sectors of activity are identified by indices s and t, with S representing the set of all industries so that $s, t = 1, \ldots, S$. S is partitioned into the subset of competitive constant returns-to-scale sectors, denoted C, and the subset of non-competitive increasing returns-to-scale industries, denoted $\bar{C}$. Countries are identified by indices i and j, with $i, j = 1, \ldots, W$ and $W = EU \cup ROW$, where the first subset represents the EU10, and the last subset represents the OECD countries that do not belong to *EU*. In a multicountry, multisector framework, it is necessary to keep track of the trade flows by their geographical and sectoral origin and destination. Thus, a subscript *isjt* indicates a flow originating in sector *s* of country *i* with industry *t* of country *j* as recipient. Since it will be necessary more than once to aggregate variables with respect to a particular subscript, to avoid unnecessary proliferation of symbols, occasionally I shall substitute a dot for the subscript on which aggregation has been performed; for instance, $c_{.si}$ is an aggregate of c_{jsi} with respect to the first subscript.

3.1 Households

Final consumption decisions in each country are made by a representative consumer whose preferences are given by:

$$U_i = \sum_{s \in S} \rho_{si} \log(c_{.si}) \sum_{s \in S} \rho_{si} = 1, \tag{3.1}$$

$$c_{.si} = \left(\sum_{j_w} \delta_{jsi} c_{jsi}^{\sigma_s - 1/\sigma_s} \right)^{\sigma_s/\sigma_s - 1} \quad s \in C, \tag{3.2}$$

$$c_{.si} = \left(\sum_{j \in W} n_{js} \delta_{jsi} c_{jsi}^{\sigma_s - 1/\sigma_s} \right)^{\sigma_s/\sigma_s - 1} \quad s \in \bar{C} \tag{3.3}$$

where δ_{jsi} are share parameters and σ_s are substitution elasticities and where $c_{.si}$ and $s \in C$ is a composite good of domestic and imported goods and $c_{.si}$, $ss \in \bar{C}$ is a composite good of products of individual firms. Consumption decisions are made at two levels. At the first level, the consumer chooses the optimal amount of a composite good $c_{.si}$ given constant expenditure shares (ρ_{si}). At the second level he/she chooses the optimal composition of the composite good in terms of geographic origin for the competitive industries (the Armington specification) and in terms of individual firms products for the non-competitive industries (the Dixit–Stiglitz specification). Final demands c_{jsi} are given by maximization of (3.1), subject to (3.2), (3.3) and to the consumer's budget constraint, that is, the sum of wage earnings, capital rentals and pure profits,

$$Y_i = \sum_{j \in W} \sum_{s \in C} p_{js.} c_{jsi} + \sum_{j \in W} \sum_{s \in \bar{C}} p_{jsi} n_{js} c_{jsi} \tag{3.4}$$

$$= \sum_{s \in S} w_i L_{is} + \sum_{s \in S} (r_i K_{is} + \Pi_{is}), \tag{3.5}$$

where *p* denotes prices and L_{is}, K_{is} labour and capital supply, respectively.

This type of formulation recognizes the possibility for non-competitive firms to price discriminate between countries (p_{jsi}) but not for competitive industries ($p_{js.}$). Also I assume that both capital and labour are mobile between sectors but not between countries.

3.2 Firms

3.2.1 *Competitive industries*

In competitive industries, input demands by producers result from minimization of variable unit costs v_{is}.

$$v_{is}Q_{is} = \sum_{j\in W}\sum_{t\in C} p_{jt.}\, x_{jtis} + \sum_{j\in W}\sum_{t\in \bar{C}} p_{jtis}x_{jtis} + w_i L_{is}^v + r_i K_{is}^v \tag{3.6}$$

subject to the production function

$$\log(Q_{is}) = \alpha_{Lis}\log(L_{is}^v) + \alpha_{Kis}\log(K_{is}^v) + \sum_{t\in S}\alpha_{tis}\log(x_{.tis}) \tag{3.7}$$

where

$$x_{.tis} = \left(\sum_{j\in W}\beta_{jtis}x_{jtis}^{\sigma_t-1/\sigma_t}\right)^{\sigma_t/\sigma_t-1} \qquad t\in C$$

and

$$x_{.tis} = \left(\sum_{j\in W} n_{jt}\beta_{jtis}x_{jtis}^{\sigma_t-1/\sigma_t}\right)^{\sigma_t/\sigma_t-1} \qquad t\in \bar{C},$$

where $x_{.tis}$, $t\in C$, $x_{.tis}$, $t\in\bar{C}$ are composite intermediate inputs of goods produced in the competitive sectors (the Armington specification) and the imperfectly competitive firms (the Ethier specification), respectively. To guarantee homogeneity of degree one of the unit costs in prices, I set

$$\alpha_{Lis} + \alpha_{Kis} + \sum_{t\in S}\alpha_{tis} = 1,$$

where α and β are share parameters and $\beta_{jtis} = 0, \forall j \neq i$ if t is non-traded. Profit maximization implies marginal cost pricing in the competitive sectors so that

$$p_{is.} = v_{is}, \quad s\in C.$$

3.2.2 Non-competitive industries In the non-competitive industries, individual firms face fixed primary factor costs. Thus, total unit costs V_{is} and marginal costs v_{is} are no longer equal. Total unit costs are given by

$$V_{is} = v_{is} + \frac{(w_i L_{is}^F + r_i K_{is}^F)}{Q_{is}}, \quad s \in \bar{C} \tag{3.8}$$

where Q_{is}, L_{is}^F, K_{is}^F denote, respectively, the *individual* firm's output, fixed labour and fixed capital.

When markets are initially segmented, firms charge a different price in each market according to the Lerner formula

$$\frac{p_{isj} - v_{is}}{p_{isj}} = \frac{-1}{E_{isj}}, \quad s \in \bar{C} \tag{3.9}$$

$$Q_{is} = \sum_{j \in W} \left(c_{isj} + \sum_{t \in S} x_{isjt} \right), \quad s \in S,\ i \in W \tag{3.12}$$

$$L_i^{sup} = \sum_{s \in C} L_{is}^v + \sum_{s \in \bar{C}} (L_{is}^v + L_{is}^F), \quad i \in W \tag{3.13}$$

$$K_i^{sup} = \sum_{s \in C} K_{is}^v + \sum_{s \in \bar{C}} (K_{is}^v + K_{is}^F), \quad i, j \in Wj \tag{3.14}$$

where L_i^{sup} and K_i^{sup} represent fixed primary factor endowments; and

- profits equal zero in all competitive industries;
- firms in non-competitive industries mark up prices over marginal costs according to (3.9). The perceived elasticity E_{isj} is evaluated at equilibrium prices and demands, so that, even though the firm may be slightly mistaken on the true demand curve it faces, it correctly perceives the prices that will clear the markets for the quantities actually produced;
- in non-competitive sectors, the number of firms n_{is} may be either fixed, in which case profits may be different from zero, or alternatively endogenously determined, in which case profits are nil.

The Rest-of-the-World (ROW) wage rate is chosen as the numéraire.

4 Data set and calibration procedure

4.1 Data set

The base year is 1982; EU therefore is actually EU10. Greece, Great Britain, Germany, Italy and France are identified separately, whereas the

Table 3.1 Sectoral breakdown of activities

Agriculture and primary products	$\in C$	(SITC: 2, 3, 4)
Food, beverages and tobacco	$\in C$	(SITC: 1, 0)
Pharmaceutical products	$\in$	(SITC: 54; Nace-clio: 257)
Chemicals other than pharmaceutical products	$\in C$	(SITC: 5-54)
Motor vehicles	$\in$	(SITC: 78; Nace-clio: 350)
Office machinery	$\in$	(SITC: 75; Nace-clio: 330)
Other machinery and transport materials	$\in$	(SITC: 7–75–78)
Other manufacturing industries (textiles, wood, paper, metallurgy, minerals)	$\in C$	(SITC: 6, 8, 9)
Transport and services	$\in C$	

Notes: C = competitive, $\bar{C}$ = non-competitive.

rest of the European countries are aggregated as RE. The adopted sectoral breakdown of activities is detailed in Table 3.1. The elasticities of substitution used in the model are given in Table 3.2. The database includes bilateral trade flows, separate input–output tables for domestic and imported inputs, final demands by type and sectoral origin, production and labour earnings figures. In the case of Greece, some of this data was sent to us by the Bank of Greece. The rest was collected from standard international publications. A reply on Monday (RAS) procedure was used to provide consistency of the input–output table of 1980 with the other sources.

Table 3.2 Elasticities of substitution σ_s

Agriculture and primary products	2
Food, beverages and tobacco	2
Pharmaceutical products	5
Chemicals other than pharmaceutical products	5
Motor vehicles	10
Office machinery	10
Other machinery and transport materials	7
Other manufacturing industries (textiles, wood, paper, metallurgy, minerals)	4
Transport and services	2

4.2 Calibration procedure

The calibration of the competitive side of the model is quite standard (see, for instance, Srinivasan and Whalley 1986). More subtle is the joint determination of the base-year price system and cost structure, consistent with the base-year data set, with the optimal price discrimination by individual competitors and with the free-entry equilibrium concept. The procedure followed is the one devised by Mercenier (1995) and consists of the joint determination of the price system and of the variable unit costs of individual producers. In Table 3.3 I report the calibrated price spread between average domestic (the first row) and average export prices (the second row) for the non-competitive sectors in the Cournot–Nash case. As expected, export prices are consistently lower than domestic ones in all countries, reflecting the smaller market power of firms in their export relative to their domestic market. Furthermore, the above price spread is larger for Greece than for the other member countries of the EU. One may, therefore, expect that if there are benefits from Europe 1992, these will be higher for Greece than for the rest of the European Community, indicative of the less competitive structure of Greek industry. The initial price spread for the Bertrand case is not reported, as it is insignificant. Therefore, none of the calibration and simulation results henceforth will include the case where firms compete in prices, since the move to a single European market will have only extremely modest consequences.

In the zero-profit equilibrium, the firm's total unit cost V_{is} and average selling price $\bar{p}_{is}$ are equalized, which, using (3.8), determines the firm's fixed costs $(w_i L_{is}^F + r_i K_{is}^F)$. Therefore,

$$w_i L_{is}^F + r_i K_{is}^F = v_{is} Q_{js} \left(\frac{V_{js}}{v_{js}} - 1 \right), \quad s \in \bar{C}. \tag{3.19}$$

Because of the lack of reliable data on the composition of fixed costs, I assume that, in each country, fixed and total costs have the same share of capital and labour inputs. Table 3.4 reports on the calibrated ratios of marginal to average costs (the inverse of the scale elasticities). We observe that this ratio for Greece is systematically smaller than that of the other EU countries in all oligopolistic industries by values ranging from 0.08 for the pharmaceutical sector to 0.003 for the other machinery and transport materials sector.

4.3 Design of the experiment

The experiment of market integration consists of assuming a single perceived elasticity based on an EU-aggregated demand for all firms in

Table 3.3 Calibrated price spread (Cournot–Nash)

	Pharmaceuticals	Chemicals	Motor vehicles	Office machinery	Other machinery and transport materials
Greece	1.000	1.000	1.000	1.000	1.000
	0.62594	0.98296	0.58182	0.76088	0.96862
GB	1.001	1.000	1.004	1.001	1.000
	0.98668	0.99714	0.78062	0.97064	0.998401
Germany	1.001	1.000	1.006	1.001	1.000
	0.99249	0.99715	0.90428	0.96871	0.99842
France	1.000	1.000	1.016	1.003	1.000
	0.99542	0.99831	0.76488	0.97162	0.99665
Italy	1.000	1.000	1.010	1.003	1.000
	0.99259	0.99682	0.68709	0.89961	0.99725
RE	1.000	1.000	1.010	1.014	1.000
	0.988582	0.99793	0.91208	0.97913	0.99826
ROW	1.000	1.000	1.000	1.001	1.000
	0.99726	0.99892	0.82370	0.99076	0.99947

Table 3.4 Calibrated ratios of marginal to average costs (Cournot–Nash)

	Pharmaceuticals	Chemicals	Motor vehicles	Office machinery	Other machinery and transport materials
Greece	0.709	0.797	0.837	0.872	0.853
GB	0.798	0.800	0.873	0.897	0.857
Germany	0.799	0.799	0.886	0.897	0.857
France	0.799	0.800	0.865	0.895	0.857
Italy	0.799	0.799	0.855	0.889	0.857
RE	0.798	0.800	0.886	0.897	0.857
ROW	0.799	0.800	0.879	0.899	0.857

the non-competitive sectors, that is,

$$E_{isj} = E_{isEEC}, \quad i \in W, \quad s \in \bar{C}, \quad j \in EU$$

The aggregate-demand-based elasticity will typically be larger than the one used for pricing in the pro-integration equilibrium. Therefore, the move to a single price strategy within the Community will induce a reduction of the price charged on the own market together with an increase in export prices. The conjecture is that average prices charged to the EU will decrease and more output will be produced at lower average costs, the pro-competitive effect. Despite output expansion, firms may not be able to cover average costs of production at these lower average selling prices and might incur negative profits.

5 Results: effects to Greece of Europe 1992

5.1 Fixed number of firms

The results from the case of a fixed number of firms are presented in Table 3.5. I then highlight some sectoral variables of special interest, in addition to the standard aggregate indicators. All results are percentage deviations from the initial segmented equilibrium. The first thing to observe is that most notable changes are experienced in the sectors of pharmaceuticals and motor vehicles. A glance at the calibrated price spread within the EU (Table 3.4) indicates that indeed these are the sectors that one expects to be most affected by the 1992 programme: these are the sectors where price discrimination is more important. As predicted from the theoretical discussion, switching from the segmented to the integrated market induces a notable drop in the within-Europe average selling prices of the above sectors, and to a lesser degree of the office machinery sector. The decrease in average prices induces an increase in demand and a net increase in real output, reaching an approximate 32 per cent and 30 per cent increase in the pharmaceutical and motor vehicle sectors, respectively. However, this cost-saving output expansion is not sufficient to compensate for the loss in revenues so that firms in these sectors experience economic losses in the post-integration equilibrium.

A second inspection reveals that in the transport and the chemical sectors, prices charged within the integrated EU will increase (when compared to the numéraire) (as is also the case in all competitive sectors), while the output expansion is only minimal. Given the initial calibrated price spread, these sectors are indeed the ones that should be the least affected from the 'internal' market experiment, according to a partial-equilibrium-based intuition. As these sectors have an initially weak

Table 3.5 Effects of the 1992 programme, fixed number of firms (% changes, Cournot–Nash)

Aggregate indicators	
Welfare (% equiv. var.)	0.48
Wage rate	2.02
Rental rate of capital	2.43
Cost-of-living index	1.60
Terms of trade	0.96
Efficiency gains (%)	3.21

	Agri-culture	Food, beverages	Pharma-ceuticals	Chemicals	Motor vehicles	Office machinery	Other machinery	Other manufacturing	Services
Av. sale price to EC (% change)	2.18	2.32	−13.47	1.43	−9.99	−1.10	0.20	1.91	2.31
Profits (% of value added)			−4.36	−0.66	−0.94	−2.48	−2.13		
Output (% change)	−0.43	−0.41	31.80	0.07	28.90	3.31	1.77	−0.71	−0.23
Efficiency gains (%)			13.40	0.02	10.68	1.05	0.42		

domestic market share and therefore already before the 1992 programme a relatively high elastic demand curve, the integration process will only make this elasticity slightly larger. Thus, other general equilibrium effects, such as the increase in aggregate income, the increase in price of factors of production and that of intermediate import prices, seem to counterbalance the partial equilibrium effect, leading to a small increase in the average selling prices to the EU and only a minor increase in total output. Overall, the individual firms in these sectors will not be induced to better exploit the potential economies of scale, but there will be some real cost savings due to the small but positive output expansion. Despite the increase in prices for chemicals, average costs increase more, so firms in this industry will also experience negative profits. Similar remarks hold for the transport materials sector which, however, experiences a larger output expansion so that the cost savings due to a better exploitation of scale economies are more significant.

Overall, there is a clear shift of resources from the competitive to the non-competitive sectors, reflected by the drop of real output in the former sectors. This means a shift of resources to the most capital-intensive sectors as indicated by the relative increase of the rental rate of capital. As returns to the factors of production increase by more than the cost of living index, consumers in the country experience a net welfare gain. Overall there is a net gain in felicity (measured in terms of equivalent variation),[2] which, however, remains modest at 0.48 per cent. Also, the Greek economy has become globally more efficient, as shown by the aggregate efficiency gains. These gains, which in fact report the real cost savings achieved due to increased scale on initial output, are particularly high for the pharmaceutical and vehicle sectors.

5.2 Variable number of firms

Table 3.6 reports the results in the alternative case where the number of firms is endogenous. This scenario could be interpreted as a 'long-term equilibrium' (even though there is no capital accumulation) since the entry and exit of firms takes time. Given that profits in the 'short run' are negative in all imperfectly competitive sectors, there will be exit of firms. As one expects, the percentage change in the number of firms in an industry is inversely related to the degree of market concentration and positively related to the magnitude of negative economic profits. Therefore, the largest exit takes place in the pharmaceutical (largest negative economic profits) and transport materials (less concentrated) sectors.

Naturally the motor vehicles sector, which is both very concentrated and has been affected the least from negative economic profits, will experience a rather minimal loss of firms and will remain rather

Table 3.6 Effects of the 1992 programme, variable number of firms (% changes, Cournot–Nash)

Aggregate indicators	
Welfare (% equiv. var.)	0.45
Wage rate	1.21
Rental rate of capital	1.78
Cost-of-living index	1.14
Terms of trade	0.39
Efficiency gains (%)	4.21

	Agri-culture	Food, beverages	Pharma-ceuticals	Chemicals	Motor vehicles	Office machinery	Other machinery	Other manufacturing	Services
Av. sale price to EC (% change)	1.62	1.69	–12.63	0.92	–9.81	–0.58	–0.21	1.23	1.69
Profits (% of value added)			–7.24	–2.50	–0.70	–4.78	–9.60		
Output (% change)	–0.27	–0.22	27.275	0.01	28.11	2.19	–0.09	–0.28	–0.09
Efficiency gains (%)			15.54	0.61	10.78	2.26	2.36		

Table 3.7 Effects of the 1992 programme, comparisons with other EU countries, variable number of firms (% changes)

	Welfare	Efficiency gains
Greece	0.45	4.20
GB	0.44	1.72
Germany	0.13	0.55
France	0.37	0.10
Italy	0.66	1.01
RE	0.18	0.39
ROW	−0.01	−0.07

concentrated. We immediately observe that welfare effects in this scenario are more modest, reflecting the cost for consumers of fewer varieties. Higher concentration implies a smaller number of varieties available for consumption and therefore a deepening effect on consumer satisfaction.

Finally, when compared with the other countries of the EU I find that the industry reallocation effects are of greater magnitude in Greece, reflecting the fact that the Greek economy was more strongly shielded against foreign competition. Efficiency gains are almost four times those of Italy, and welfare effects are also higher than for the other countries with the exception only of Italy (Table 3.7). These results are consistent with both the predictions of the European Commission,[3] and with the results of Gasiorek et al. (1992). Even though a rigorous comparison is difficult to make because of differences in sectoral disaggregation and country breakdown, their results indeed suggest that the aggregate region of 'Greece and Ireland' will benefit the most from the completion of the internal market.[4]

6 Conclusion

I have estimated the effects of Europe 1992 in a context of a general multicountry, multisector equilibrium model. Europe 1992 has been interpreted as the halting of the individual firm's price discriminating behaviour following the dismantling of non-tariff trade barriers.

The country disaggregation that was adopted has singled out Greece from the rest of the European Community. This has been shown to be of significant consequence since Greece has a particular industrial structure that sets it apart from the rest of the member countries. As shown by the results, Greece's relatively lesser competitive structure in the pre-1992 equilibrium makes this country most likely to benefit from the EU integration effort: according to the model, it would benefit more than most other EU partners, with the exception of Italy.

Notes

1. To the above list, Greece has added export subsidies as an important trade barrier. The sectors that were mostly affected by these barriers were identified to be the steel, aluminium and leather sectors.
2. Using the price vector that existed before the introduction of a specific policy, the equivalent variation measure of utility asks what income change at the current prices would be equivalent to the prices and income that the consumer will face after the policy change.
3. *Social Europe*, p. 180.
4. One may expect that had Greece been aggregated with the rest of the member countries of the EU, that is, with countries with more competitive industrial structure such as Belgium, the results would be of a lesser magnitude. In Mercenier (1995) where the country breakdown scheme includes Greece in the rest-of-the-EU aggregate (RE) aggregate the welfare gains are among the lowest in the EU (0.15 per cent).

References

Bourgignon, F., S. Lolos, A. Suwa-Eisenmann and N. Zonzilos, 'Evaluating the Community Support Framework with an Extended Computable General Equilibrium Model: The Case of Greece (1988–1995)', DELTA, Documents de Travail, No. 9221.

Brander, J. and B. Spencer (1985), 'Tacit Collusion, Free Entry and Welfare', *Journal of Industrial Economics*, **33**, 277–94.

Dixit, A. and J. Stiglitz (1977), 'Monopolistic Competition and Optimal Product Diversity', *American Economic Review*, **67**, 397–408.

Ethier, W.J. (1982), 'National and International Returns to Scale in Modern Theory of International Trade', *American Economic Review*, **72**, 389–414.

Gasiorek, M., A. Smith and A. Venables (1991), 'Completing the Internal Market in the European Community: Factor Demands and Comparative Advantage', in A.J. Venables and L.A. Winters (eds), *European Integration: Trade and Industry*, Cambridge: Cambridge University Press.

Gasiorek, M., A. Smith and A. Venables (1992), '1992: Trade and Welfare, a General Equilibrium Model', *CEPR*, WP 672, London.

Mercenier, J. (1995), 'Can "1992" Reduce Unemployment in Europe? On Welfare and Employment Effects of Europe's Move to a Single Market', *Journal of Policy Modeling*, **17**, 1–37.

Pratten, C. (1988), 'A Survey of the Economies of Scale', *Economic Papers*, **67**, October, European Commission.

Smith, A. and A. Venables (1988), 'Completing the Internal Market in the European Community', *European Economic Review*, **32**, 1501–25.

Srinivasan, T.N. and J. Whalley (1986), 'General Equilibrium Trade Policy Modeling', Cambridge, MA: MIT Press.

4 NAFTA, the EU and agricultural trade

Bala Batavia, Nicholas A. Lash and A.G. Malliaris

1 Introduction

For decades governments have imposed complex sets of interventions that have restricted agricultural trade. Agriculture has traditionally been treated differently from other industries in the General Agreement on Trade and Tariffs (GATT) rules, and the rules have been adjusted to fit the different national programmes. In the early 1950s, the US objected strongly to including agriculture in postwar GATT agreements. This was because political realities required price supports at levels that would have drawn large imports of grain, dairy products and other commodities. Several escape clauses inserted by the US exempted nations from the strictures of GATT against quantitative restrictions to trade, and export and internal subsidies. Therefore, from the very beginning of GATT, agriculture was a special case. Since the 1950s, the US has been increasingly reliant on agricultural export markets and this has led to a turnaround in the US position. By 1962, Europe had set up the Common Agricultural Policy (CAP) which established a system of internal price supports (target prices), variable import levies, and export subsidies without supply control.

The subsequent GATT Rounds (Dillon Round, 1960–62, Kennedy Round, 1963–67, Tokyo Round, 1973–79) did not bring about any progress in the liberalization of agriculture primarily because non-tariff barriers in agriculture were integral parts of domestic policies. The history of agricultural negotiations in the Kennedy and Tokyo Rounds of multilateral negotiations was shaped basically by conflicts between the US and the European Union (EU). The US, as a net agricultural exporter, had a strong interest in trade liberalization. For the EU, the CAP was considered a cornerstone of integration efforts and in this context not negotiable. The GATT approaches, particularly the Kennedy and Tokyo Rounds, have failed to bring about significant changes even after strong statements that progress in agriculture is an essential prerequisite to broader agreements.

By the early 1980s, world trade in agriculture began to fall after nearly two decades of expansion. The share of world trade values accounted for by agricultural products has declined from 32 per cent of trade volume in

1960 to about half that in the early 1990s. The EU, despite its inefficiency, became a significant exporter of subsidized agricultural products in the 1980s, partially at the expense of the US. In response, the US undertook several steps. It retaliated by adopting explicit subsidies for its agricultural exports – the Export Enhancement Program was introduced in 1985 which, along with the EU's subsidies, ultimately resulted in increasingly costly government programmes that drove down world prices. The US, frustrated with the slow pace of agricultural liberalization under GATT, called for the Uruguay Round of the GATT in 1986. In addition, the US started to pursue regional trade agreements with its immediate neighbours, first Canada, in the Canadian–United States Free Trade Agreement (CUSTA) and soon after with both Canada and Mexico in the North American Free Trade Agreement (NAFTA). In this chapter, we wish to investigate the internal agricultural policies of the EU and NAFTA in greater detail and their implications for agricultural trade.

2 Common Agricultural Policy of the EU

The 1957 Treaty of Rome provided the basis for a common market, thus removing trade barriers between member states and establishing a common external tariff. European agriculture posed a problem. Existing national support systems were not compatible with a common market in agricultural products, but continued support to farmers was a political necessity.

During the 1950s, governments of the prospective member states of the EU had increased the degree of government intervention in agriculture in order to support farm incomes. The purpose of these policies was both to prevent prices from being depressed by a rapid rise in output and to enable farm incomes keep pace with other incomes because of the relatively low income elasticity of demand for agricultural products.

Given the desire to bring agriculture within the common market and maintain a degree of government intervention in this sector, the EU created the CAP. The objectives and main features of the CAP were stated in Articles 39 and 40 of the Treaty of Rome. Five objectives were adopted: (i) raising productivity; (ii) ensuring a fair standard of living; (iii) stabilizing markets; (iv) food security; and (v) reasonable prices for customers. Depending upon the product, the CAP would entail common rules on competition and compulsory coordination of the various national market organizations. We shall examine CAP briefly as it evolved historically. The first period extended until 1968, the second period covers the years 1968–80 and the third period starts from 1981 onwards. A further presentation of these issues is in Batavia and Malliaris (1996).

During the first period, a broad set of objectives were decided upon which European agriculture was to be reformed and made competitive but without prejudicing the family character of the farm unit. Common agricultural prices which were to be established progressively and expected to settle slightly above world market prices, were to remunerate farmers adequately without encouraging overproduction.

The final policy emerged and came into force in 1962 after several proposals which were initiated in the conference in Stresa, Italy, in 1958. The three principles of the CAP were: (i) a unified market, implying common prices and free circulation of goods; (ii) union preference which was to protect the unified market from imports and price fluctuations in world markets by subjecting imports to levies that would ensure that their prices exceed Union prices; and (iii) financial solidarity, whereby funding would be transferred from the national to the community level through the European Agricultural Guidance and Guarantee Fund (EAGGF). By 1962, the new CAP began to replace the plethora of support schemes used in the six member states.

The goal of the CAP was to reduce the price variation among the member countries to one of common prices. However, this was not an easy task, with each member being reluctant to implement the application, instead clinging to existing national policies. This resulted in slow progress during the first two years. Therefore the Commission proposed that common price levels should be established for cereals, pigmeat, poultry-meat and eggs for the 1964/65 harvest year. Since there were differences on the price level, the unified prices did not come into force until 1 July 1967. Eventually, the Commission agreed on prices for fruits and vegetables and other major products. However, the high prices agreed for the cereals set the trend for higher price levels for beef and veal, milk and dairy products, sugar, olive oil and oil seeds. The Council went a step further by adopting even higher prices for milk, sugar, olive oil and oil seeds than those proposed by the Commission.

The period 1968–80 saw the beginning of inconsistencies in the CAP. This was a result of the very policies that were designed to promote further European unification. The combination of high and guaranteed prices for unlimited amounts of production, stringent protection against imports and technical progress was bound to lead to overproduction. Common financing ensured that the financial consequences of overproduction were not met directly by the member states responsible for them. The 1960s witnessed the diminishing of the initial political momentum, which in some instances was enough to overcome economic conflicts. This was a period characterized by steady growth in supply which tended to surpass that of demand. It was primarily during this period that the CAP had its significant impact upon world agricultural trade. Put it differently, one may argue that the EU as a regional integration scheme has played an important role in world agricultural trade almost exclusively because of its CAP.

The 1980s were characterized with high CAP costs and therefore with growing realization of the inevitability of change. The EU reached a turning-point in 1982–83 when it became a net exporter of grain. In 1977–78 it had net imports of 18 million tons; in 1988–89 it had net exports of approximately 25 million tons. As a result, export subsidies increased from ECU 1076 million in 1985 to ECU 3518 million in 1988. Agriculture was absorbing more than 60 per cent of the EU budget, with spending doubling between 1980 and 1986. This was largely because of increasing costs for market intervention, storage and surplus disposal.

Intervention becomes expensive as producers unload their output on intervention agencies instead of finding a market. Generous price awards in 1981 and 1982 ensured an upward trend in production, just as world markets became saturated. The EU found itself having to compete for markets for its surplus cereal and other products, against countries that had a more legitimate claim to being exporters from principles of comparative advantage. This surplus production thus contributed to lowering world prices and forcing exporting countries like Canada, the US, Australia and New Zealand into developing domestic policies of agricultural adjustment or attempting to protect their farmers through increased subsidies. This is further evidence of EU's distorting role of world agricultural trade.

Finally the 1990s have been a period when considerable effort has been put towards the CAP reform. The second CAP reform adopted in 1992, supported direct income subsidies to the agricultural producers with policies aimed at production ceiling and favourable treatment to farmers who are able to diversify their overcapacity into non-farm production. Export subsidies will become a less important part of the EU budget under CAP reform, because lower EU prices reduce the gap with world prices and reduce the per-unit export subsidy needed to place surplus EU agricultural commodities on to third markets. Export subsidies have fallen from 30 per cent in 1992 to less than 17 per cent, or ECU 6 billion ($7 billion), in 1994 appropriations. The EU faces two major changes in 1995: implementation of the Uruguay Round and the admission of new members. The main impact of the Uruguay Round will be the limits imposed on the EU's subsidized exports. The target goods are wheat, coarse grains, pork, beef, poultry and cheese. The EU also has to convert all non-tariff barriers, such as variable levies and import quotas, to equivalent tariffs and establish tariff-rate quotas to ensure current and minimum access. Thus for the first time, over a period of almost 40 years, the EU's role as a leader in world agricultural trade is being changed from a negative to a positive one.

3 NAFTA and agricultural trade

This section investigates the world's largest regional trade pact, NAFTA, to analyse the following: the motivations of the three countries to become regional partners, the provisions of NAFTA on agricultural exports and imports, the expected impact of NAFTA upon agricultural trade, and the implications for the three partners and the rest of the world.

3.1 CUSTA

The first major step towards a free-trade area in North America began with CUSTA in 1989. The United States, perhaps because of its frustration with what it perceived as widespread evasion of GATT and its desire for greater integration with Canada and Mexico, two of its largest trading partners, has increasingly emphasized regional trade liberalization in the 1980s. Canada, fearing a growing dependence to its southern neighbour, had more ambivalent feelings towards free trade. None the less, aware of the advantages of penetrating the United States' enormous markets and concerned over protectionist pressures in the US, Canada decided to enter into a free trade agreement.

CUSTA represents the world's largest bilateral trade, amounting to more than US $150 billion on the eve of its birth. For the United States, Canada accounts for almost one-quarter of US exports and almost one-fifth of US imports. Although Canada is the world's second largest country, only 8 per cent of its land is suitable for agricultural production and 3 per cent is available for grazing. In contrast, for the US, the figures are 29 and 20 per cent, respectively. Bilateral trade is significantly more important for Canada than for the US, accounting for almost three-quarters of Canadian exports and two-thirds of Canadian imports. Canada's exports comprises almost 20 per cent of Canadian GNP. Canada sends one-third of her farm exports to the US, primarily feeder cattle, meat products, particularly pork, grain and oilseed products.

CUSTA would eliminate virtually all tariffs between the two countries over a ten-year period starting with 1989. At that time, tariffs on agricultural products levied by Canada against US imports averaged 6.1 per cent while US tariffs on Canadian imports averaged 4.7 per cent. None the less, tariff reduction is restricted by 'snapback provisions' that allow either country to reinstate tariffs on horticultural products whenever it appears that imports have pushed domestic product prices or planted acreage levels below certain levels. Canadian horticultural interests, fearing competition from more efficient US producers, insisted upon the snapback provisions.

Both countries levelled their highest non-tariff barriers on agricultural products, 8.6 per cent in Canada and 10.7 per cent in the US in 1988. These countries support and protect their agricultural sectors through agricultural subsidies, such as quotas, import licences and non-tariff border measures of phytosanitary regulations that include most major crops, livestock and dairy goods.

The issue of export subsidies has been contentious. The US, which competes with subsidized wheat exports from the EU, wanted to maintain its own subsidies. Although the implementation of the Export Enhancement Program in 1985 was targeted at the EU, it has proven injurious to Canada. For example US export subsidies to third countries, such as in North Africa, have hurt Canadian exports. The CUSTA partners have reduced some agricultural protection by prohibiting subsidies for agricultural exports destined for each other. Moreover, health and other regulations were harmonized. The two partners also agreed to harmonize their interpretation of subsidy legislation. Also, CUSTA has arranged for settlement of trade disputes regarding unfair competition to be heard by a joint panel to determine whether national laws have been applied fairly. None the less, CUSTA has left many of the subsidies to be handled by the GATT negotiations because of the importance of EU subsidies of agricultural exports. In summary, while CUSTA is scheduled to eliminate all tariffs by 1999, some non-tariff barriers will remain.

Studies by Karemera and Koo (1994) and Koo et al. (1991) found that US imports of agricultural and industrial goods from Canada were more responsive to import, domestic and world price changes than were Canadian imports. This difference was attributed to the greater amount of substitutes available for US consumers. They also estimated that the trade diversion effects would be modest, amounting to only approximately 15 per cent of total trade expansion. During the first two years following CUSTA, farm exports to each country went up by 30 per cent, even though exports to other countries remained approximately unchanged.

3.2 NAFTA

Soon after CUSTA was established, Canada, Mexico and the US entered into two years of negotiations before signing the NAFTA on 17 December 1992. Although the impact on the US was expected to be far smaller than on Mexico, the US ratification of NAFTA faced vehement opposition. NAFTA supporters included exporters such as US producers of oilseeds, livestock, grains and horticultural products. Agricultural interests opposed to NAFTA were producers of wheat, sugar, peanuts, and winter fruit and vegetables.

A particularly sensitive issue in the US was possible job loss as expressed by the American Federation of Labor-Congress of Industrial Organizations (AFL-CIO) and presidential candidates Pat Buchanan and Ross Perot, the latter with his 'giant sucking sound' criticisms of NAFTA. In response, President Bill Clinton made the case for NAFTA on a job-creating basis, and he discussed withdrawing from it in three years if it led to job loss. President Carlos Salinas even discussed raising the minimum wage so as to counter predictions that cheap Mexican labour would take away US jobs.

Following prolonged debate and narrow US Congressional ratification, NAFTA became operative on 1 January 1994. NAFTA is essentially an improved and expanded version of CUSTA, which centres on liberalizing trade between Mexico and the US. NAFTA represents the largest regional trade pact in the world, encompassing 360 million people and a gross product of approximately $7 trillion. It also marks the first regional trade agreement between advanced and less-developed countries (LDCs).

For the US, NAFTA was a natural extension of CUSTA to Mexico, the fourth largest market for US agricultural exports. Incentives for entering into a free trade pact with Mexico may have included improving its competitive position with a low-cost supplier, slowing the flow of illegal migration, and reinforcing Mexico's democratic institutions and market reforms.

Canada, given the small volume of trade with Mexico of which more than 85 per cent of her agricultural exports already entered Mexico duty free, may have had the least to gain. She may have entered NAFTA to ensure that the Mexican–US deal did not displace Canadian exports to these two countries. NAFTA reinforces and even strengthens CUSTA preferences in the US market and improves Canada's access to the Mexican market.

For Mexico, NAFTA represents a continuation of economic and trade liberalization reforms initiated in 1985. By the early 1990s, Mexico was touted as an LDC role model for its monetary and fiscal discipline, its privatizing of state enterprises and its trade liberalization. During the first half of the twentieth century, Mexican agriculture was one of its most dynamic and prosperous sectors, but pervasive government intervention, coupled with a highly regulated system of land tenure and support mechanisms, restricted its restructure and modernization thereby contributing to rural poverty. This factor, along with growing disillusionment with its policy of protectionism and import substitution, encouraged Mexico to undertake liberalization reforms in the mid-1980s.

Since accession to GATT in 1986, Mexico has significantly lowered tariffs and eliminated import-permit requirements for most agricultural products, but some goods including livestock and dairy products still need import licences. Mexico exports more than three-quarters of her farm goods to the US including fruits and vegetables, fruit juice, coffee, sugar and feeder cattle. Non-tariff barriers are far more significant to Mexico than the US's very low tariffs. For example, quality, health and sanitary standards play an important role in limiting US imports of Mexican horticultural and livestock products.

3.3 Provisions of the agreement

NAFTA maintains CUSTA between Canada and the US while extending a free trade agreement between Mexico and both Canada and the US. Agriculture is the only area where NAFTA does not involve a trilateral agreement between the three partners. Instead, with CUSTA applying to Canadian–US trade, two separate bilateral agreements were negotiated: one between the US and Mexico and the other between Canada and Mexico. This provision reflected Canada's reluctance to enter a more comprehensive agreement. NAFTA's biggest impact will be on Mexican–US trade. The comprehensiveness of the Mexican–US agreement can be credited to Mexico's willingness to remove protections from maize. CUSTA will continue to apply to US–Canada, while Canadian–Mexican trade is expected to remain small. It was agreed that the less comprehensive CUSTA left non-tariff barriers intact for dairy, poultry and other sectors and would remain in effect for bilateral Canadian–US trade. Mexico and Canada negotiated a similar agreement. In addition, NAFTA has retained rigorous health and safety standards on imports.

Within 15 years, all non-agricultural and 94 per cent of agricultural tariffs are scheduled to be eliminated. The US–Canada bilateral tariffs are to be phased out according to the CUSTA schedule by January 1998. Otherwise, NAFTA's tariff removal separates agricultural products into five classes, with tariffs on the most trade sensitive products removed last.

Schedule A immediately eliminated tariffs on 57 per cent of US–Mexican trade. This group includes Mexican tariffs on US exports of livestock, fresh fruits and vegetables and US tariffs on Mexican exports of most livestock, poultry and eggs. Schedule B eliminates tariffs within five years on 6 per cent of US–Mexican trade and includes some US tariffs on fresh fruits. Schedule C, which encompasses 23 per cent of Mexican–US farm trade, eliminates within 10 years Mexican tariffs on US out-of-season soybeans, wheat, rice and selected horticulture products and US tariffs on vegetables and fruits. Schedule C+ covers only one per cent of bilateral trade and is limited to a small number of Mexican exports of fruits and vegetables.

The final group refers to the most trade sensitive farm goods, which account for about 13.5 per cent of bilateral trade. For these products, non-tariff barriers are immediately transformed into tariff rate quotas and phased out over 10 to 15 years. Because of their transparency, tariffs are the easiest to ultimately eliminate. The most important products are US imports of sugar, orange juice and peanuts and Mexican imports of US corn and dry beans.

In addition to the above, a country can impose special safeguards such as tariff quotas during a 10-year transition period for listed products. For the US, the list includes seasonal vegetables and fresh watermelons; for Mexico, swine, certain potatoes and fresh apples; and for Canada, certain vegetables, fresh cut flowers and frozen strawberries. Moreover, NAFTA establishes a tariff snapback to the pre-NAFTA level for up to three years for most products and up to four years for the most sensitive products where imports cause or threaten serious injury. Canadian farmers had snapbacks included in the CUSTA agreement and the US farmers had similar provisions extended to NAFTA. The snapback provision covers about 15 per cent of Mexican exports to the US in products such as tomatoes, onions, eggplants, Chili peppers, squash and watermelons. For Mexico, live swine, pork, apples and potato products, which comprise about 3 per cent of imports from the US, are covered.

While NAFTA makes significant progress in liberalizing trade, protection still remains. For example, NAFTA includes strong 'rules of origin' that are intended to prevent non-NAFTA countries from unfairly benefiting from reduction in trade barriers in a free trade area. These rules allow only products having a substantial amount of Canadian, Mexican or US value added to enter second markets. For example, the US has been concerned over Mexico transhipping orange juice from Brazil and peanuts from Argentina and the Caribbean. The rules of origin would allow the US to apply its tariffs because the products did not originate in Mexico.

Unfortunately, NAFTA does little to eliminate farm subsidies. Despite the objections of Canada and Mexico, the US has retained the ability to retaliate against EU export subsidies to Mexico. Also intact are 'hidden subsidies' by the Canadian Wheat Board and transportation policies. There are two types of farm assistance: domestic supports, which encourage excess production and export subsidies, which push farm products on to world markets at discount prices. The NAFTA parties have committed themselves to prior consultations with each other before providing such assistance to agricultural commodities. Moreover, a Working Group has been established to endeavour to eliminate such subsidies among the three countries. The agreement offers little reduction but defers the issue to the Uruguay Round of GATT.

3.4 Impact of NAFTA on Mexican–US trade

Major differences between the economies of the US and Canada versus Mexico suggest that there may be some major gains from trade. Although the impact on Canada is expected to be modest, many analysts have been bullish about NAFTA's impact on Mexican–US trade. Mexico's growth, rising incomes and population have created a strong market for many US agricultural exports. Since 1986, US exports have been growing at an annual rate of about $42 billion and NAFTA is expected to reinforce this trend.

US producers have a comparative advantage in agriculture in general and in grains and oilseeds in particular as was borne out by the pre-NAFTA pattern of trade where the US exported grains and oilseeds to Mexico while importing horticultural products. NAFTA is expected to improve Mexico's position of being the leading exporter of horticultural products to the US. Mexico has a comparative advantage in producing winter vegetables that are out of season in the US. Moreover, increased US investment in the Mexican food-processing industry could raise imports of canned and frozen fruits and vegetables.

Grennes and Krissoff's (1993) model, which implicitly holds technology and national incomes constant, suggests that NAFTA will increase agricultural exports of both the US and Mexico. US exports are expected to increase most because Mexico has had a higher level of protection. Increased specialization is anticipated with the US exporting more grain (rising by more than 50 per cent), especially corn, oilseed and livestock to Mexico in exchange for more horticultural products and live cattle from Mexico.

Assuming that NAFTA would raise Mexico's growth rate and therefore its demand for income-elastic livestock and poultry exports from the US, the US Department of Agriculture (1992) estimated that NAFTA would have an even greater impact on trade than do Grennes and Krissoff. Davison and Arnade (1991) also estimate that growing incomes in Mexico could significantly increase US exports of corn, wheat and soybeans because of the high income elasticity of demand for these products.

The elimination of Mexican restrictions along with the expected surge in the Mexican standard of living is expected to substantially raise food demand, especially for meat. US grain and oilseed exports could benefit as more grain would be necessary to feed livestock. Mexican consumers should benefit from access to cheaper food as prices of US crops such as corn and other coarse grains are estimated to fall by 30 per cent.

Under NAFTA, the biggest winners may be US feedgrain producers with exports to fuel larger meat and poultry production in Mexico while the US horticultural industry might have minor losses. An increase in Mexican farm imports is likely. Of the partners, some believe that Mexico will be the biggest winner from NAFTA because its economy is smaller and until recently the most protected, and the US is a major factor in its economy. Grennes and Krissoff, among many other analysts, anticipate that NAFTA will not significantly divert trade excepting the market for frozen concentrate orange juice where US consumers would substitute Mexican imports for that of other countries. Moreover, efficiency gains to the NAFTA partners could improve their international competitiveness. Otherwise, however, trade diversion should be minor for a combination of factors. First, NAFTA simply reinforces much of the access that Mexico's importers had to the US market. Second, the expected increase in Mexican incomes should raise its total imports. Third, the NAFTA members appear committed to lowering most favoured nation tariffs, and finally, sectors where the potential for greatest diversion such as agriculture, have been liberalized somewhat by the Uruguay Round of GATT. GATT may have made it easier for NAFTA's partners to accept NAFTA which in turn may ease acceptance for future liberalization under GATT.

Agricultural trade liberalization poses the greatest political and social risks to Mexico. Although it contributes less than 8 per cent of Mexico's GDP, agriculture, especially maize production, was a major obstacle to Mexican acceptance of NAFTA. The Mexican government has a long tradition of safeguarding small farmers. About a third of the population lives in rural areas and a quarter of Mexico's workers are employed in agricultural production. The primary purpose of protection was to raise farm incomes thereby reducing rural unrest and deterring migration into Mexico City and other overcrowded cities. Agricultural products were protected with a combination of tariffs (averaging 5 per cent on US farm exports) and licence requirements. Maize is Mexico's key crop, occupying the largest acreage, and is typically produced by small farmers on rain-fed land. Approximately 30 per cent of the 6 million rural workers are employed in the maize sector and maize protection costs most in terms of fiscal subsidies. There has been a major concern that sharp declines in maize prices would reduce living standards, increase underemployment and cause a significant migration of rural farmers to Mexico's cities and to the US.

Levy and van Wijnbergen (1995) demonstrate that the efficiency gains from unleashing agricultural trade are large for both Mexico and the US, but that freeing up maize will trigger rural–urban migration of 700 000 workers in the first year and eventually will reach 1.9 million cumulatively.

Moreover, the gains of trade may not trickle down to lower-income groups and subsistence farmers. In fact, it is difficult to design compensation schemes to losers from trades without creating the wrong incentives. The authors' model suggests the need to invest more in the rain-fed land used for maize growing. Their results also suggest that the compensation programme would work best if liberalization were gradually implemented as the loss in efficiency would be modest. There may be a lesson here for other countries, especially LDCs, in implementing liberalization policies.

However, de Janvry and Sadoulet (1995) find that the majority of maize producers are not producing for the market and thus will not be directly affected by the drop in maize prices. None the less, there is an important minority at risk who are not diversified and so depend heavily on the price of maize. The authors recommend diversification towards high-value crops and modernization of maize production, but point out the importance of supporting institutions for marketing, credit and technical assistance. NAFTA represents only the latest reforms affecting Mexican farmers. Since the late 1980s, Mexico has undertaken a number of reforms that affected the agricultural sector and maize producers, which included privatization of the land.

In autumn 1993, Mexico initiated a programme of direct payments to cereal and oilseed producers, called Procampo, that was designed to fully replace the existing system of price support for maize, beans, oilseeds and other cereals by 1996. Its goals are to compensate producers for removal of trade barriers while ensuring that domestic markets reflect world prices. The decoupling of direct payments from commodity production may improve resource efficiency. However, what ultimately happens to displaced maize producers also depends heavily upon employment opportunities in the horticultural and non-agricultural sectors and also foreign investment in Mexico.

Coincidentally, on the day NAFTA took effect, the Chiapas uprising of Mexican peasants began. Critics have blamed NAFTA both for sparking the Chiapas uprising and for contributing to the capital flight that caused the Mexican peso crisis. Regardless of the dubious validity of these claims, Mexico's experience helps exemplify the potential political and social disruptions that can accompany free trade agreements.

4 Summary and conclusions

This chapter analyses the developments of agricultural policies in the EU and NAFTA, and their impact on world agricultural markets.

There have been substantial distortions to agricultural incentives across countries and over time (Anderson 1992). In advanced industrial economies, agricultural protection has been growing steadily for decades but it accelerated markedly in the 1980s. The most elaborate schemes of protection have actually occurred in the EU because of the CAP. The EU, in its continued efforts to develop a successful customs union, coordinated agricultural subsidies among its members which resulted in excess supplies. The CAP has been costly to the EU, particularly to the consumers and taxpayers, and involves large transfers to EU farmers. Evidence also shows that the CAP has caused more trade diversion than creation. This differentiated effect for agriculture results from the impact of domestic distortions in addition to trade distortions. This suggests that regional arrangements which do not remove domestic distortions are likely to be trade diverting (McCalla 1992). Also, once the CAP was in place it became hard to change because of vested interests and capitalization of Community preference benefits into land values and quota rents. Temporary efforts to stabilize domestic prices are likely to lead to outright protection.

In the 1980s, the US introduced an explicit system of export subsidies to regain its share of the market. These subsidies involved high government outlays and also imposed considerable losses on other countries heavily dependent on agricultural exports. The US then pursued regional trade agreements with Canada and Mexico. In promoting agricultural trade, NAFTA provided bilateral agreements for Canada and the US and also for Canada and Mexico, while maintaining the CUSTA arrangements between Canada and the US. NAFTA concentrates on the issues of market access for internal trade, avoiding conflicts with domestic policies. Tariff and non-tariff barriers are to be phased out over the next 15 years, leading to a relatively free internal market for agricultural products.

As a regional trade agreement, NAFTA is of particular interest because it creates a partnership between two wealthy nations and an LDC with all the strains, and potentially explosive issues of employment, rural poverty, social interest and dependence. Because it is estimated to create trade with little trade diversion, in the long run, NAFTA is a major move for trade liberalization. In the short and intermediate run, however, the record is far less positive. There was little reform of US and Canadian agricultural support programmes during the lengthy transition periods, and the quantitative impediments to dairy, poultry and some other products under CUSTA remained intact, as did the Canadian and US wheat subsidization programmes. Moreover, US sugar remained protected from Mexican competition. Thus, while NAFTA moves towards the ultimate objectives of GATT, a lengthy period of protection remains.

The Uruguay Round of GATT was completed in 1993 and was a modest success in the area of agriculture. The agreements called for reductions in domestic market supports and export subsidization. This should reduce the distortions in world markets and increase export opportunities for more efficient producers. The Uruguay Round's true significance is not in terms of its effect on price changes in world markets, but in laying the foundation for future liberalization. The tariffication will make market access more secure and facilitate future negotiations on trade liberalization.

References

Anderson, Kym (1992), 'Analytical Issues in the Uruguay Round Negotiations on Agriculture', *European Economic Review*, **36**, 519–26.

Batavia, B. and A.G. Malliaris (1996), 'The Common Agricultural Policy of the EU and Developing Countries', in Paraskevopoulos et al., Ch. 16, pp. 193–205.

Davison, Cecil W. and Carlos A. Arnade (1991), 'Export Demand for U.S. Corn, Soybeans, and Wheat',' US Department of Agriculture Economic Research Service, Technical Bulletin No. 1784.

de Janvry, Alain and Elisabeth Sadoulet (1995), 'NAFTA and Mexico's Maize Producers', *World Development*, **22** (8), 1349–62.

Goldin, Knudsen and Van der Mensbrugghe (1993), *Trade Liberalization: Global Economic Implications*, Paris–Washington: OECD–World Bank.

Grennes, Thomas and Barry Krissoff (1993), 'Agricultural Trade in a North American Free Trade Agreement', *World Economy*, **16** (4), July, 483–502.

Hathaway, D. (1987), *Agriculture and the GATT: Rewriting the Rules*, Washington, DC: Institute for International Economics.

Hufbauer, Gary Clyde and Jeffrey J. Schott (1993), *NAFTA: An Assessment*, Washington, DC: Institute for International Economics, February.

Karemera, David and Won W. Koo (1994), 'Trade Creation and Diversion Effects of the U.S.–Canadian Free Trade Agreement', *Contemporary Economic Policy*, **XII**, January, 12–23.

Koo, Won W., Ihn Ho Uhm and Joel T. Golz (1991), 'Bilateral Trade Relationship between the United States and Canada: Implications of the Free Trade Agreement', *Contemporary Policy Issues*, **IX**, 56–69.

Levy, Santiago and Sweder van Wijnbergen (1995), 'Transition Problems in Economic Reform: Agriculture in the North American Free Trade Agreement', *American Economic Review*, September, 738–54.

McCalla, Alex F. (1992), 'GATT, Preferential/Regional Trading Blocs and Agricultural Trade', *Review of International Economics*, **1** (1), 73–89.

McCalla, Alex F. (1993), 'Agricultural Trade Liberalization: The Ever-Elusive Grail', *American Journal of Agricultural Economics*, **75**, December, 1102–12.

OECD (1995), *Agricultural Policies, Markets and Trade in OECD Countries*, Paris: OECD.

Orden, David (1994), 'Agricultural Interest Groups and the North American Free Trade Agreement', National Bureau of Economic Research, Inc., Working Paper No. 4790, July.

Paraskevopoulos, C.C., R. Grinspun and T. Georgakopoulos (1996), *Economic Integration and Public Policy in the European Union*, Cheltenham, UK and Brookfield, US: Edward Elgar.

United States Department of Agriculture (1992), *Agriculture in a North American Free Trade Agreement: Analysis of Liberalizing Trade Between the United States and Mexico*, Washington, DC, July.

5 The state of the welfare state in the EU, anno 1992*

Jozef Pacolet and Katia Versieck

1 Introduction and methodology

The year 1992 was significant in the European integration process; important steps had to be taken in the direction of completing the establishment of the 'internal market'. Efforts towards this goal, however, were causing growing concern about the creation of a 'Social Europe', which in several respects was developing at a slower pace. The realization of European monetary union (EMU) and the convergence criteria of Maastricht were putting new constraints upon the national social protection systems.

An analysis of internationally comparative figures in the field of social protection was prepared. In addition, research institutes from the EU member states were asked to describe in which direction(s) the social protection systems were evolving and how the evolution of these systems was being influenced by economic, demographic and political forces. The aim of the research project was to study initiatives influencing the level and structure of social expenditures and the ongoing political discussion of the previous issues.

The scope of the research was to discover in which direction(s) the social protection systems were evolving and how was the evolution of the

* The European Centre for Workers' questions (Europäisches Zentrum für Arbeitnehmerfragen, EZA) commissioned the Higher Institute of Labour Studies (Hoger Instituut voor de Arbeid, HIVA) of the Catholic University of Leuven (Katholieke Universiteit Leuven, Belgium) to set up a network of research institutes for the purpose of studying to what extent the creation of a 'Social Europe' is succeeding (or failing), within the context of the European research project 'The State of the Welfare State anno 1992'. We thank EZA, and especially Mr J. Herudek and the EU for the research possibilities. The focus of the project, originally on the 12 EU member states in 1992, has been extended to include the three new members of the EU. Austria, Sweden and Finland have contributed to the project on a voluntary basis on a colloquium on 'The State of the Welfare State anno 1992', March 1995. The following researchers all contributed to the project: J. Pacolet, K. Versieck, K. De Brabander (Belgium), V. Talpale (Finland), E.B. Hansen (Denmark), M. Kemperman (The Netherlands), G. Schaber (Luxembourg), T. Nicolosl, A.-M. Guillemard (France), E. Paliginis (United Kingdom), E. O'Shea (Ireland), Ch. Wilk (Germany), R. Keckeis (Austria), F. Belletti (Italy), X. Rambla (Spain), A. Mateus (Portugal), J. Yfantopoulos (Greece) and J. Edling (Sweden). The results of this project are published in three volumes (see Pacolet and Versieck 1997a, 1997b and 1997c).

systems influenced by economic forces and economic reasoning. A wide definition of social protection is used to describe the trends, although special attention is given to health-care and pension schemes.[1] Since trends of privatization were one of the research questions, even wider definitions of alternative (occupational, private) solutions for those risks should be considered. Other aspects of social protection schemes for labour (labour conditions, working time, and so on) should also be included since they can all be confronted with the same reasoning of for instance less regulation, less state. The 'welfare state' refers to this complete set of (social) protection schemes, including other categories of public spending such as education.

All areas of social protection or welfare have implications for the spending and distribution of national income. In several public discussions, the cost impact and the negative impact of welfare expenditures on competitiveness of an economy are underscored. The project wanted to have a critical analysis of this reasoning about conflict between social policy and economic growth, illustrated by the 'public choices' made in the political debate on the welfare state.

In particular, the increased competition and industrial change expected from the creation or completion of the internal market in 1992 in Europe, and the convergence criteria (the so-called Maastricht norms) of the path towards a European monetary union created the fear in social movements of increased social dumping and substantial cutbacks in the welfare state programmes.

Since then, new studies, even those presented within the official fora of the Presidency of the EU, or documents prepared by the European Commission, have supported the *convivialité* of a strategy of growth towards high levels of social protection, instead of the common wisdom claiming the opposite.[2]

This is in line with what emerges from the description of the political–economic debate in 15 member states of the EU, presented hereafter: a welfare state at the beginning of the 1990s which was alive and well, in reality not so much (until 1992) disturbed by the discourse on monetary union and the internal market, but much more by a critical reflection on some basic principles of the internal organization of social protection schemes. Those problems of competition versus public provision, selectivity versus universal systems, funded or pay-as-you-go schemes, decentralization or centralization, privatization or not, earnings and growth of national income related moral hazard aspects were emphasized more than the impact of the creation of the internal market and EMU. What the future trend of social protection will be is not clear; it gave the impression of 'alive and well', but it could have gone either way. The above-mentioned recent initiatives (1997), however, also point in the direction of maintaining those systems.

On the basis of the contributions of the different countries, the main trends in the European social security and welfare systems are identified and the development of the European welfare states up to the present time and into the near future are summarized. Not only are national trends discussed, but also the influences of European integration, the conditionalities of EMU and the pressure of European objectives on national choices.

National experts were asked to document the facts and ongoing political debate/discourse on the level and structure of social protection, and especially how this was influenced by the debate on the completion of the internal market (the Europe 1992 project) and the preparation of EMU.[3]

In the next pages, the most important trends and policy issues dominating the European welfare states are summarized. The summary illustrates which issues are predominantly discussed in which countries. The topics discussed are grouped around four major themes:

1. the direction in which the social protection systems are evolving: further expansion and diversification, and differentiation (no essential changes) or contraction;
2. the situation of the beneficiary and the provider of certain forms of protection;
3. topics related to the organization of the social protection systems;
4. topics related to the macro-economic context.

Each country's social security system seems to develop in a distinctive way and therefore, at European level, opposite trends can be observed (centralization versus decentralization, further expansion versus contraction).

2 The direction in which the social protection systems are evolving

2.1 Expansion

Even in mature welfare states new forms of protection are being defined and created. Some of these new forms of protection might be wide-ranging and substantial. This is the case with the 'long-term care' insurance. That expansion in reality is illustrated by the figures on the real growth rate of social protection expenditures between 1982 and 1992 (about 40 per cent increase in the EU member states).

2.2 Contraction

The list of examples of EU member states where contraction occurs is however, longer, pointing to the fact that contraction is more widespread: control of supply and demand of services, cost control, tightening of eligibility rules, reduction of benefits, more means-testing of benefits, abolition of income-related supplements to flat-rate benefits and so on. A potential reduction of the protection is also present in issues such as selectivity and the failure to keep pace with the real standard of living of the nation.

In general, the 1980s were characterized by a further expansion of social security systems. New rights and even new subsystems were developed; new groups becoming eligible for existing systems of protection. Most of the European member states, however, now face budgetary problems. The social protection systems suffer in the first place from cyclical problems: deterioration of the labour market situation has led to both an increase in expenditures (high unemployment) and a narrowing of the income base (total wage mass). Expenditures on social protection are influenced by economic crisis. The systems are also confronted with structural problems such as the ageing of the population, leading to increasing demand for health and social care and putting pressure on the pay-as-you-go pension system. These and other conditions (for example, changes in family structures) have put pressure on the European welfare states. It is mentioned frequently that the social protection systems have been designed for different social structures and under different conditions (such as full employment). The economic problem of high unemployment has frequently been responded to by introducing early retirement systems, leading to a lowering of the average age of retirement, but this solution only enhances the problems experienced in the pension system.

It is remarkable that even with budgetary constraints, further expansions of some subsystems are feasible. Sometimes, however, there are important cutbacks. It is not clear whether the systems have become so highly developed and robust that the level of social protection as it is felt by the population changes only slowly. Changes in the UK emerged gradually, but they occurred and are now manifested in a lower level of care and (a suspicion of) lower quality of care.

Fear for increased dualization has now become present even in highly developed systems, where the incidence of poverty is low. Is this a confirmation of an inefficient system or of changes and cutbacks? Are cutbacks so large that even when the systems are designed for the poor, they make the poor even poorer and risk the creation of new poverty and exclusion? In Denmark this is already a point of concern, and Denmark is a country with a low poverty rate.

Let us look at the mature welfare states of the Scandinavian countries. The Nordic countries do not give a uniform picture. From Finland the image of a sustainable and effective welfare state is still projected. But even Finland mentions some dualization, along the gender line, after *decennia op* emancipation strategies. In Sweden, after probably two decades of a highly developed welfare state, we find a system in trouble because it is confronted which such huge adverse performance. Denmark is confronted with the dual labour market. There is acquiescence and acceptance of the new reasoning that the welfare state was constructed at a moment when its use was underestimated, and now has to be reorganized to stimulate responsibility, active job search and the ethos that 'benefits must be earned'.

This brings us to changes in the expected performance standards of the welfare systems *vis-à-vis* the individual and the society in general.

2.3 Announcement of reform

In many countries, although no substantial increase or decrease can be observed, the concerns about the efficiency and effectiveness of social protection, the affordability and the impact on economic performance, persuaded policymakers to announce fundamental reforms of social protection, sometimes called 'plans of modernization'.[4] In terms of this comparative study, the breadth and depth of this reform is not always clear, but it could be a precursor of substantial change in the coming years.

3 Performance of the welfare systems

The performance of the social protection schemes usually means the ability to meet the objective of safeguarding the standard of living of those confronted with the contingencies of life and, in narrower terms, to reduce and avoid poverty. In the first sense, universal protection is linked to previous earned income and the safeguarding of replacement income (and in-kind support in order to be in line with the general evolution of income and economic growth. In the latter sense we enter the rationality of basic provisions, approaching social assistance. Effectiveness is sometimes also taken together with increased attention to selectivity and control of misuse.

3.1 Poverty and social exclusion, income inequality

The final aim of various aspects of social security in several countries is discussed. Is the system specifically meant to combat poverty by providing a good minimum protection and selectivity, or is it a collective insurance system with a close relationship between premiums and benefits, between earnings and benefits?

It seems that many systems are criticized for being ineffective in combating poverty and exclusion. The Irish system is said to have failed in combating poverty and income inequality. In Denmark the welfare system has survived up to now but it has not prevented the community from being split into the haves and have-nots, into rich and poor people. Income and wealth inequality have also been increasing in the UK since 1979 and even though pensioners' income increased rapidly in the period 1979–92, the distribution among pensioners is unequal.

In several countries the attention shifts towards performance in the battle against poverty. In Belgium, for instance, it became the priority of the new government in 1994; whereas in France attention was paid early to the issues of social exclusion and the fight against poverty.

3.2 Selectivity and targeting

More targeting and selectivity are introduced in family policies (poor families and single parents). In Ireland, family benefits are used as an instrument to combat poverty. In Belgium, poverty is now put on top of the political priority list. The focus on social exclusion and poverty creates some preference for selectivity, that is, benefits are directed to the needy groups. Because of financial problems, several countries mention targeting and conditionalities. Home-help resources (such as in Denmark) are an example of a service for the total population that has been targeted to those most in need and to the most vital activities (personal care). In traditional parts of social security (work injury in Sweden, unemployment in Spain) elements of selectivity are introduced. New systems of social protection, such as long-term care insurance in Germany, are designed to properly assess the need for care.

3.3 Indexing benefits according to prices or standard of living

Other important issues proposed in the 1980s, such as individualization and relation with real income, are being discussed. Some of those issues might change the nature of social protection: selectivity, minimal protection (both important to combat poverty), increased personal responsibility and private topping up of cash benefits are proposed.

Most of the benefits are indexed to the evolution of prices. But in many systems there is no guarantee that benefits are linked to the standard of living. This is especially important for future social risks such as pension schemes and health expenditures. In many countries (for example, the United Kingdom, Spain, Germany, Belgium and the Netherlands) the linkage of benefits and the standard of living is no longer guaranteed, so that replacement ratios are declining and approaching basic benefits. In the Netherlands, the debate had already started in 1983 that this link was not sustainable. In Belgium the conclusion was reached that financial equilibrium of the system cannot be guaranteed when there is a close link to the evolution of general income. In the UK, unemployment benefits became taxable and their real value decreased as a consequence of the erosion of flat-rate benefits. Earning-related supplements to benefits were abolished. In other countries, new links with previous earnings are introduced in benefit schemes.

Elements such as indexing according to the real standard of living make social protection more of an insurance policy, guaranteeing a return related to previous income or a constant replacement ratio. For such approaches there is less support and interest than before (compare the discussion on the Netherlands and Belgium), illustrating the potential for serious change in the character of the system. Is the system to be allowed to degrade to a minimum one? In Austria, under the current pension system the present standard of living is still ensured through the relationship with pre-retirement earned income, but employers have demanded that the pension should be reduced to a basic income. It should be left to the individual if he/she chooses to purchase retirement insurance at his/her own cost. In Germany, there is still a strong preference for the previous income-related pension.

Eligibility to insurance-related benefits has become tighter and values reduced. In the UK, the unemployment benefit will be replaced by the job seeker's allowance, paid for a shorter period of time. More people will be forced into means-tested benefits.

3.4 Improper use and control

Some countries report that a kind of mistrust of the policymakers has come to the surface. In many countries increased attention is paid to the issue of 'social fraud'. In the Netherlands, the debate existed for more than a decade; in Belgium the battle against 'social fraud' was mentioned in the plan for modernization of social security (1996) and in 1996 the UK government launched a programme to stimulate informers on fraud ('beat-a-cheat'). Not only have benefit earners or users taken advantage of social protection, but in many countries the providers themselves are targeted for better control, namely in health care (for example, France, Belgium). The control can range from control of prescription behaviour to complete control of supply. Also employers (the sickness insurance in the Netherlands) are identified as potential misusers of the social protection schemes. The mistrust is partly related to improper use or misuse of social protection, but there is also criticism of the discouraging nature of unemployment benefits, that is, the disincentive nature of social benefit schemes themselves. This goes hand in hand with inactive income market policy, and 'activating' unemployment benefits by combining them with work subsidies. The new ideology is from 'welfare' to 'workfare'. 'Benefits must be earned' is mentioned even in countries (such as Denmark) where more universal and generous benefit schemes (in terms of replacement ratio) existed previously. In Germany, for instance, work 'duty' is also introduced for those benefiting from minimum income. This activating policy is also becoming the answer to the macroeconomic problem of massive unemployment. In the Netherlands, as in Denmark, the strategy of stimulating independence is explicitly mentioned. In Denmark, unemployment rules are tightened to restrict the choice between work and unemployment.

4 Organizational changes

Devolution and decentralization are traceable in the member states to different degrees. Sometimes both are present in different forms. They have a strong theoretical–ideological basis in the principle of 'subsidiarity', encouraging responsibilities to be assigned to the level where they are taken most efficiently (scale) and most effectively (in accordance with individual preferences). In a certain way, these responsibilities may be situated in the market (privatization) or in the hands of the individual (stimulating individual responsibility).

4.1 Sectoral devolution

The opinion is gaining ground that the public pensions (funded by the pay-as-you-go system) should be kept to a minimum and can be topped up by occupational and individually funded pensions (capitalization system). This might lead to higher intersectoral and personal income inequality.

In several countries (such as Italy and Greece) there is a tendency to harmonize and unify the fragmented systems of protection in the area of health care. In Belgium as well, it is mentioned that sectoral funds are sometimes important and this hinders the financing and solidarity and responsibility in the universal system.

The conclusion is that there is certainly not a univocal trend towards sectoral devolution and that if decentralization occurs it is not without problems. On the contrary, sometimes a movement towards centralization is taking place.

4.2 Regional devolution

The same opposing trend can be observed where regional (d)evolution is concerned. In some member states, increasing attention is paid to regional responsibilities in social protection. However richer and poorer regions have (temporary?) opposing interests. This seems to be the case in Italy,

Spain and Belgium. In several other (less thriving) countries, huge regional differences occur, for example, between cities and rural regions. In several Scandinavian countries and the UK, where local responsibility is high, there is a tendency towards centralization in funding and control. In Germany the newly installed long-term care insurance means a centralized solution for the coverage of home care and the cost of old-age homes. These have more and more become the responsibility of (local) social assistance. These trends of centralization are essential for compensating the inequalities between regions. At the same time, in many countries steps forward and backward can be observed on the issue of regional devolution, indicating perhaps that several technical solutions or a combined responsibility (local provision and central funding?) are possible. It also demonstrates that a growing sector is still looking for organizational equilibrium.

Regional differences, however, remain a problem and may be caused by technical (how can the coverage of certain services existing in cities be guaranteed in rural regions?) and/or economic factors. For Ireland, large differences in terms of provision of several services (especially health and elderly care and education and training) between rural and urban regions are reported, creating a vicious circle of depopulation, poverty and a further lowering of the level of provision.

4.3 Privatization and competition

A major shift towards more privatization has not occurred. In countries where there is much discussion on privatization, the realization is only limited. There is, however, an important distinction between privatization in the provision of services and the privatization of the financing of social protection. There seems to be only one important achievement in the direction of privatizing the financing of social protection: the growing acceptance of occupational and individually funded pension systems. Except for a growing co-insurance of the individual (which usually remains marginal), the financing of and control over the provision of health care remain public. There are, however, attempts to introduce more privatization and competition in the provision of health care in Beveridge-orientated systems. In the UK, quasi-markets and contracting-out have been introduced to increase efficiency. In Denmark, the idea of market orientation in health care gained ground in the 1980s. Citizens were given the possibility of choosing among a wider range of services and institutions. All in all, however, widespread privatization of large parts of social services remains limited.

It is remarkable that relatively little attention is paid to efficiency in the contributions of the member states. One explicit example mentioned was the public sector in southern parts of Italy, which has poor standards of efficiency. Improvement of the efficiency of the existing systems of service provision (technical efficiency) is not expected, at least it is not mentioned. This is surprising since 'value for money' might be a good answer to the problem of increasing needs and budgetary constraints. More is expected from reforms of the present systems of service provisions. The introduction of quasi-markets in the Beveridge-orientated welfare systems and increased competition is expected to lead to more efficiency. In Denmark and the UK, it is hoped that the reforms in the provision of hospital care will lead to shorter waiting lists. In Bismarck-orientated systems, such as Belgium and France, more is expected from control of the labour supply and avoidance of overconsumption, than from progress in new knowledge and technology (of physicians, for instance).

5 Macroeconomic context

5.1 Employment and economic growth

There has been a crisis in macroeconomic performance, especially where the relationship between growth and employment is concerned (mentioned by both Belgium and France). In those countries, it is pointed out that 'full employment' is no longer realizable. In Belgium that period had already ended in the early 1970s. In Sweden it continued to exist until the early 1990s, even combined with a very high level of labour market participation. In many countries, unemployment continues to exist, even after periods of higher growth rates.

Now, active labour market policies focused on integration, concern about labour costs and about budget objectives are predominantly present. Discussions, however, differ from sector to sector. Active labour market policies are mentioned by many countries (for example, Belgium, Germany, the Netherlands and Luxembourg) as a remedy for unemployment.

The burden placed on wages for the financing of social protection is criticized and said to have a negative influence on employment. Efforts have been made to reduce this burden by changing the financing structure. It is the case that in many countries the lowering of employers' social security contributions can encourage employment. Another alternative is reducing social expenditures. Cost control in the health sector and increased occupational pensions and private savings can cope with demographic pressure without increasing public spending. In many countries the emergence of a 'dual' labour market is signalled, especially in countries where it was previously avoided (for example, Denmark and Finland).

5.2 Discussion of the welfare state, the completion of the internal market and the realization of EMU

The main objective of the research 'The State of the Welfare State Anno 1992' was to identify the transformation process of the 'welfare states' of the EU; the public discourse about it; the impact of the completion of the internal market; and the creation of monetary union. Less than the expected reference is made to those two changes. The public discourse is much more concentrated on the internal mechanisms of social protection. Perhaps there is no direct need to expect many influences. Social protection remains, to a large extent, a decision on how to spend the national income, and on redistribution, within the subsidiarity of the national state.

Discussions in the member states do not seem to be influenced to a large degree by the completion of the internal market and the realization of EMU. In several countries, even without the convergence criteria of Maastricht, the constraints of public finances would urge restrictive policies. In many countries, the budgetary constraints, the labour market situation and the demographic pressure led to similar policy choices, with or without European convergence criteria. This does not seem to be different for the new members of the EU. Certainly there are no common driving forces and it is not the EU agenda that determines the discussion on social insurance. Does this mean that the fear that EMU and the completion of the internal market are not compatible with social protection, was unfounded? The discussion in the 1980s and until 1992 was perhaps not yet adapted to the new EU momentum. Perhaps the EU momentum might spread a common wisdom on how social protection should be organized in the next decades. Future discussion will be on whether the older principles are still valuable or whether a new system with new characteristics should emerge.

5.3 Attention to economic aspects and financing of social security

There is no general and drastic reduction in social protection. On the contrary, there is convergence at a higher level. In several countries the direct link with public financing, however, is determining choices. Increased competition will also strengthen the attention for the competitiveness of each country and thus for social protection.

6 Conclusions

Until 1992, there are no clear indications in the 15 member states of the EU that the present systems of the welfare state are not sustainable. At least their principles are still valuable. However, it is often said that social protection systems were designed for different social structures and under different conditions (such as full employment). This has led to fears about maintaining the same level of social protection in the future. The European welfare systems are under pressure because of cyclical and structural problems such as the ageing of the population. The fear has grown for dual systems and that the policy options might change the nature of social protection systems. The trend towards selectivity, targeting, means-testing and personal responsibility is apparent.

There is no consensus about whether we can adhere to the same principles and the reality of plans to change the system drastically. The huge amount of often underestimated labour reserve in unemployment and underemployment (as opposed to lack of qualifications) needs a structural answer (where reduction of working time and redistribution of labour is important to free the rest of the system of the demographic pressure and without acknowledging that unemployment is not to a large extent a consequence of demographic factors). There is also the question of changes to the retirement age (it is an issue of heated debate in Italy, and in Belgium there has been a strike for an earlier pension at age 55 instead of 57). This illustrates that we expect either changes in those characteristics of the labour market that determine social expenditures, or changes in the system itself. The choice has not been made definitively.

Certain facts illustrate at this moment the robustness of the status quo. In most of the EU member states and at European level, there is a continued political will and convincing arguments showing the viability of those systems. The threat does not (or need not) come from European integration. It comes from doubts among many whether social protection and social security can continue to be organized along the same principles as when they were first established. The answer for the moment is that they can. The picture we obtained from '15 fair faces of the welfare states' of the EU in the beginning of the 1990s, and reflecting the trends and emerging changes of the 1980s, showed their own momentum of (self)-critical reflection, transformation and modernization. The systems were presented as robust and viable, little influenced by further European unification. The implications of those processes are perhaps too new, and in a starting phase. How convergence criteria of Maastricht can act as an alibi for the national policymakers, even if there is no mechanic impact on the development and criteria of social security, is one way in which the impact can be larger then expected. The way in which competition rules the EU can clear the way for private providers in pension and health-care schemes; competing public systems is another way.[5]

We probably observed those impacts at the onset of the process. The intention was to use this 'portrait' as a benchmark for the year 1992 and to repeat the exercise five years later, to assess the real impact of the internal market and the start of EMU coming closer and closer. It remains an interesting next research step.

Notes

1. In the European debate and statistics, the following elements of social protection are included: sickness, invalidity, occupational accidents and diseases, old age, survivors, maternity, family, unemployment, placement and vocational guidance, housing and so on.
2. See, for instance, European Commission (1997): Beck et al. (eds) (1997); Dutch Ministry of Social Affairs and Employment (1997).
3. The papers were written mostly by academics, but even so they reflect only the opinions of the authors. The summary of issues presented here is a selection made by us of already selective views. The papers were mostly submitted around the beginning of 1995, so they contained the opinion and debate up to that time, concerning trends up to 1992 and the ongoing discussion on the deepening of the EU.
4. See also the title of the recent Communication from the Commission, 1997: 'Modernising and Improving Social Protection in the European Union'.
5. Pacolet (1997).

References

Beck, W., L. van der Maesen and A. Walker (eds) (1997), *The Social Quality of Europe*, The Hague: Kluwer Law International.

Dutch Ministry of Social Affairs and Employment (1997), *Dutch Presidency Conference on 'Social Policy and Economic Performance'*, Amsterdam.

European Commission (1997), 'Modernising and Improving Social Protection in the European Union', Communication from the Commission, Brussels: European Commission.

Pacolet, J. (ed.) (1996), *Social Protection and the European Economic and Monetary Union*, Aldershot: Avebury.

Pacolet, J. (1997), 'Conclusions of the Rapporteur', in A. Bosso and M. Hutsebaut (eds), *Social Protection in Europe. Facing up to Changes and Challenges*, Brussels: European Trade Union Institute, pp. 371–8.

Pacolet, J., R. Bouten, H. Lanoye and K. Versieck (1997), *The State of the Debate on Social Protection for Depending in Old Age in the 15 EU Member States and Norway*, Leuven: HIVA.

Pacolet, J., E. Gos and E. O'Shea (1993), *EMU, Social Protection, Social Charter and Regional Social Cohesion*, Leuven: HIVA.

Pacolet, J. and K. Versieck (eds) (1997a), *The State of the Welfare State Anno 1992. Volume 1: Comparative Report*, Leuven: HIVA.

Pacolet, J. and K. Versieck (eds) (1997b), *The State of the Welfare State Anno 1992. Volume 2: Report on the Member States, EU12 B, D, DK, E, F, G, I*, Leuven: HIVA.

Pacolet, J. and K. Versieck (eds) (1997c), *The State of the Welfare State Anno 1992. Volume 3: Report on the Member States, EU12 IRL, L, NL, P, UK; EU15 A, FIN, SWE*, Leuven: HIVA.

Pacolet, J., K. Versieck and R. Bouten (1994), *Social Protection for Dependency in Old Age*, Leuven: HIVA.

6 Economic integration and regional economic convergence in NAFTA and the EU

Elias G. Carayannis, Rajiv Mallick and George K. Zestos

1 Introduction

This chapter focuses on the varying experiences of the three North American members of NAFTA (the US, Canada and Mexico) with respect to sectors of spatial convergence (divergence) and then looks at convergence patterns in terms of per capita gross domestic product (GDP), unemployment rates and wages at the national level among the nation members of the European Union. Differences in the 'convergence experiences' of the three NAFTA countries are documented (based on synthesized evidence), and illustrated by drawing on tenets of economic theory, such as the impact of mobility of factors of production, the role of transportation and communications infrastructure, the significance of natural resources and amenities and their impact on industries such as agriculture and hotels/tourism.

Economic convergence across geographical subdivisions has been treated in the context of both open and closed economy analysis. Open economy analysis has focused on intra-national convergence, that is, the growth experience of individual states or subdivisions of specific countries (Amos 1989 and 1991; Barro and Sala-i-Martin 1991; Carayannis and Mallick 1996; Mallick 1993; Mallick and Carayannis 1994). Closed economy analyses have estimated the rate at which relatively poor countries have converged towards more affluent countries (Baumol 1986; De Long 1988).

As shown by Smith (1975) and McCombie (1988), factor mobility is expected to diminish regional differences. Yet, empirical studies have shown that long-term rates of intra-national convergence have been weaker than would have been anticipated on the basis of economic theory (Barro and Sala-i-Martin 1991).

2 The US experience

In the US, state per capita incomes have converged since the beginning of this century. Only briefly in the 1920s and, more recently, in the 1980s, was this process reversed as per capita incomes of richer states grew faster than those of the poorer states. Yet the speed of convergence has been extremely slow compared to that predicted by conventional theory.

Convergence of per capita incomes across US states has not been as rapid as would be expected in an open economy with near-perfect mobility of capital and labour. Barro and Sala-i-Martin (1992) point out that if capital were to account for about 30 per cent of the nation's assets, convergence should have occurred at the rate of about 12 per cent per year, rather than the 2 per cent rate actually observed. Once the notion of capital is broadened to include not only physical but also human capital, its share is about 70 per cent and a lower convergence rate is more easily explained. However, wage convergence has been too anaemic to explain in terms of a human capital bias in migration, as pointed out above. It is suggested here that one must, at minimum, also examine labour market influences such as the rapid growth in low-wage labour markets in the South in order to fully understand the reasons for the relatively slow pace of convergence in state incomes (see Table 6.1).

The model used to estimate convergence in wage rates is as shown in (6.1) (Mallick 1993). Growth in per capita income is a function of growth in each of its components and growth in wage rates is related to growth in employment rates:

$$(1/T)\log(w_{it}/w_{i,t-T}) = a'_w - [\log(w_{i,t-T})](1 - e^{-B'_wT})(1/T) + c^*[(1/T)\log(e_{it}/e_{i,t-T})] \quad (6.1)$$

where $w = (W/E)$ and $e = (E/P)$ (W is wages, E is employment and P is population) and the coefficient 'c' in (6.1) estimates the employment elasticity of wage growth.

In the 1960s, employment rate (ER) growth had a negative effect on wage rate growth and per capita income growth, as in the 1950s and over the 1951–89 period. The adjusted wage convergence coefficient is marginally greater (2 per cent) than when ER growth is not controlled for (1.6 per cent). Also, per capita incomes would have converged faster had there been no across-state differences in ER growth during the 1960s. Instead of converging at 2.4 per cent during this period, per capita incomes would have converged at 3.4 per cent during the 1960s.

Results for the 1970s are intriguing at first sight. ER growth has no significant effect on wage growth, but a positive effect on per capita income growth, contrary to results for the full period and both the 1950s and 1960s. In the 1970s, while female ERs continued to grow and male ERs continued to decline, the increase in female ERs was no longer dominated by women with low levels of schooling (US Department of Commerce). Adjusting for ER growth, per capita incomes converged slightly slower and wage rates marginally faster than the unadjusted estimates suggested. But unlike previous periods, there was no dramatic impact of ER growth on convergence tendencies during the 1970s; this reinforces the conclusion that the skill levels of new entrants were no longer a wage-depressing influence in the poorer states. In addition, the 1970s were characterized by two major influences: (i) the energy crises of the early and late 1970s, and (ii) net out-migration from the states of the Northeast and North-Central regions to the Sun-Belt states.

Results for the 1980s show that there was no convergence, but rather a divergence, in wages, adjusting for ER growth. Further, employment growth was positively associated with both wage rate growth and income growth. This is consistent with the gradual increase in actual female work experience, as well as a skilled-labour demand bias in employment growth in the 1980s. What characterizes the non-convergence of the 1980s is greater defence spending in the relatively affluent Northeast as well as the decline in energy prices (Coughlin and Mandelbaum 1989, 1988), contributing to faster growth in the high-income, industrialized states relative to the low-income, energy-producing states, in particular.

3 The Canadian experience

Unlike the US experience, Canada has been characterized by consistent, albeit gradual, economic convergence, including during the 1980s (see Table 6.2). No leading sectors of regional importance emerge, but based on available data, federal programmes of regional equalization may be at least partly responsible for continued regional convergence in Canada.

Canada provides an interesting case study of trends in regional economic disparities for an additional reason as well. Canada is unique in that regional economic equalization has been recognized as an explicit federal policy goal. In the US, by contrast, regional equalization is recognized as a social objective only to the degree that the federal contribution to states for Medicaid is based on per capita income for the state. The same is true of federal contributions to localities for development programmes.

We may summarize our major findings and implications as follows:

1. There is virtually no convergence in the 'primary' or 'natural resource-based' industries – agriculture and forestry, fishing, and mining. Indeed, regional inequality increased in these industries, especially in the 1970s and early 1980s before declining somewhat in the late 1980s and early 1990s. The non-convergence of per capita income

Table 6.1 Income per capita, employment rates, wage rates and growth of each by state, 1951–1989

State	Income per capita	Growth in PCI	Employ-ment rate (ER)	Growth in ER	Wage rate	Growth in wage
1. Alaska	2 724	18.28	*	*	*	*
3. Arkansas	945	33.27	16.78	3.19	3 556	14.32
5. California	2 041	23.06	31.60	0.97	5 010	15.02
7. Connecticut	2 139	27.73	40.86	0.70	4 145	19.09
9. Florida	1 366	31.37	25.49	1.65	4 007	14.48
11. Hawaii	1 577	28.21	*	*	*	*
13. Idaho	1 481	21.72	23.54	1.40	4 032	13.90
15. Indiana	1 691	21.92	33.03	0.90	4 081	14.03
17. Kentucky	1 136	29.19	20.36	2.34	3 953	13.85
19. Massachusetts	1 800	29.78	39.08	0.90	3 770	19.33
21. Maine	1 308	30.08	29.67	1.30	3 384	17.43
23. Minnesota	1 563	27.11	27.74	1.92	3 940	15.40
25. Mississippi	840	34.08	15.43	3.35	3 411	14.65
27. North Carolina	1 176	31.37	23.96	2.50	3 526	15.75
29. Nebraska	1 622	22.42	25.60	1.89	3 851	13.72
31. New Jersey	1 974	29.06	35.32	0.92	4 414	17.00
33. Nevada	2 178	20.65	34.86	1.32	4 761	12.38
35. Ohio	1 808	21.20	36.64	0.54	4 147	14.41
37. Oregon	1 805	20.57	29.69	1.17	4 696	11.98
39. Rhode Island	1 698	25.20	39.30	0.47	3 715	16.49
41. South Dakota	1 483	21.66	18.56	2.84	3 773	12.32
43. Texas	1 460	25.66	25.93	1.45	4 239	14.98
45. Virginia	1 392	33.15	25.32	2.25	4 232	15.16
47. Washington	1 847	22.51	30.31	1.11	4 705	13.38
49. West Virginia	1 166	25.22	27.09	0.58	3 711	14.81

Note: * 1951 data for Alaska and Hawaii for ER and wage rate not available.

Source: Adapted from Mallick (1993).

within these sectors is consistent with our expectations since, by definition, these industries are relatively immobile across space; therefore, regional differentials are not expected to narrow over time in the absence of diversification of the resource-based economies.

Table 6.1 (continued)

State	Income per capita	Growth in PCI	Employment rate (ER)	Growth in ER	Wage rate	Growth in wage
2. Alabama	1 029	32.19	21.67	2.10	3 634	15.40
4. Arizona	1 255	23.39	23.01	2.04	4 596	12.59
6. Colorado	1 773	23.42	29.97	1.29	4 169	15.49
8. Delaware	2 145	20.04	39.07	0.82	4 157	15.93
10. Georgia	1 188	32.93	24.70	2.24	3 639	16.67
12. Iowa	1 619	22.54	24.10	1.98	3 909	13.47
14. Illinois	2 002	22.11	37.69	0.49	4 295	16.19
16. Kansas	1 580	24.85	26.25	1.61	4 128	13.86
18. Louisiana	1 188	25.98	24.17	1.19	3 650	16.00
20. Maryland	1 776	28.49	31.47	1.21	4 279	15.64
22. Michigan	1 857	22.09	34.87	0.56	4 482	15.04
24. Missouri	1 534	25.31	31.44	1.12	3 738	16.19
26. Montana	1 784	18.12	25.04	1.16	4 317	11.81
28. North Dakota	1 432	22.30	18.19	3.07	3 881	12.33
30. New Hampshire	1 490	33.16	33.46	1.13	3 370	19.47
32. New Mexico	1 325	23.47	22.46	1.68	4 241	12.61
34. New York	1 978	25.40	38.65	0.50	4 329	18.10
36. Oklahoma	1 267	26.77	22.82	1.53	4 031	14.47
38. Pennsylvania	1 689	24.27	36.70	0.43	3 880	16.54
40. South Carolina	1 100	29.99	23.34	2.18	3 518	15.25
42. Tennessee	1 105	32.35	23.90	2.20	3 524	16.17
44. Utah	1 510	20.16	29.37	1.00	3 974	13.38
46. Vermont	1 322	29.97	26.41	1.97	3 646	15.52
48. Wisconsin	1 710	22.68	31.15	1.25	4 151	13.11
50. Wyoming	1 927	17.16	28.48	1.12	4 342	12.56

2. There is some convergence in manufacturing gross domestic product per capita (GDPC), as evidenced by a consistent decline in the regional inequality index for goods-producing industries. This evidence is consistent with an earlier finding that in the 1961–75 period, the Atlantic states witnessed highest rates of productivity growth in manufacturing activity (Denny and May 1981). Evidence of convergence in manufacturing output per capita is in concordance with our expectations since manufacturing is a basic (national) industry,

Table 6.2 Regional economic convergence in Canada: a cross-classification table

1961–1992 (Sample period)	Below average 1961 GDPC	Above average 1961 GDPC
Below average GDPC growth	Downward divergent Manitoba	Downward convergent Ontario, British Columbia
Above average GDPC growth	Upward convergent Newfoundland Prince Edward Island, Nova Scotia, New Brunswick, Quebec, Saskatchewan	Upward divergent Alberta

1961–1971	Below average 1961 GDPC	Above average 1961 GDPC
1960s below average GDPC growth	Downward divergent Manitoba	Downward convergent Ontario, Alberta, British Columbia
1960s above average GDPC growth	Upward convergent Newfoundland, Prince Edward Island, Nova Scotia, New Brunswick, Quebec, Saskatchewan	Upward divergent

1971–1981	Below average 1971 GDPC	Above average 1971 GDPC
1970s below average GDPC growth	Downward divergent Nova Scotia, New Brunswick, Quebec, Manitoba	Downward convergent Alberta, Ontario
1970s above average GDPC growth	Upward convergent Newfoundland, Prince Edward Island, Saskatchewan	Upward divergent British Columbia

Table 6.2 (continued)

1981–1992	Below average 1981 GDPC	Above average 1981 GDPC
1980s below average GDPC growth	Downward divergent	Downward convergent Saskatchewan, Alberta, British Columbia
1980s above average GDPC growth	Upward convergent Newfoundland, Prince Edward Island, Nova Scotia, New Brunswick, Quebec, Manitoba	Upward divergent Ontario

Source: Adapted from Carayannis and Mallick (1996).

which is responsive to interregional wage differentials (Bartik 1991; Wasylenko and McGuire 1985); accordingly, mobility of manufacturing capital should ensure that regional wage differentials narrow over time. Further, if manufacturing activity has attained the status of a mature industry in most industrially advanced nations, then one should expect manufacturing to be in the phase of reversal of regional polarization.

3. Unlike the US experience, Canadian provinces seem to have converged throughout – including the 1980s – especially in the 'new leading industries' such as finance, transportation and communications, and wholesale trade which, by contrast, were the engine for US regional economic divergence (repolarization) in the 1980s (Amos 1991). It is interesting to note, therefore, that earlier studies had found that, even by the late 1970s, there existed significant provincial differences in the rate of adoption of new technology (Martin et al. 1979; Economic Council of Canada 1977) as well as in capital per worker (Auer 1979), with the Atlantic provinces consistently lagging behind the rest of the country. If so, the observed convergence of the leading sectors of the economy may reflect growing regional diffusion of technology in Canada. However, it may also be due to growing public investments and we return to this issue below.

4 The Mexican experience

As late-comers to the technological innovations of the late twentieth century, and with growing global interdependence, less-developed countries (LDCs) are more subject to frequent technological shocks. The technological shocks imply regionally concentrated investment spurts in the traditional growth poles, perhaps furthering regional inequality. Moreover, the relative underdevelopment of transport and communication infrastructure in LDCs could hinder factor mobility. Further, in an *export* economy, mobility incentives may be distorted by the need for *export* industries to locate in border states.

There is also a second set of reasons that dictates differences across industries in rates of regional equalization. Empirical evidence indicates that industries differ in terms of mobility. Industries that serve a *national* market, such as manufacturing, have been found to be more mobile than *local* industries such as services (Testa 1989; Gyourko 1987; Wasylenko and McGuire 1985). Industries that are based on natural resource endowments, such as agriculture and mining, or fixed locational amenities, such as tourism, should also be less mobile than manufacturing. It would be interesting to see if these findings are replicated in Mexico, given the predominance of *maquiladora* manufacturing.

Convergence in a national economy implies that:

$$d(g_Y)/d(Y^0) < 0, \tag{6.2}$$

namely, that the derivative of gross state product (GSP), or g_Y, over the original GSP per capita, or Y^O, is negative, that is, states with low (high) original GSP per capita (Y hereafter) grow faster (slower); this is estimated by the following log-transformation:[1]

$$(1/T)^* \log(Y^F/Y^O) = a_0 + a_1^* \log(Y^O), \tag{6.3}$$

where O is the original and F the final year, T is the duration over which convergence is estimated, and a_1 is the log-linear convergence coefficient which is expected to be negative for convergence (Mallick and Carayannis 1994).

Similarly, we estimate rates of *within-industry* convergence from:

$$(1/T)^* \log(Y_i^F/Y_i^O) = a_{0,i} + a_{1,i}^* \log(Y_i^O), \tag{6.4}$$

where i = agriculture and mining, manufacturing, hotels and transportation, and other industries (ibid).

The absence of any statistically significant regional convergence in agriculture and mining product per capita is consistent with our prior expectations. As these activities are based on permanent or semi-permanent natural resource endowments, regional reallocation of resources is less likely to occur over time. Consequently, interregional differentials in factor returns will persist. We find that, adjusting for growth in border states, per capita manufacturing output did not converge any faster (see Table 6.3). The absence of convergence in manufacturing is, it seems, not due to locational advantages of Mexican border states.

The relatively strong convergence in hotels and transportation-related activity is striking, especially for the 1980s. The data does not allow us to separate convergence in hotels/tourism from convergence in transportation activity, so that we can offer only somewhat tentative explanations. One conjecture, already made, is that part of the measured convergence in hotels and transportation may reflect growth of transportation-related

Table 6.3 Topology of five top Mexican states by predominant industrial activity

1970s	
Predominantly agriculture	Tabasco, Chiapas, Zacatecas, Nayarit, Oaxaca
Predominantly manufacturing	Mexico, Nuevo Leon, Queretaro, Tlaxcala, Puebla
Predominantly hotels and transportation	Aguascalientes, Guerrero, Temaulipas, Baja California, Norte, Distrito Federal
Other	Quintana Roo, Colima, Distrito Federal, Baja California Norte, Guerrero
1980s	
Predominantly agriculture	Tabasco, Chiapas, Zacatecas, Campeche, Durango
Predominantly manufacturing	Nuevo Leon, Queretaro, Hidalgo, Coahuila, Jalima
Predominantly hotels and transportation	Quintana Roo, Distrito Federal, Geurrero, Jalima, Aguascalientes
Other	Guerrero, Zacatecas, Mexico, Tamaulipas, Yucatan

Note: Predominant industrial activity is defined as being ranked among the top five states in terms of the GSP share of each particular industry.

Source: Adapted from Mallick and Carayannis (1994).

infrastructure in the relatively less-developed regions. As noted earlier, the US experience suggests that transportation-related growth and convergence historically precedes overall economic convergence (Nordhaus and Baily 1991).

Part of the convergence in hotels and transportation in Mexico, may be attributed to the hotel industry. Recent studies have shown that in an economy, the regional hotel industry depends on the growth of tourism (Jeffrey and Hubbard 1988). Since tourism has traditionally been driven by regional climate and/or natural beauty, one is less likely to observe a strong regional economic convergence in this industry. However, one may speculate that if tourists' preferences change over time, then one may conceivably observe the tourism industry of the traditionally non-tourist states growing rapidly.

5 The European Union countries' experience

In 1957 with the Treaty of Rome, six European countries formed a customs union and a common market, the European Economic Community (EEC). By 1995, the number of member countries increased to 15 and the EEC is now called European Union (EU) indicating a higher level of integration. The EU introduced many programmes to facilitate and accelerate the integration process. The most important among these programmes are: the single market, or Europe 1992, as it is widely known, and the Maastricht Treaty (1991). The latter provides for the formation of an economic and monetary union and the adoption of a common currency by 1 January 1999.

To evaluate the relative success or failure of the EU programmes to bring about harmonious development and balanced growth, we examine three economic variables to study whether there is evidence towards economic convergence among the EU countries. The three variables are: real gross domestic per capita product, the unemployment rate and real manufacturing wage rate. Historical data for the three variables mentioned above are presented utilizing a simple diagrammatic analysis.

5.1 Real gross domestic per capita

In Figure 6.1, the real gross domestic product per capita in 1990 US dollars, purchasing power parity (PPP), is presented in groups of three or four countries. Careful examination of Figure 6.1 reveals that there was no tendency for convergence in the real per capita GDP of the member countries. In Figure 6.1, the real per capita GDP of each country can also be compared with the average EU per capita GDP which appears as a shaded area. The latter was constructed as a weighted average, the weights were assigned according to the size of each country's GDP in relation to the entire EU GDP. The same conclusion is reached by examining the coefficient of variation (CV) of the real per capita GDPs. The CV does not decline with time and this is evidence of non-convergence in the real per capita GDPs.

5.2 Unemployment rate

The next macroeconomic variable is the unemployment rate for the entire economy of each EU country. Examining the unemployment rate for the period 1960–95, we observe one characteristic common to all countries, which is the relatively low rate of unemployment for all countries for the first ten years (1960–70) of our sample. In the early 1970s, the unemployment rate began rising for all of the 15 EU countries. This can be seen in Figure 6.2, where the time plots of all EU countries are presented in groups of four or three countries in conjunction with the EU average, which is indicated by the shaded area.

To show whether convergence or divergence occurred in the unemployment rate in the EU, the coefficient of variation is calculated and presented graphically for the same period (1960–95). The coefficient of variation is calculated for four different groups of EU countries, the same groups as for the coefficient of variation of the real per capita (GDP). An interesting characteristic is that all four graphs of the coefficient of variation follow the same pattern. The pattern indicates a decline until the early 1980s, a small increase during the late 1980s and decline thereafter. This must be interpreted as a convergence in the unemployment rate of the EU countries. An explanation for this is that the ongoing European integration for the past 39 years and the opening of these countries to trade led the EU economies to similar cyclical fluctuations.

Real wage rate

Lastly we compare the manufacturing real wage rates of all the EU countries, which are presented graphically in groups of three or four in Figure 6.3, and are expressed in 1990 US dollars utilizing PPP exchange rates for private consumption expenditures. By examining the data carefully, a few observations can be made. The real manufacturing wage rate for every country is increasing during the period 1975–95. This constitutes evidence that the standards of living are rising in the EU countries during the last two decades. In Figure 6.4, the coefficient of variation of the real manufacturing wages indicates that there is no convergence. It is interesting to note that while the coefficient of variation first declined, implying a tendency for convergence, this did not last for long, since in the early 1980s it started rising.

6 Conclusions

In the US, while per capita incomes of states have converged in the last forty years, as has recently been documented (Barro and Sala-i-Martin 1991), the evidence on wage rate convergence is mixed, at best. Wage rates converged in the 1960s and marginally in the 1970s, but not in the 1950s or 1980s.[2] However, employment rates did converge strongly across states and largely accounted for the observed income convergence.

Canada was characterized by continued regional convergence in the 1980s, and in sectors such as transportation and communications, finance,

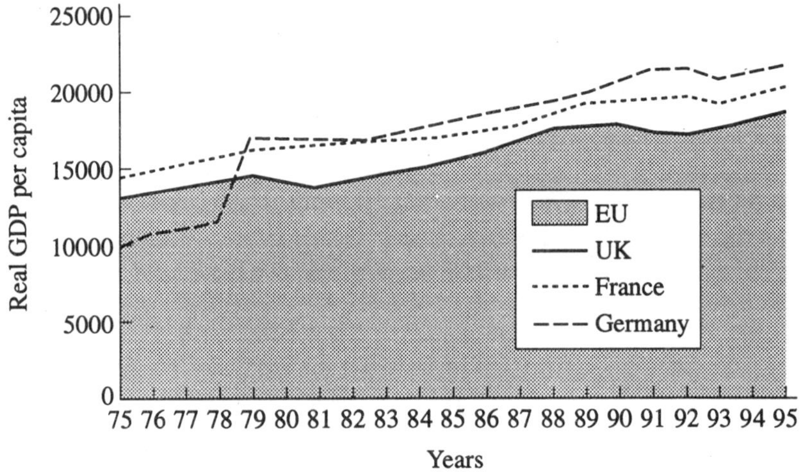

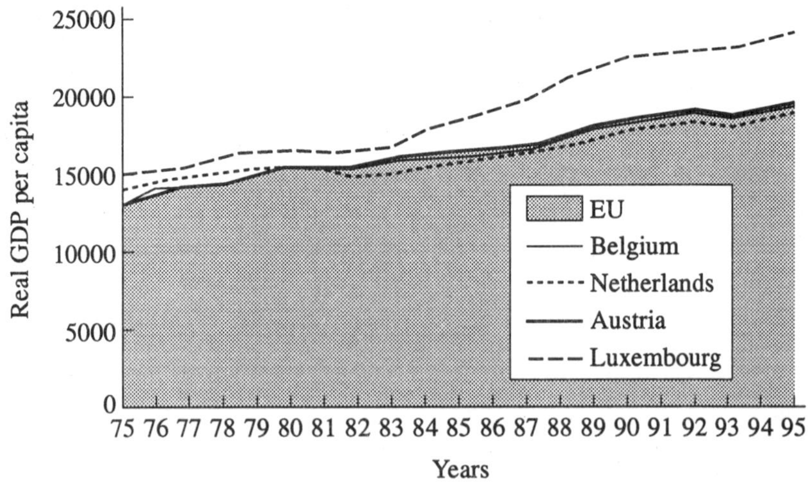

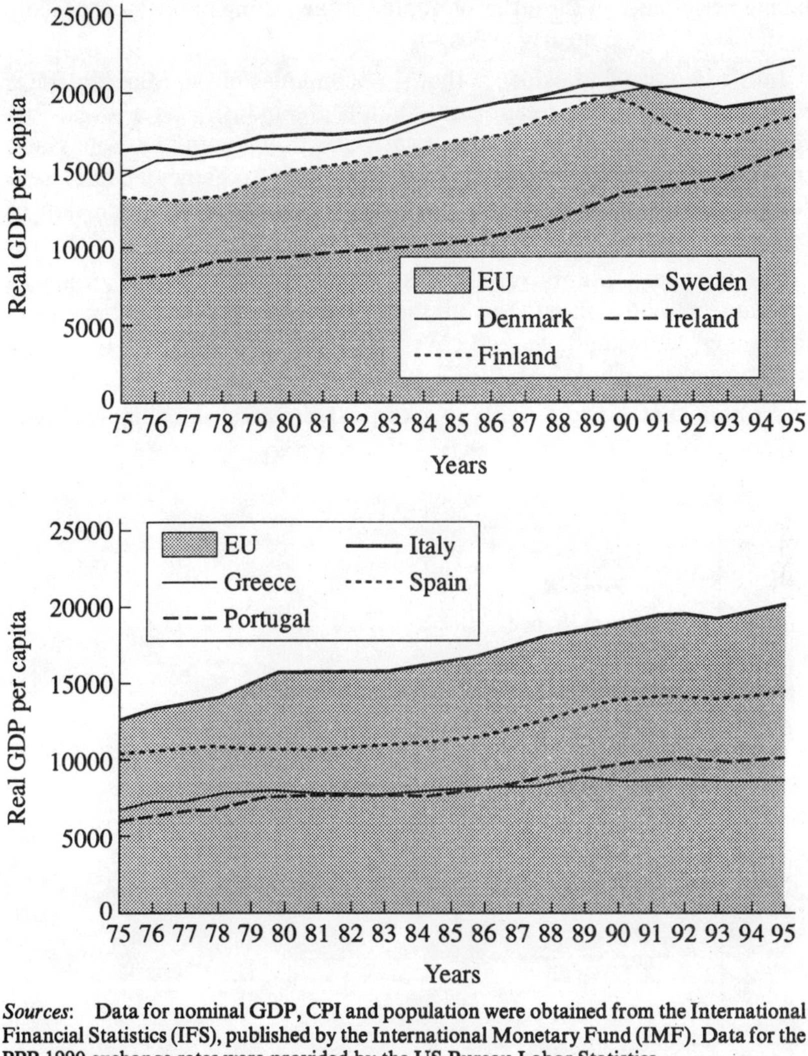

Sources: Data for nominal GDP, CPI and population were obtained from the International Financial Statistics (IFS), published by the International Monetary Fund (IMF). Data for the PPP 1990 exchange rates were provided by the US Bureau Labor Statistics.

Figure 6.1 Real gross domestic product per capita, 15 European Union countries

and wholesale trade, which were the engines of regional repolarization in the US during the 1980s. The continued regional convergence in Canada was led by the strong economic performance of the Atlantic provinces and Quebec during the last decade, despite the adverse impact on the former of falling prices and on the latter of quotas in the fishing industry, especially in the late 1980s and early 1990s.

In Mexico, we find evidence that the economies of the Mexican states have converged in the recent past. Data at the industry level reveal that regional convergence in Mexico has been strongest in the hotels and transportation sector. We believe this may reflect changing preferences towards less traditional tourist regions, as well as greater dispersion of transportation-related activity.

The European Union countries have converged only within groups as the data presented show. The southern European economies have been increasingly slowing down and have impeded any convergence to appear for Europe as a whole.

We hope that this study will provoke greater interest in regional analysis

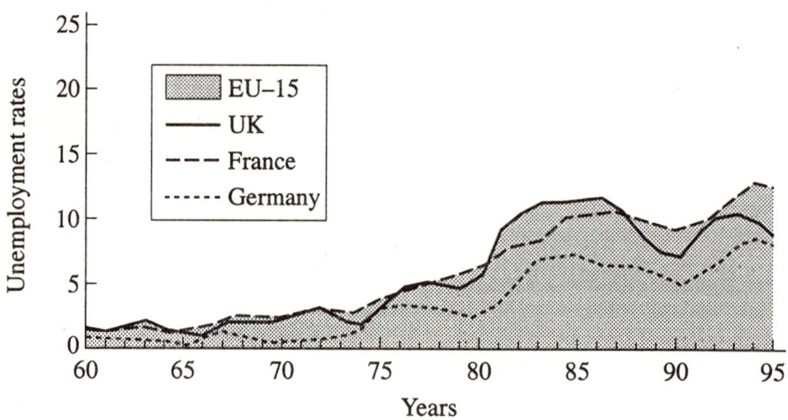

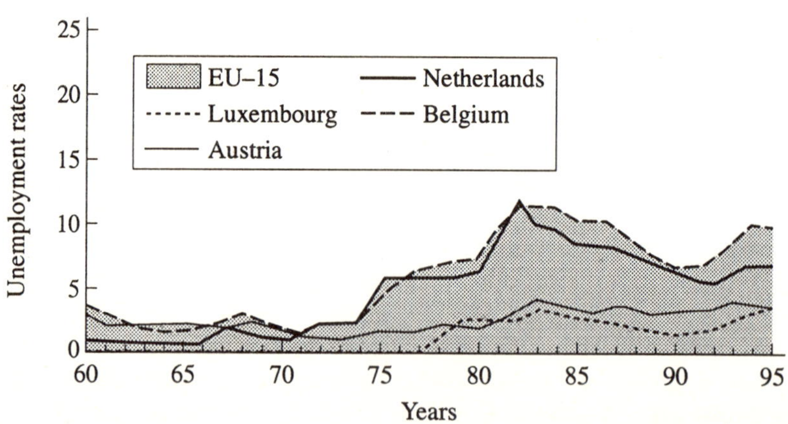

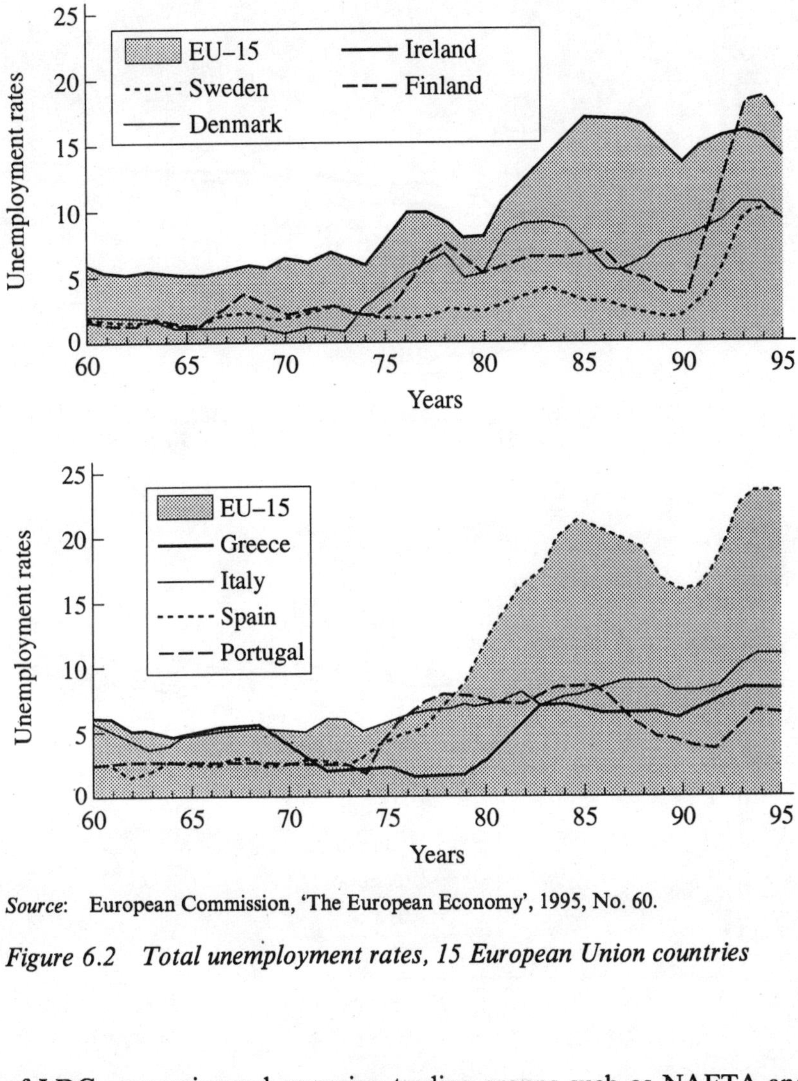

Source: European Commission, 'The European Economy', 1995, No. 60.

Figure 6.2 Total unemployment rates, 15 European Union countries

of LDC economies and emerging trading groups such as NAFTA and the European Union which are in the process of regional dispersion of infrastructural developments in sectors such as transport and communications. Further studies should explore whether countries converge regionally in infrastructure-related activities – which facilitate mobility – before they converge in manufacturing activity, whose mobility is presumably enhanced by well-developed transportation and communication networks.

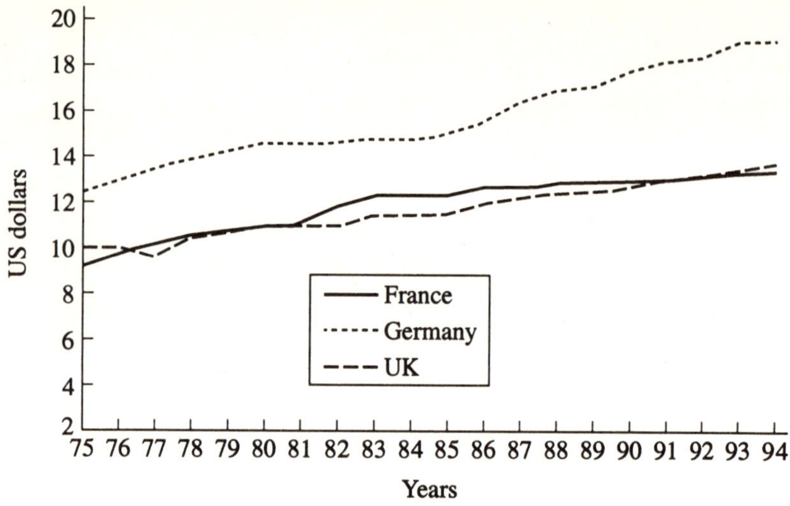
20
18
16
14
12
10
8
6
4
2
US dollars
France
Germany
UK
75 76 77 78 79 80 81 82 83 84 85 86 87 88 89 90 91 92 93 94
Years

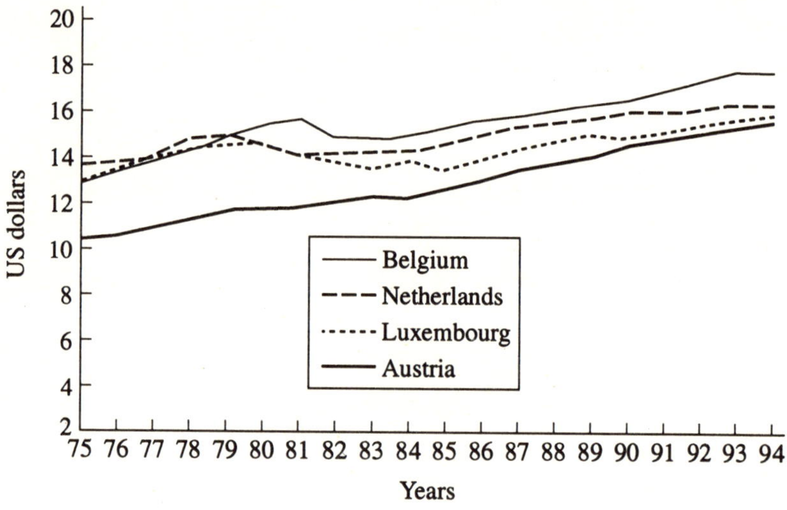
20
18
16
14
12
10
8
6
4
2
US dollars
Belgium
Netherlands
Luxembourg
Austria
75 76 77 78 79 80 81 82 83 84 85 86 87 88 89 90 91 92 93 94
Years

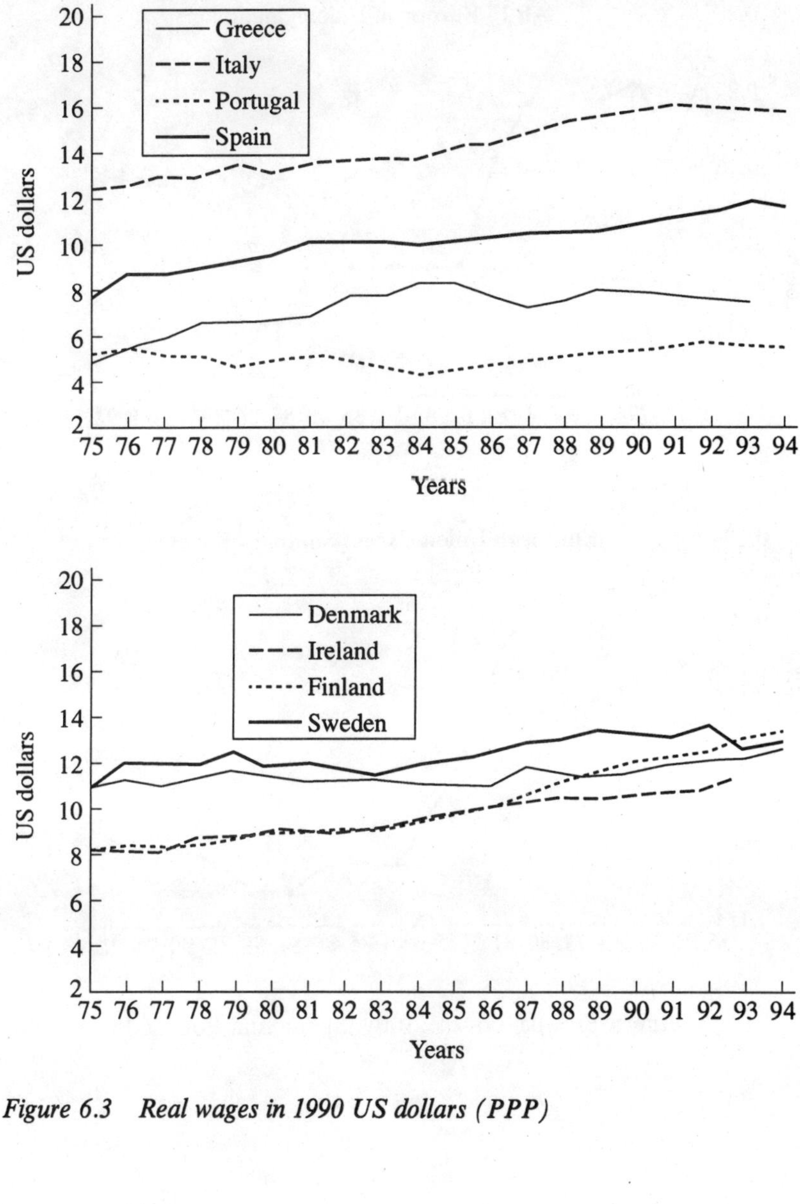

Figure 6.3 Real wages in 1990 US dollars (PPP)

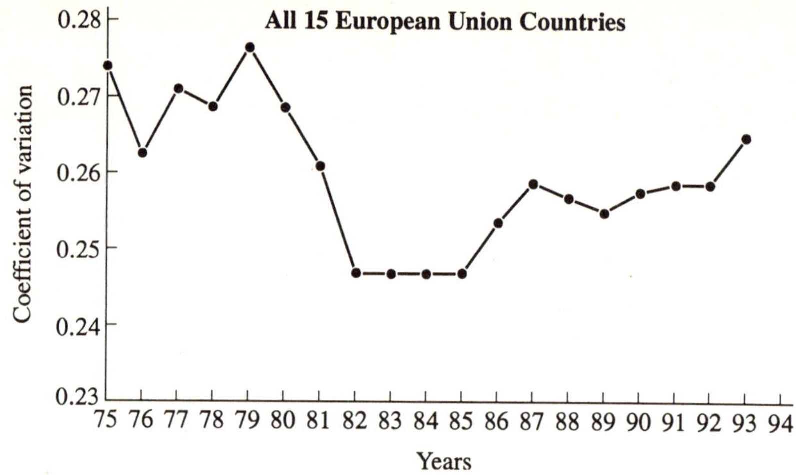

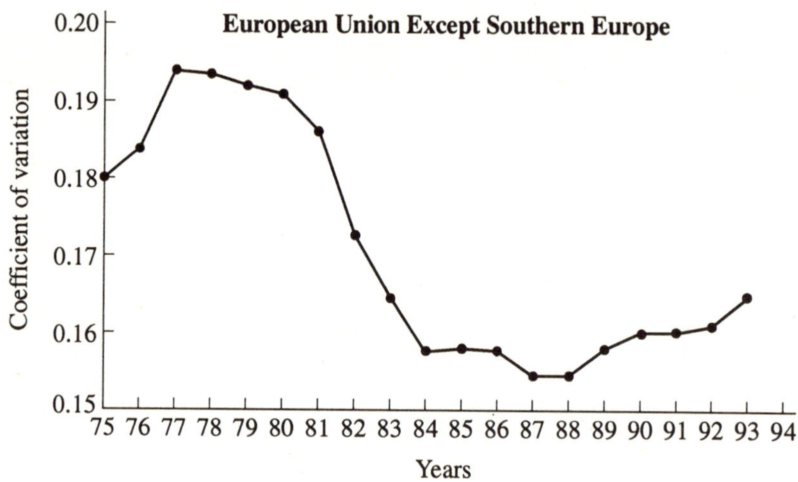

Southern Europe: Greece, Italy, Spain, and Portugal

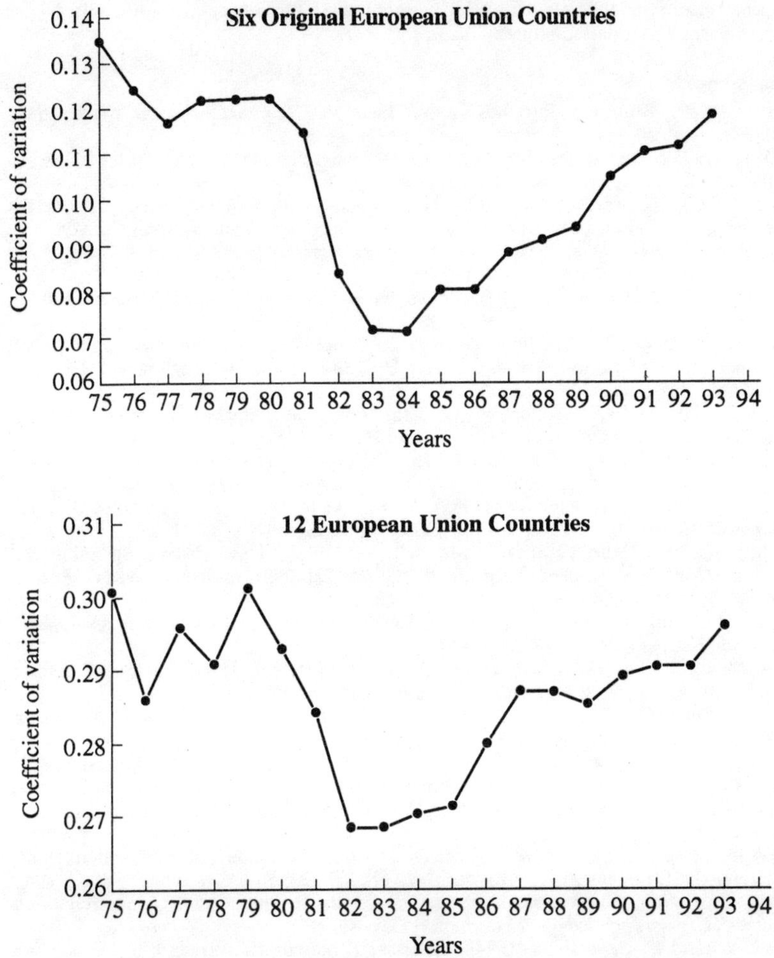

Figure 6.4 Coefficient of variation, real hourly compensation costs of manufacturing workers, 1990 US dollars (PPP)

Notes

1. Since the log-transformation is positive monotonic, a negative coefficient a_1 still indicates convergence.
2. Indeed, the *Wall Street Journal* (23 December 1996) recently reported that lifetime wages like annual wages may be becoming unequal as well, making the rich richer and the poor poorer: 'Rapid technological change is bringing increasing rewards to skill and education, and trade and immigration may also play a part'. Individual workers' total inflation-adjusted earnings in the 1970s were compared with those in the 1980s and it was found that low-wage earners 'are worse off over the long term, not only relative to those at the top, but also compared to similarly situated workers in previous decades'. During the 1980s, a worker in the 10th percentile suffered a 17.6 per cent drop in inflation-adjusted

income compared to the 1970s, while a worker in the 90th percentile experienced a 4.7 per cent increase in inflation-adjusted income.

References

Amos, O. (1989), 'An Inquiry into the Causes of Increasing Regional Income Inequality in the United States', *Review of Regional Studies*, **19** (2), 1–13.

Amos, O. (1991), 'Divergence of Per Capita Real Gross State Product by Sector – 1963 to 1986', *Review of Regional Studies*, **21**, 221–34.

Auer, L. (1979), *Regional Disparities of Productivity and Growth in Canada*, Study prepared for the Economic Council of Canada, Ottawa: Minister of Supply and Services Canada.

Barro, R. and X. Sala-i-Martin (1991), 'Convergence Across States and Regions', *Brookings Papers on Economic Activity*, No. 1, 107–82.

Barro, R. and X. Sala-i-Martin (1992), 'Convergence', *Journal of Political Economy*, **100** (2), 223–51.

Bartik, T.J. (1991), *Who Benefits From State and Local Economic Development Policies?*, Appendix 2.4, Kalamazoo, Michigan: W.E. Upjohn Institute for Employment Research, pp. 254–8.

Baumol, William J. (1986), 'Productivity Growth, Convergence, and Welfare: What the Long-Run Data Show', *American Economic Review*, **76**, 1072–85.

Carayannis, Elias and Rajiv Mallick (1996), 'Regional Income Disparities in Canada: Implications for Theories of Regional Convergence', *Review of Regional Studies*, Summer.

Coughlin, C. and T.B. Mandelbaum (1988), 'Why Have State Per Capita Incomes Diverged Recently?', *Review of the Federal Reserve Bank of St. Louis*, No. 70, 24–37.

Coughlin, Cletus C. and Thomas B. Mandelbaum (1989), 'Have Federal Spending and Taxation Contributed to the Divergence of State Per Capita Incomes in the 1980s?', *Federal Reserve Bank of St. Louis Review*, **71** (4), 29–42.

De Long, J. Bradford (1988), 'Productivity Growth, Convergence, and Welfare: Comment', *American Economic Review*, **78**, 1138–54.

Denny, M. and J. May (1981), 'Intertemporal Changes in Regional Productivity in Canadian Manufacturing', *Canadian Journal of Economics*, **14**, 390–408.

Economic Council of Canada (1977), *Living Together: A Study in Regional Disparities*, Ottawa: Minister of Supply and Services, Canada.

Gyourko, J. (1987), 'New Firm Activity and Employment Changes Among the Localities in the Philadelphia Area, 1980–83', in A. Summers and T. Luce (eds), *Economic Development within the Philadelphia Metropolitan Area*, Philadelphia: University of Pennsylvania Press, pp. 110–30.

Jeffrey, D. and N. Hubbard (1988), 'Foreign Tourism, the Hotel Industry, and Regional Economic Performance', *Regional Studies*, **22** (4), 319–29.

Mallick, R. (1993), 'Convergence of State Per-Capita Incomes: An Examination of its Sources', *Growth and Change*, **24** (Summer), 321–40.

Mallick, R. and E. Carayannis (1994), 'Regional Economic Convergence in Mexico: An Analysis by Industry', *Growth and Change*, **25** (Summer), 325–34.

Martin F., N. Swan, I. Banks, G. Barker and R. Beaudry (1979), *The Interregional Diffusion of Innovations in Canada*, Study prepared for the Economic Council of Canada, Ottawa: Minister of Supply and Services, Canada.

McCombie, J.S.L. (1988), 'A Synoptic View of Regional Growth and Unemployment: The Neoclassical Theory', *Urban Studies*, No. 25, 267–81.

Nordhaus, W. and M. Baily (1991), 'General Discussion (on Barro and Martin, *Convergence Across States and Regions*)', *Brookings Papers on Economic Activity*, No. 1, 107–82.

Smith, D.M. (1975), 'Neoclassical Growth Models and Regional Growth in the U.S.', *Journal of Regional Science*, No. 15, 165–81.

Testa, W.A. (1989), *Metro Area Growth from 1976 to 1985: Theory and Evidence*, Working Paper, Federal Reserve Bank of Chicago, January.

US Department of Commerce (Various years), *Statistical Abstract of the United States*. Washington, DC: US Government Printing Office.

Wasylenko, M. and T. McGuire (1985), 'Jobs and Taxes: The Effect of Business Climate on States' Employment Growth Rates', *National Tax Journal*, **38** (4), December, 497–512.

PART II

IMPACT OF ECONOMIC INTEGRATION ON INDUSTRIAL ORGANIZATION

7 The role of small and entrepreneurial firms in achieving economic integration during the transition from command to market-based economies

Allan Young

1 Introduction

Experience has shown that as an economy moves in transition from a command to a more market-based status a significant array of economic dislocations are likely to arise. Unemployment is normally an unhappy byproduct of privatization as are inevitable strains upon a frequently immature financial infrastructure. Accordingly, human and capital resource pricing and allocation frequently face misspecification as the economy fuelled by inflation spins towards serious disequilibrium.

Few indigenous resources are normally available to an economy in such a condition, and it is indeed rare that external entities can be relied upon for significant amelioration. One of the prime sectors which can play a useful role in this situation is that of small and entrepreneurial enterprises. The activities of such entities may be usefully engaged in order to enhance employment, growth and creative possibilities. Their competitive aspects can also be of value in helping to retard inflationary pressures. Further, a well-functioning small and entrepreneurial sector can be invaluable in the development of a more effective financial infrastructure.

Regrettably, however, it is usually just this sector which is most seriously disadvantaged by the pressures of transition, so that their service to overall economic growth is hindered as their own ability to effectively function in the transitory economic environment is hampered by the forces normally at play. This chapter proposes to examine the forces discussed above and then offer a set of public policy recommendations for countries undergoing the transition from a command to a market basis so that the benefits which small and entrepreneurial firms can bring to this process can be effectively harnessed.

As the former command economies of Central and Eastern Europe and the former USSR seek to shed the shackles of trade tied to a barter-orientated transfer pricing system as practised by the moribund COMECON bloc, the inefficiencies of their former operations have been exposed with attendant unemployment and other negative consequences as modernization has proceeded. That the small and entrepreneurial business sector is an excellent source for securing employment increases and other benefits in an economy is beyond doubt, as shown by Western economies in recent decades. For example, in the United States, 90 per cent of the employment increase which occurred during the 1980s and thus far in the 1990s is directly attributable to the small-business sector. Hence, the notion of the growth of small and entrepreneurial businesses in Central and Eastern Europe and the former USSR ameliorating unemployment and other negative consequences resulting from the movement to a market economy is highly tenable and viable.

In Section 2 of this chapter we look at some of the advantages of a vital small and entrepreneurial business sector as an economy attempts to emerge from a command status. We are concerned with the ways in which these market economy changes can present unique opportunities or advantages to the small and entrepreneurial business sector so that the benefits of a vibrant small-business sector can accrue to an economy undergoing this change. Section 3 will deal with the disadvantages of small-business operation in the current climate in transition economies and develop some of the present concerns in the small-business community. Finally, Section 4 will present a set of public policy recommendations to assist the small and entrepreneurial sector so that its benefits to the transition and integration process can be brought to fruition.

2 The benefits of the small and entrepreneurial sector in achieving economic integration during the transition process from command to a market-based economy

First, as to the benefits of a vibrant small-business sector, there is little doubt that one of its primary advantages is in terms of the employment opportunities it can offer. This is particularly significant at the present time because of the major potential unemployment consequences inherent in the economic changes currently taking place. In the shift from a command to a market economy, many former skills can become outdated with the danger of unemployment increases. Additionally, as privatizations are an integral part of the shift we are discussing, it should be noted that, in the wake of this change from state to private ownership, cost-cutting measures such as staff reductions and division eliminations with attendant increases in unemployment often follow. Privatizations often result in a greater concern with profit generation than job creation, at least in the short run, with frequent undesirable effects upon the employment situation. To the extent that small businesses mean at least a job for the owner entrepreneur, if not additional job creations as well, the process of small-business growth can be one of the significant avenues to combat the unemployment which often follows the conversion from a command to a market economy.

Another major advantage of small and entrepreneurial enterprises in Central and Eastern Europe and the former USSR at the present time stems from their potential flexibility, vitality and ability to react rapidly to changing opportunities. Smaller firms normally require far fewer players in the decisionmaking loop than their larger counterparts. This frequently has the effect of speeding up the reaction time of the business entity. Additionally, smaller firms are usually less burdened with 'standard operating procedures' and their attendant bureaucracy than their larger counterparts, offering such firms the potential for more flexible reactions to business opportunities. Each of these advantages, greater speed and flexibility in confronting a changing business environment on the part of the small and entrepreneurial firm, is particularly significant at the present time in the area of the world under consideration, as it seeks to deal with this transitory phase of its economic and political life. Changes are occurring very rapidly and in ways heretofore unknown in Central and Eastern Europe and the former USSR, and those businesses which are better positioned to take advantage of desirable situations as they arise, while rapidly avoiding potential pitfalls, will not only profit themselves handsomely, but also most greatly assist their overall economy in achieving a smooth and beneficial transition.

From what has already been said it can be seen that small-business entrepreneurship may well be a more rapid route to success and autonomy than through employment in a large firm in the part of the world we are discussing. Particularly if the firm is a state-owned enterprise facing privatization at some time in the future, the degree of uncertainty surrounding the employment situation would appear to be considerable. Impending privatization of an enterprise places an aura of uncertainty around its employees which often results in stagnation at best and debilitating infighting at worst. The small-business person on the other hand, particularly when he/she is characterized as possessing an 'entrepreneurial state of mind', may be in a far better position to be 'master/mistress of his/her own fate' and achieve not only greater financial success, but far more control and autonomy. That these potential virtues of small and entrepreneurial business ownership might be particularly valuable in Central and Eastern Europe and the former USSR at the present time stems, among other considerations, from the highly educated and literate population of the region who are likely as a result to be able to be readily trained in Western business techniques and methodologies. Additionally, the high level of education of the population tends to make one believe that the people of the area could well value the potential autonomy which small-business entrepreneurship frequently brings.

3 Current disadvantages and concerns of small and entrepreneurial firms in the transition process

Now that we have looked at the advantages of small-business ownership in the part of the world we are considering and the contributions this can make towards the movement to a market economy, we can review some of the disadvantages or hurdles which such firms face at the present time which are particular to their current environment.

There seems little doubt that one of the major disadvantages with which small business must cope at the present time in Central and Eastern Europe and the former USSR is the lack of a genuine financial infrastructure in the region. The absence of a modern banking system means that for virtually all but the largest transactions, a physical exchange of cash is required. This necessitates that a large pool of liquid resources must be maintained on hand simply to make transactions. The effect is increased labour costs from the making of transactions as well as increased capital costs which result from the maintenance of extended balances of barren liquid assets which bring no monetary return. Obviously, the burden of this tends to weigh more heavily upon smaller firms than larger ones since for the former type of enterprise all of their transactions are small. A similar problem results from the lack of capital, which largely derives from the nature of the planned economy which held sway in the region for about fifty years in some areas and considerably more in others. Little real savings were created, the middle class was virtually eliminated, and a high level of illiquidity and a lack of capital formation in private hands resulted. A banking system which was highly fluid and operated effectively in its loan-granting functions would have alleviated this problem considerably. Regrettably, however, such a banking system is not present – the lack of which seems to fall far more heavily upon small firms than large ones, especially if the large firm in question is still state owned and has access to the funds of the state to meet its banking needs. Added to the above concerns are the extremely high interest rates which are currently operative in the region.

Hungary, for example, had to live through a period during which interest rates for business loans ran at about 40 per cent for 1991 and most of the first half of 1992. Moreover, even for such high interest rate loans when they could be obtained, in the vast preponderance of cases only short-term maturities prevailed and 90-day money was by far the rule rather than the exception. All of the above problems are compounded even further upon the small entrepreneur who, especially in relation to his/her larger-firm counterpart, rarely has the collateral which banks frequently require before a loan can even be seriously considered. Thus, while for larger firms the lack of a well-developed banking system or financial infrastructure can be a considerable burden, for smaller enterprises, without the ability to obtain funds from the state or the size to even consider a joint venture with a foreign partner in order to relieve the liquidity shortage, the problems posed by this financial institutional void can frequently appear insuperable.

But on top of this, there are additional problems with which small and entrepreneurial businesses must cope at the present time in transition economies. Most of these additional difficulties stem from the fact that such firms generally have far less political power than large ones and, regrettably, this difference is magnified at the present time in Central and Eastern Europe and the former USSR during this transitory phase of their economic development. At the present time in this region there still exists many state-owned, dinosaurlike, behemoth firms which may or may not be awaiting privatization, but which in one way or another are able to attract the attention of the government and receive greater favour than their counterpart smaller firms. At the very minimum, as noted above, state-owned enterprises may at least have access to the funds of the state, whereas smaller firms find capital raising far more difficult as it is a task they must undertake on their own, often with little or no direct state assistance. On the other hand, at least in some of the countries of this region, there exist a number of both state-supported and private small-business associations which attempt to foster the interests of small businesses and their entrepreneurs. For example, in Hungary there is a Small Business Administration which operates much like the similarly named governmental organization in the US. In addition, Hungary also has a number of small business development centres and a private foundation devoted to supporting the interests of small and entrepreneurial firms, the Foundation for Small Enterprise Economic Development (SEED). In general, however, notwithstanding the efforts of the small-business support organizations noted above, such firms are at a considerable political and economic disadvantage *vis-à-vis* larger firms, and this unfavourable situation would appear to be greater at the present time than is normally the case in the area of the world we are considering.

The final area of disadvantage for small firms which we shall consider stems from the general lack of market-orientated business, finance and economic training in this region. While it is surely true, as noted above, that the general literacy rate is quite high in this part of the world, education and training in those disciplines which are necessary for success in a market-based economy are woefully lacking. This absence of highly trained professionals in market-orientated economics is prevalent not only among small-business people, but in large firms as well and even in most of the universities and training centres of the region. The prime disadvantage for small firms in relation to their larger counterparts stems not simply from a major differential in the knowledge of either entity as to the main subdisciplines of business (for example, finance, accounting, marketing and management) as these fields are professionally practised in the West, but in an inability to compensate for their lack of these skills by hiring individuals who are qualified to perform them. Lacking the ability to pay or even find outsiders who are competent to practise professionally in the fields noted above, small businesses are at a considerable further disadvantage at the present time in this region.

In general, we saw in Section 3 of this chapter that while small businesses and their entrepreneurs in Central and Eastern Europe and the former USSR can offer many advantages to the region and represent a major catalyst in its change to a market economy, we find in Section 4 that such enterprises and individuals are particularly disadvantaged from a number of different perspectives in this part of the world at the present time. It is in the best interests of Western economies as well as the region under discussion that the transition in question succeed. Failure could run the risk of a return to totalitarianism, planned economies and the cold war or even worse. Accordingly, it is incumbent upon the governments of the region as well as upon Western economies and governments to do all they can to foster the healthy development of small and entrepreneurial businesses in the area. It is only in this way that the inherent benefits of such enterprises can fruitfully be brought to bear upon the economic problems in question in the current phase of economic transition. It is in the above spirit that in the following section some public policy recommendations are offered for possible adoption by countries currently in transition.

4 The need for an advocate for small and entrepreneurial firms

As noted above, the small-business sector of any economy is almost always at a serious competitive disadvantage *vis-à-vis* its larger enterprise counterparts. The resources at the command of larger firms, such as financial, technical, legal, economies of scale and other such assets often simply dwarf and overwhelm those normally at the disposal of smaller enterprises, to say nothing of the far greater contacts and political muscle giant companies are frequently readily able to utilize and bring to bear to their often considerable advantage. This comparative disadvantage of smaller enterprises is almost always prevalent. However, it is typically exacerbated during turbulent or transitory economic periods when a scarcity of most resources characteristically prevails, and at times the ethical dimension of business affairs as well as the fairness and evenness of government in dealing with the business community is most amenable to compromise. Nevertheless, it is particularly during such difficult and transitional economic eras, such as in the movement from a command to a market-orientated economic system, when, as noted above, the benefits which the small and entrepreneurial firm, if given relatively free rein and an evenhanded economic environment, can most valuably accrue to the overall benefit of the country. The recent experiences of the Czech Republic, Hungary and, to a lesser extent to date, Poland, all testify to the considerable and valuable role a well-functioning small entrepreneurial sector can play in this command to market transition. Privatization frequently entails at least short-run economic pain, sacrifice, hardship and inevitable dislocations. Accordingly, the policies of transitional economic governments should explicitly recognize the unique and especially valuable role that small and medium-sized enterprises alone can play in ameliorating some of the worst and most difficult aspects of this transition. The remainder of this chapter will outline some of the issues the governments of transition economies might consider in order to be of greatest value in satisfying the needs of the small and entrepreneurial business community.

It should be noted at the outset that most, if not all, of these considerations can best be implemented through the formation of an agency patterned after the US Small Business Administration. The role and functions of this agency might, among other things, be:

- To represent the interests and voice the concerns of the small and entrepreneurial business community in the councils of government. In pursuit of the above mission, to seek the passage of legislation and the allocation of government funding which is consistent with the best interests of this sector of the economy.
- To provide statistical analyses of business opportunities focused at the small and entrepreneurial firm level. This should include both data relevant to domestic business affairs and information useful to foreign joint-venture partnering. The latter would have the added benefit of assisting the development of the critical export sector, which would greatly speed the maturation of the financial infrastructure of the economy.
- To administer training programmes focused at small and entrepreneurial business. Some such training programmes are available at present. However, a review of many of these programmes in a number of countries by the author showed that, at least with respect to course

material, the programmes appeared to be excessively orientated towards the legislative enactments of the country and written in rather arcane and complicated legal jargon. Accordingly, the present utility at the grass roots level of such programmes seems dubious at best. These training programmes need to be refocused so as to concentrate upon financial management, accounting and other such issues of immediate concern. Moreover, the course materials should be simplified and brought to a level congruent with the concerns and background of the entrepreneur. Further, to the extent that these training programmes are centrally run, rather than the regional focus which seems to currently exist in many countries, there will be far broader dissemination of the informational content of the course as well as the achievement of economies of scale and time effectiveness with their attendant cost savings. A national focus would also allow televised presentations (perhaps patterned after the Sunrise Semester format).

- To encourage the formation of local organizations, such as chambers of commerce, Rotary and Lions clubs, in the various districts of a country, all coordinated and controlled under the auspices of the country's Small Business Administration.
- To press the national government to increase the fund pool available for direct lending to small and entrepreneurial firms. For this purpose, the utilization of funds generated by the state from the proceeds of privatizations seems highly appropriate. However, transparency in the access and commitment of this privatization fund pool is essential if the programme is to operate fairly and effectively. The proposed Small Business Administration could direct this lending programme or, if the private commercial banking sector could be developed sufficiently, government funding could be provided to the commercial banks for onlending to qualifying small and entrepreneurial firms.
- To call for an offshoot of the above programme under which the country's Small Business Administration would administer a loan guarantee programme. Under this latter programme (successfully run in the US since the origination of the US Small Business Administration in 1954), private banks investigate the credit worthiness of a potential small-business borrower. Qualifying borrowers then have their loan substantially guaranteed (in the US 90 per cent of the loan is government guaranteed) by the governmental agency. In this manner, the loan exposure of the private bank is substantially reduced, yet the bulk of the credit investigation is in private hands. Should the loan be fully serviced and the borrower prosper, subsequent lending would likely be forthcoming from the participating private bank without the

need for government guarantee. Accordingly, all parties to the original transaction could eventually find it a profitable one, with the government benefiting through an increased tax base arising from successful businesses. (In the US the government loan guarantee programme can only be accessed by a small enterprise which has been denied a loan commitment by at least two private banking institutions.)

- To institute a Small Business Development Centre (SBDC) where those enterprises in need of managerial assistance and counselling as to managerial techniques and processes useful in the running of a business can receive appropriate help. While such a centre would be open to all small businesses, it is normally particularly valuable to fledgling enterprises in the startup phase of operations.
- To encourage relations between the SBDC, called for in the above recommendation, and business incubators also to be created in the various major population centres of the country. However, the efforts of these various business incubators should also be coordinated and controlled by the Small Business Administration. If both SBDCs and business incubators are placed in the major population centres throughout the country, all coordinated and controlled by the Small Business Administration, considerable economies of scale could be achieved, all eventually accruing to the benefit of the small and entrepreneurial business community as well as to the country at large.
- To pursue the development of a computerized information-gathering, storage and retrieval network specifically focused at the small and entrepreneurial firm level. The potential benefits of such an undertaking with respect to both the national and international arenas are incalculable. These benefits are especially significant in an economy seeking integration and/or a major transition. Not only is information transfer within the country greatly enhanced by such a system, but international business relations can be significantly improved as well. This is particularly significant in the region under consideration with its antiquated telecommunication system making exporting, foreign investment, joint ventures and other such international partnering arrangements difficult to arrange effectively, even when they are economically and technically feasible. A computerized information-gathering, storage and retrieval network, such as that proposed here, would not only address the above problems, it would, by inclusion of that segment of the economy with the greatest needs in this respect and at the same time the least abilities – the small and entrepreneurial business sector – greatly enhance the functioning of their businesses and allow them to focus their efforts on those opportunities of

potentially greatest value both to themselves and to the economy at large. (It should be noted that feasibility studies encompassing a number of recent investigations of the utility of data-gathering networks of this kind have been undertaken. One recent such effort was sponsored by UNIDO in Sri Lanka, *The Industrial Technology and Market Information Network*, DP/SR/(91/007).

8 Trade liberalization in Eastern European countries and the prospects of their integration into the world trading system

*Jaleel Ahmad and Jing Yang**

1 Introduction

A challenging task facing the Eastern European countries is the integration (or the 'reentry' as some would like to call it) of their economies into the world trading system. Credible liberalization of trade and payments regimes in Eastern Europe, as part of overall economic reforms, is a precondition for their fuller participation in trade with the rest-of-the-world (ROW). By the same token, the speed and the 'quality' of domestic reforms would themselves depend crucially on how fast and on what terms these economies can be drawn into the mainstream of the multilateral trading system. The lack of progress in this important task may slow down the speed of economic reform in Eastern Europe.

The purpose of this chapter is to explore the short- and long-run prospects of integrating the transitional economies of Eastern Europe into the mainstream of world trade. This is attempted in a quantitative framework which considers the relative merits of three possible options, namely, the revitalization of intra-Council for Mutual Economic Assistance (CMEA) trade (following its collapse in 1992); entry into an enlarged European Union (EU), and a more active pursuit of multilateral trade through non-conditional membership in the World Trade Organization (WTO). These options, of course, are not mutually exclusive.

The plan of the chapter is as follows. Section 2 briefly discusses the progress of economic reforms in Eastern Europe in so far as they relate to openness of the economy to trade with the rest-of the-world. Section 3 analyses the future prospects of a fuller participation in world trade in the context of the three broad and non-competing alternatives that are feasible. Section 4 presents a quantitative assessment of these options based on an econometric estimation of long-term trends. Some conclusions are offered in Section 5.

2 Trade-related reforms

While the extent and the speed of economic reforms has varied

* The authors wish to thank the participants at the Athens conference for helpful suggestions that emerged from the discussion.

considerably across individual countries, all countries in the region have substantially liberalized their trade and payments regimes since 1990. In most countries, state monopoly of foreign trade has been virtually eliminated. This is accompanied by a significant reduction in quota restrictions (QRs) on imports, as well as in export subsidies and export-licensing arrangements. An indication of the depth of these reforms is a steady rise in the share of liberalized imports in the total to an average of between 75 and 80 per cent. These reforms are most advanced in three of the countries, namely, Hungary, Poland and the Czech Republic, but are being pursued in all transition economies.

The overall picture of trade that emerges from these reforms is, however, a paradoxical one. While trade with the West has expanded rapidly, trade with other Eastern European countries and with the Commonwealth of Independent States (CIS) has all but collapsed because of the demise of earlier CMEA arrangements. Rodrik (1992) estimates that the collapse of the CMEA has contributed to a loss of real income to the tune of 3.5 per cent of GDP in Poland and 7.8 per cent of GDP each in Hungary and the Czech Republic.

The dramatic changes in trade policy, none the less, underestimate the task of realigning the transition economies into the world trading system. Historically, the levels of tariffs and QRs in Eastern Europe have been relatively low. The principal means of protection there has been the central planning mechanism which in its wake has created widespread distortions in relative prices and has contributed to an inefficient functioning of labour and capital markets. Factor subsidies in one form or another, particularly to the state-owned enterprises, are still common. The practice of trading at domestic prices and absorbing the difference between domestic and world prices in fiscal budgets has largely disappeared. But it has left a legacy of non-diversified and overextended production structures that inhibit trade with the rest-of the-world. The dissonance between production structures and underlying resource endowments caused by central planning was further aggravated by payments mechanism in the former Ruble Zone. As a result, the more difficult tasks of integration into the world trading system still lie ahead. The prospects of success in this more difficult task depend crucially on the evolution of future trading arrangements with the West. This is because closer ties with world markets help to establish a rational set of relative prices and promote a more efficient allocation of resources.

3 Feasible trade options

Following the collapse of the CMEA, individual countries in Eastern

Europe have devised various *ad hoc* schemes for maintaining some minimum level of trade with former CMEA partners, particularly with those that are now part of the CIS. But, by and large, such arrangements are confined to trade in a limited number of products (the 'indicative list') and involve barter and other countertrade arrangements. By their very nature, these arrangements are bilateral rather than multilateral. In the chaotic conditions of the early 1990s, these patchwork arrangements were considered necessary to maintain some level of trade to prevent further disorganization of the economic system, even though barter deals create their own distortions. More importantly, some trade outside of a country's borders was deemed necessary to prevent closure of state enterprises, since much of the barter trade was, in fact, interenterprise trade. There is some indication that intra-CMEA trade in the 1980s was larger than predicted on the basis of economic variables, since it was determined by political considerations (Havrylyshyn and Pritchett 1991).

The combined external trade of Eastern Europe and of the former USSR was estimated to be about 10 per cent of world trade in 1988. While the combined market size of the transition economies is relatively small, it is not unreasonable to visualize a modest free trade area or a customs union between them on lines that are radically different from the earlier CMEA. Such an arrangement is feasible, at least temporarily, between the Eastern European countries and as many CIS countries as are interested in negotiating modest tariff preferences. It will permit individual countries, particularly those in the CIS, to adjust gradually to their long-run comparative advantage. The more comprehensive the arrangement in terms of countries and coverage of commodities, the more likely it is to reduce transition costs in the short and medium runs. There may be some reluctance on the part of some countries to join preferential trading arrangements because they may regard trade diversion costs as excessive. However, a cursory examination of commodity composition of trade and its direction (for example, in Rodrik 1992) leads one to believe that intra-trade in the ex-CMEA countries does not overlap with their trade with the West. An indirect evidence of this is the fact that East European exporters have had little success in finding Western markets for exports they have lost in the Eastern markets.

In visualizing a possible arrangement for revitalizing intra-trade between individual countries of Eastern Europe and the CIS, certain considerations should be kept in mind. First, any revival of intra-trade should be structured on the lines of a preferential trading area (with or without a common external tariff) in the neoclassical sense, with transparent rules-of-the-game and without regard to non-economic considerations. Second, any enlargement of the intra-Eastern trade beyond the meagre current magnitudes would not be feasible without cumbersome clearing and payments arrangements. Third, any emerging free trade arrangement should be designed in a way that it represents a coherent and unified approach to eventually joining the larger European market.

Even if workable intra-Eastern preferential trading arrangements can be devised in the foreseeable future, it is clear that any significant expansion of Eastern Europe's trade without an accommodation by major Western industrial countries would not be possible. In this regard, the role of the EU is likely to be crucial. Beginning in 1988, the then European Community (EEC) entered into separate 'cooperation agreements' with individual Eastern countries, most notably Czechoslovakia, Hungary and Poland, for phasing out all selective QRs against their exports. In 1990, much earlier than the original timetable, the EEC abolished the application of all selective QRs against Eastern Europe, except in 'sensitive' sectors, such as agriculture, textiles, apparel, coal and steel products. It also granted generalized preferences (GSP) treatment to all Eastern countries. More recently, the EU has concluded 'association' agreements with the Czech Republic, Hungary and Poland as the basis for a move towards full membership. However, separate 'protocols' have been devised for agriculture, textiles and apparel, and steel products. The protocols are expected to contain provisions on safeguards, rules of origin, anti-dumping, subsidies, intellectual property rights and adherence to EU competition policy, all of which will restrict trade with Eastern Europe.

Of all the products included in the separate protocols, agriculture appears to be the most troublesome. The main problem is that any attempt to cover free trade in agriculture without a reform of the Common Agricultural Policy (CAP) would almost certainly result in surplus in the enlarged EU production and increase the budgetary cost of the CAP. The steel protocol stipulates free trade in steel products only if the Eastern countries abide by the EU rules on prices and subsidies. It also stipulates capacity reduction in order to achieve a subsidy-free steel industry in Europe. For textiles and apparel, the EU markets will continue to be protected by extensive product-specific and country-specific VERs under the Multi Fibre Arrangement (MFA).

Despite some market opening, Eastern European economies face formidable barriers to their exports in the EU, as they do in all other industrial country markets. These barriers are in precisely those products which are potentially important Eastern products for exports to the West. Nevertheless, all recent empirical estimates suggest that Eastern Europe and the EU are 'natural' trading partners.[1] Therefore, the urgency of market opening in the EU cannot be minimized.

All Eastern European countries joined GATT (now the World Trade Organization: WTO) at different times and, as a result, conditions of membership differ significantly. All of Eastern Europe now enjoys most favoured nation (MFN) treatment in all OECD countries. Major OECD countries have also extended GSP coverage to Eastern European countries, but restrictions remain. In the case of Poland, Hungary and Romania, 'discriminating safeguards' were instituted which allow the contracting parties to restrict imports from these countries if they cause 'injury' or threaten domestic producers. In addition, Romania and Poland were required to increase their imports from the contracting parties at an annual rate not lower than the minimum stipulated. Only Romania and Hungary were able to negotiate progressive elimination of QRs against their exports, if deemed inconsistent with GATT Article XIII. It is hoped that these restrictions are transitional. Membership in the WTO on normal terms is essential to provide Eastern Europe with assured access to industrial country markets. Without this assurance, the transitional economies of Eastern Europe may find it difficult to lock in economic reforms in their own countries.

4 Quantitative analysis

The quantitative analyses of the Eastern European countries' trade to date have been based on some variant of the 'gravity' model for estimating the gap between potential and actual trade. These gaps are almost always estimated only for trade with the West (Van Bergeik and Oldersma 1990; Biessen 1991; Collins and Rodrik 1991; and Wang and Winters 1991). This chapter departs from this tradition in two respects. First, it undertakes an analysis of time-series fluctuations in trade data to estimate long-run trends in exports and imports of Eastern Europe. Second, it does so with respect to Eastern Europe's trade, both exports and imports, with four bilateral 'addresses' namely, Eastern Europe itself, the former USSR, the European Community and the rest-of-the-world. Without investigating the trend properties of Eastern Europe's trade in all directions, it is not possible to evaluate the hierarchy of options and their relative importance.

The analysis contained in this section has undertaken three econometric tasks.[2] First, it employs trend stationary and difference stationary statistical approaches to estimate long-run trends from time-series data. Second, with a view to identify the appropriate class of series, an Augmented Dickey–Fuller (ADF) test for unit roots is applied. The ADF tests the null hypothesis as to whether the series are trend stationary or difference stationary. Identifying the appropriate class of series has important implications for determining long-term trends. Third, we employ Box–Jenkins methodology to estimate an ARIMA (p, d, q) model for forecasting of trade volumes under the options identified in Section 3.

The backdrop for our econometric analysis is provided by the plots of raw data on Eastern European countries' trade with other Eastern countries, with the former USSR, with the EU and with the rest-of-the-world. This initial data analysis reveals that total exports of Eastern Europe have suffered a significant decline since 1988. This decline is most dramatic for exports to the former USSR, as well as to other Eastern countries. Within this overall decline, however, Eastern Europe's exports to the European Community have increased steadily. This pattern is duplicated in the behaviour of imports of Eastern Europe. They decline both from the former USSR as well as from other Eastern countries, but have expanded greatly from the EC.

The estimation of time trends is based on a consistent data set for the years 1973 to 1993. Tables 8.1 and 8.2 give estimates of trend stationary (TS) and difference stationary (DS) representations estimated from equations (8.1) and (8.2), shown below.

$$\begin{gathered} LY_t = C + T + u_t \\ \Phi(B)u_t = \psi(B)a_t \\ a_t \sim iid(0, \sigma^2) \end{gathered} \tag{8.1}$$

$$\begin{gathered} DLY_t = LY_t - LY_{t-1} = C + v_t \\ \Phi(B)v_t = \psi(B)e_t \\ e_t \sim iid(0, \sigma^2). \end{gathered} \tag{8.2}$$

In the trend stationary approach, the log of Y (denoted by LY) is regressed on the constant and the time trend. In the difference stationary approach, the first difference of L (denoted by DLY) is regressed on the constant. The residuals from both regressions are then interpreted as the cyclical component. Table 8.3 presents the results of the ADF test for unit roots. An examination of p-values at significance levels of 0.05 per cent reveals that the null hypothesis that these series have unit roots cannot be rejected. The difference stationary representations are, therefore, the appropriate class of series for further analysis.

The next step was to identify the best ARIMA (p, q) model for estimation. The three variables to be estimated are:

$Y1$: total trade between Eastern Europe and the EEC/EU

Table 8.1 The TS and DS representation: exports and imports of the USSR

Exports of USSR	TS	DS
1. Total exports	$LY_t = 10.365 + 0.071t + u_t$ (66.95) (5.259)	$DLY_t = 0.04268 + v_t$ (0.783)
2. Exports to EEC	$LY_t = 8.345 + 0.106t + u_t$ (52.97) (7.129)	$DLY_t = 0.1044 + v_t$ (2.6749)
3. Exports to EE	$LY_t = 9.454 + 0.08t + u_t$ (88.14) (8.96)	$DLY_t = 0.076 + v_t$ (2.103)
Imports of USSR	**TS**	**DS**
1. Total imports	$LY_t = 10.316 + 0.056t + u_t$ (91.22) (5.678)	$DLY_t = 0.0534 + v_t$ (1.7826)
2. Imports from EEC	$LY_t = 8.339 + 0.071t + u_t$ (88.3) (8.534)	$DLY_t = 0.094 + v_t$ (2.7425)
3. Imports from EE	$LY_t = 9.690 + 0.033t + u_t$ (50.55) (1.990)	$DLY_t = -0.010 + v_t$ (−0.1738)

Note: Numbers in parentheses are *t*-statistic values.

$Y2$: total trade between Eastern Europe and the former USSR

$Y3$: total trade between the Eastern European countries themselves.

We use the Box–Jenkins methodology to select the appropriate values of p and q by examining the pattern of autocorrelations (ACF) and partial autocorrelations (PACF). They suggest that $Y1$, $Y2$ and $Y3$ are all ARIMA (1, 1, 0), since ACFs are declining in sine wave while PACFs are significant at first lag.

We also did the diagnostic test on two overfitting models which are ARIMA (0, 1, 1) and ARIMA (1, 1, 1), using likelihood ratio (LR):

$$LR = N^* \ln(\sigma^2/\sigma^2)$$

$H0$: $Y1$, $Y2$ and $Y3$ are ARIMA (1, 1, 0).

$H1$: $Y1$, $Y2$ and $Y3$ are ARIMA (0, 1, 1) or ARIMA (1, 1, 1).

On the basis of these results, we accept the null hypothesis that $Y1$, $Y2$ and $Y3$ are ARIMA (1, 1, 0) in all cases since none of the LR-statistics are significant at 5 per cent level.

Table 8.2 The TS and DS representation: exports and imports of Eastern Europe

Exports of EE	TS	DS
1. Total exports	$LY_t = 10.7 + 0.038t + u_t$ (84.21) (3.45)	$DLY_t = 0.028 + v_t$ (0.591)
2. Exports to EEC	$LY_t = 8.55 + 0.086t + u_t$ (139.09) (12.05)	$DLY_t = 0.084 + v_t$ (3.093)
3. Exports to USSR	$LY_t = 9.69 + 0.033t + u_t$ (50.50) (1.99)	$DLY_t = -0.010 + v_t$ (−0.174)
4. Exports to EE	$LY_t = 9.454 + 0.022t + u_t$ (75.42) (1.94)	$DLY_t = 0.219 + v_t$ (0.048)
5. Exports to ROW	$LY_t = 9.14 + 0.060t + u_t$ (82.57) (5.86)	$DLY_t = 0.065 + v_t$ (2.155)
Imports of EE	**TS**	**DS**
1. Total imports	$LY_t = 10.688 + 0.045t + u_t$ (94.03) (4.55)	$DLY_t = 0.0351 + v_t$ (1.020)
2. Imports from EEC	$LY_t = 8.785 + 0.042t + u_t$ (79.16) (4.332)	$DLY_t = 0.0775 + v_t$ (2.177)
3. Imports from EE	$LY_t = 9.454 + 0.022t + u_t$ (75.43) (1.940)	$DLY_t = 0.00219 + v_t$ (0.048)
4. Imports from USSR	$LY_t = 9.450 + 0.089t + u_t$ (88.14) (8.967)	$DLY_t = 0.0757 + v_t$ (2.102)
5. From ROW	$LY_t = 9.105 + 0.044t + u_t$ (91.0) (4.80)	$DLY_t = 0.057 + v_t$ (1.570)

Note: Numbers in parentheses are *t*-statistic values.

The results of the LR test are shown below.

*H*1:	ARIMA (0, 1, 1)		ARIMA (1, 1, 1)	
	LR-statistics	*P*-value	*LR*-statistics	*P*-value
*Y*1	1.2693	0.2598	3.0607	0.0802
*Y*2	0.9782	0.3226	0.5595	0.4544
*Y*3	0.2323	0.6298	0.1671	0.6826

Table 8.3 Statistical output of ADF test for unit root

	Statistic value	*p*-value	Critical value (5%)
Exports of USSR			
1. Total exports	1.488	0.997	−3.711
2. To EEC	−1.537	0.712	−3.734
3. To EE	−0.762	0.906	−3.734
Imports of USSR			
1. Total imports	−0.617	0.932	−3.711
2. From EEC	−3.346	0.092	−3.711
3. From EE	2.882	0.998	−3.711
Exports of EE			
1. Total exports	1.624	0.998	−3.711
2. To EEC	−1.573	0.699	−3.734
3. To USSR	2.882	0.999	−3.711
4. To EE	0.082	0.977	−3.734
5. To ROW	1.745	0.998	−3.711
Imports of EE			
1. Total imports	0.422	0.988	−3.711
2. From EEC	−1.313	0.797	−3.711
3. From EE	0.082	0.977	−3.734
4. From USSR	0.182	0.980	−3.734
5. From ROW	−2.065	0.495	−3.734

Note: For ADF test, we regressed DLY on the constant, trend, $LY(-1)$ and $DLY(-1)$.

Using Box–Jenkins estimation, we flush out the following model for each of the variables, (the *t*-statistic values are shown in the parenthesis):

$$\Delta Y1_t = \underset{(3.453)}{0.65}\ \Delta Y1_{t-1} + u_t \qquad \text{EEC/EU}$$

$$\Delta Y2_t = \underset{(3.823)}{0.91}\ \Delta Y2_{t-1} + e_t \qquad \text{Former USSR}$$

$$\Delta Y3_t = \underset{(2.051)}{0.567}\ \Delta Y3_{t-1} + a_t \qquad \text{Intra-Eastern Europe}$$

For *forecasting* with the ARIMA (1, 1, 0) model we started from the general presentation as:

$$
\begin{aligned}
\Phi(B)(1-B)Y_t &= a_t \\
(1-\phi_1 B)(1-B)Y_t &= a_t \\
[1-(\phi_1+1)B+\phi_1 B^2]Y_t &= a_t \\
Y_t &= (\phi_1+1)BY_t - \phi_1 B^2 Y_t + a_t \\
Y_t &= (1-\phi_1)Y_{t-1} - \phi_1 Y_{t-2} + a_t
\end{aligned}
\tag{8.3}
$$

where B is the lag operator and ϕ_1 is the autocorrelation coefficient. Using equation (8.3) we can do n-step forecasting. The results of 10-step forecasting are summarized below. (Forecasting beyond a 10-year period was not deemed necessary since the trends became quite clear on this set of observations.) A comparison of the forecast value of the variables $Y1$, $Y2$ and $Y3$ shows that while in the starting period Eastern Europe's trade with the former USSR had the highest proportion of its total trade, the trade with the EU assumed the highest proportion in the end period.

	Starting period: 1990	Ending period: 2000
$Y1$	35 912	40 217
$Y2$	55 656	25 501
$Y3$	18 648	1 366

As seen in Tables 8.1–3, the only unmistakable long-run trend (on the basis of difference stationarity) is with respect to Eastern Europe's trade with the European Union.[3] Trends for both exports to and imports from the EU are significant at the 5 per cent level. Other significant trends are with respect to Eastern Europe's exports to the rest-of-the-world, and of their imports from the former USSR. But Eastern Europe's trade with the former USSR seems 'unbalanced', since USSR imports from Eastern Europe are on a continuous decline. Surprisingly, one cannot detect any long-run trend with respect to intra-trade between the Eastern European countries. This confirms the long-held suspicion that CMEA arrangements were biased towards trade of individual East European countries with the Soviet Union and against trade with each other.

The Box–Jenkins estimation and the forecasting for the ten-year period (1990–2000) confirms these trends. If these forecasts are any guide to the future, Eastern Europe's trade with the EU appears to be the most promising.

5 Conclusions

The data on Eastern Europe are notoriously scanty and unreliable, so the room for generalization is limited. Moreover, our analysis can discover only regular patterns of movement and does not include the effect of any policy initiatives that may be taken in the future. Nevertheless, it provides some insights that may be useful for future policy initiatives. The major insights that emerge from the analysis in this chapter can be summarized as follows. First, the most promising option for Eastern European countries is to strengthen their trade ties with the EU, possibly through a full membership. Second, the multilateral trading option, particularly with industrial countries of the OECD, needs to be pursued for a freer access to their markets. Third, the prospects for intra-trade in Eastern Europe or trade with the CIS, with or without preferences, do not seem promising in the short and the medium runs. It should be stressed, however, that the trade options for Eastern Europe considered in this chapter are not either–or propositions. They can be pursued simultaneously. Our analysis based on long-run trends merely suggests that some options may have a higher payoff than others.

Notes

1. Wang and Winters (1991), using a gravity model, find that potential trade between Eastern Europe and the EU (based on 1985 data) is in all cases substantially higher than the actual. The gap ranges from about 30 per cent for Hungary to almost 650 per cent for Bulgaria. Collins and Rodrick (1991), using a markedly different econometric procedure, arrive at a broadly similar conclusion.
2. A preliminary analysis of the direction of Eastern Europe's trade was done on the basis of a plot of raw data and their log values versus time trends. These plots are not included in the chapter but are available from the authors.
3. EEC and EU are interchangeable in this analysis since the data through 1993 refer to trade with the then EEC.

References

Baldwin, Richard E. (1993), 'The Potential for Trade Between the Countries of EFTA and Central Eastern Europe', Occasional Paper No. 44, Geneva: European Free Trade Association

Biessen, G. (1991), 'Is the Impact of Central Planning on Level of Foreign Trade Really Negative?', *Journal of Comparative Economics*, **15**, 22–44.

Collins, Susan and Dani Rodrik (1991), *Eastern Europe and the Soviet Union in the World Economy*, Washington, DC: Institute of International Economics.

Hamilton, Carl B. and Alan Winters (1992), 'Trade with Eastern Europe', *Economic Policy*, **14**, 77–116.

Havrylyshyn, Oleh and Lant Pritchett (1991), 'European Trade Patterns After the Transition', Policy Research Evaluation (PRE) Working Paper No. 748, Washington, DC: World Bank.

International Monetary Fund (1991), *Issues and Developments in International Trade Policy*, prepared by staff team led by Margaret Kelly and Anne Kenny McGuirk, Washington, DC: IMF.

Rodrik, Dani (1992), *Foreign Trade in Eastern Europe's Transition: Early Results*, Cambridge, MA: National Bureau of Economic Research.

Van Bergeijk, P. and H. Oldersma (1990), 'Detente, Market-Oriented Reforms and German Unification: Potential Consequences for the World Trade System', *Kyklos*, **43** (4), 566–609.

Wang, Zhen Kun and L. Alan Winters (1991), 'The Trading Potential of Eastern Europe', Centre of Economic Policy Research (CEPR) Discussion Paper No. 610, London.

9 Long-run and short-run effects of economic integration on the inflow of foreign direct investment

Petros E. Ioannatos

1 Introduction

The impact of economic integration on the locational patterns of foreign direct investment (FDI) has drawn considerable attention from FDI theorists. The majority of the empirical research on the subject has concentrated in analysing the response of the United States (US) FDI to the formation of the European Union (EU). An excellent survey on available empirical evidence from the formative years of the EU has been conducted by Yannopoulos (1990). However, the empirical evidence on the subject has produced conflicting results. Several studies have supported the hypothesis that the creation of the EU has caused a reallocation of US FDI while others have provided evidence against it. The conflicting results have been attributed to model specification errors, inappropriate estimation methods and inadequate data. Further, insufficient data have prevented comprehensive research for analysing the response of the intra-EU FDI and world FDI to the formation of the EU. As a result, the impact of European economic integration on the allocation of US FDI, intra-EU FDI and world FDI remains an open question.

The present study differs from the existing studies on the subject in that it presents a case study regarding the effects of economic integration on the inflow of world FDI into an upper-middle-income newly industrialized economy. The issue is addressed in terms of the experience of Greece with the EU. This case study is especially interesting because the accession of Greece to the EU in 1981 was unprecedented for bringing together partners with unequal levels of economic development. Greece, an upper-middle-income newly industrialized country, joined an economic union composed of high-income developed economies. Data availability for several years prior and after the Greek accession to the EU allow for *ex-post* treatment of the effects of economic integration on the inflow of world FDI into Greece.

2 Model specification

The model specification is based on the eclectic approach to international production (Dunning 1980, 1981, 1986, 1988) where FDI emerges as the result of ownership, internalization and locational advantages. The eclectic approach postulates that firms possessing only the first two advantages would tend to export domestic production. However, if locational considerations in foreign countries are favourable, firms would tend to establish international production and become multinationals. It must be emphasized that the eclectic approach utilizes extensively the research developed along the lines of the market imperfections hypothesis (Kindleberger 1969; Hymer 1972, 1976; Horaguchi and Toyne 1990). This hypothesis asserts that FDI emerges from the imperfect global market environment where it is possible for multinational firms to possess monopolistic advantages over firms in the host countries.

In view of the above considerations, a specification for the demand determinants of the inflow of world FDI into Greece has been formulated which is consistent with the existing theories of international production. Thus, the impact of the Greek accession to the EU on the inflow of world FDI into Greece is addressed in terms of a broader framework of analysis which incorporates other key determinants of FDI. The dependent variable is the inflow of world FDI into Greece. The model distinguishes three types of influences on the dependent variable. First, factors reflecting domestic economic performance, second, variables which control for economic integration effects, and third, a time-trend explanatory variable.

Domestic economic performance is expressed by the market growth and the direction of the trade flows. The former is measured by the growth rate of the gross domestic product (GDP) and the latter by the trade balance. The market growth hypothesis has been the most popular explanation of a country's propensity to attract FDI (Agarwal 1980). This hypothesis emphasizes the importance of a growing domestic market not only for initially attracting high levels of FDI, but also for maintaining the inflow of FDI at subsequent high levels. Ample evidence in favour of the market growth hypothesis has been provided by Goldberg (1972), Agarwal (1980), Lunn (1980, 1983), Scaperlanda and Balough (1983) and Tsai (1991).

The complex relationship between capital flows and trade flows has been extensively discussed in international trade theory. Trade flows and FDI may be complements as is the case with export-orientated FDI, but also substitutes when FDI is directed towards import substitution and trade discrimination policies. The former view has been convincingly supported by Mundell (1957) in terms of the Heckscher–Ohlin–Samuelson (HOS) framework. However, it has been argued (Markusen 1983; Markusen and Svensson 1985) that when some of the assumptions of the HOS framework are relaxed, trade flows and FDI may actually be substitutes. The necessary and sufficient conditions for substitutability and complementarity are derived in Wong (1986). The relationship between absolute trade flows and FDI appears to be even more complex. Trade surpluses are indicative of a healthy economy and may encourage inward FDI. Trade deficits, on the other hand, may stimulate inward FDI as a result of export diversification and import substitution policies (Torrisi 1985).

The empirical literature has addressed the effects of economic integration on the locational patterns of FDI in terms of either a tariff discrimination proxy (Lunn 1980, 1983; Scaperlanda and Balough 1983) or a dichotomous regressor indicative of economic integration status (Arge 1969; Torrisi 1985). The latter approach is used here because it provides an appropriate framework to determine whether the Greek accession to the EU has impacted the flow of world FDI into Greece by (i) a once-and-for-all effect, (ii) a more gradual change in trend, or (iii) a combination of both.

A time-trend regressor has been included in the model specification. The purpose of the time trend is to account for any non-quantifiable or unspecified factors which over time might have affected the behaviour of the dependent variable. Arge (1969) and Torrisi (1985) have used such a time-trend regressor to capture time-related effects.

From a historic perspective, it may be interesting to note that Greece pursued membership to the EU not only for economic prosperity but also for political stability and national security. In fact, by 1974 membership to the EU had become an important objective of Greek foreign policy. Official negotiations between Greece and the EU started in 1976. The treaty of accession was signed in 1979, and full membership status was granted on 1 January 1981. In anticipation of the imminent accession, this study considers 1976 the year of change in membership status.

In formal terms, the above analysis suggests the following specification:

$$FDI_t = \beta_0 + \beta_1 \delta GDP_{t-1} + \beta_2 TB_t + \beta_3 T_t + \beta_4 EU_t + \beta_5 S_t + \epsilon_t$$

where:

FDI_t = annual inflow of world FDI into Greece at time t;

δGDP_{t-1} = annual market growth rate at time $t-1$, computed as the change of the GDP between two subsequent time periods $(GDP_{t-1} - GDP_{t-2})$;

TB_t = annual trade balance (exports−imports) of Greece at time t;

T_t = time-trend variable defined by $1960 = 1$;

EU_t = intercept shift variable indicative of membership status of Greece in the EU at time t. Thus, $EU_t = 0$ for 1960–75 and $EU_t = 1$ for 1976–91;

$S_t = T_t * EU_t$, a slope-shifting variable defined by $S_t = 0$ for 1960–75 and $S_t = T_t$ for 1976–91;

ϵ_t = error term assumed to be normally distributed with mean zero and constant variance.

3 Results

The model outlined above and four of its variants are estimated by ordinary least squares (OLS). Estimation was conducted for the period 1960 to 1991 using annual data. The data are taken from the International Financial Statistics (Yearbooks of 1990 and 1992). All monetary variables are expressed in 1985 Drachmas. Estimation results are presented in Table 9.1 which reports the estimated regression coefficients, the t-statistics (numbers in parentheses), the standard error of the estimate (s), the coefficient of determination (R^2) and its adjusted version (adj R^2), the F-value (ratio of the explained variation over the unexplained), the Durbin–Watson (DW) statistic and the number of observations (N).

Five (5) alternative specifications are presented. Model I differs from Model II and Model III in that, first, the time-trend variable T_t is omitted (Model II), and then, both the time-trend variable T_t and the intercept shift variable EU_t are excluded (Model III). Model IV is identical to Model I with the exception that the market growth rate is computed as the percentage change of the GDP between two subsequent time periods, $\%\delta GDP_{t-1} - (GDP_{t-1} - GDP_{t-2})/GDP_{t-2}$. Finally, Model V differs from Model I in that it excludes the time-trend variable T_t and includes instead GDP_t in order to test for the market size hypothesis.

In all variants, the market growth rate hypothesis is statistically significant and assumes the theoretically correct sign. This result provides strong support for the view that the growth rate of the domestic economy is an important determinant regarding the ability of the host country to attract FDI. In particular, the present study indicates that the domestic market growth rate is associated with a statistically significant increase in the inflow of inward FDI in the following period. As demonstrated by Model IV, this result is robust regardless of how market growth rate is computed. Previous studies based on cross-sectional data (Goldberg 1972; and Lunn 1980, 1983) as well as time-series data (Tsai 1991) have also provided support for the market growth hypothesis.

Table 9.1 Estimation results

	Model I	Model II	Model III	Model IV	Model V
Constant	19.15*	19.48*	20.16*	15.52**	16.79**
	(4.48)	(5.32)	(5.65)	(2.82)	(2.83)
δGDP_{t-1}	0.24***	0.24***	0.27**	—	0.24**
	(1.98)	(2.01)	(2.26)		(1.96)
TB_t	0.46**	0.44*	0.48*	0.45**	0.51**
	(2.48)	(3.20)	(3.61)	(2.38)	(2.80)
T_t	0.08	—	—	0.31	—
	(0.16)			(0.58)	
EU_t	8.27	7.83	—	12.38	6.87
	(0.89)	(0.09)		(1.33)	(0.76)
S_t	2.01*	2.07*	2.40*	1.78*	2.01*
	(3.87)	(5.29)	(19.40)	(3.41)	(4.94)
$\%\delta GDP_{t-1}$	—	—	—	0.67***	—
				(1.75)	
GDP_t	—	—	—	—	0.17
					(0.58)
s	5.67	5.56	5.54	5.76	5.64
R^2	96.3%*	96.3%*	96.1%*	96.1%*	96.3%*
adj R^2	95.5%	95.6%	95.7%	95.3%	95.5%
F-value	118.62	154.54	207.39	114.80	120.29
DW	1.84	1.84	1.79	1.77	1.85
N	30	30	30	30	30

Notes: t-statistics are in parentheses. Asterisk (*), double asterisk (**), and triple asterisk (***) indicate statistical significance at $\alpha = 0.01$, $\alpha = 0.05$ and $\alpha = 0.10$, respectively.

Greece has experienced trade deficits over the entire period covered by the data. With the trade deficit measured negatively, the trade balance TB_t variable is positive and statistically significant in all variants. This implies that a deterioration of the trade balance is associated with a substantial increase in the flow of inward FDI, whereas an improvement in the trade balance would produce the opposite effect. In fact, this result supports the argument presented earlier that trade deficits may stimulate the flow of inward FDI. From a policy viewpoint, one may conclude that Greece has responded to growing trade deficits by liberalizing the treatment of FDI. A similar result has been obtained by Torrisi (1985).

The time-trend variable T_t is statistically insignificant in all variants. Thus, the data reveal the absence of time-related factors affecting the behaviour of the dependent variable. In fact, inclusion or exclusion of the time-trend regressor has no effects on the remaining regression coefficients.

The effects of the economic integration on the inflow of world FDI into Greece are captured by EU_t and S_t, respectively. The former is an intercept shift indicator variable which accounts for the event that economic integration has caused a one-time effect on the flow of inward FDI, whereas the latter is a slope-shifting regressor which controls for the prospect that economic integration has affected the flow of inward FDI by a gradual change over time. Since a time-series data set is considered, EU_t and S_t represent the short-run and long-run effects, respectively, of the economic integration on the inflow of world FDI into Greece.

In each variant, the intercept shift variable EU_t is positive but not statistically significant. This suggests that the Greek accession to the EU has caused a positive but rather weak immediate effect on the flow of inward FDI. However, the slope-shifting variable S_t is positive and statistically significant for all variants. This finding provides strong evidence that the accession of Greece to the EU has caused a considerable gradual increase over time on the inflow of world FDI into Greece. Thus, on the basis of the observed sample, the economic integration of Greece to the EU has produced limited short-run gains but substantial long-run benefits in terms of its international competitiveness to attract FDI. This is a reasonable result as economic integration is a gradual process which requires a substantial amount of time to be implemented.

Model V is a test for the market-size hypothesis. This hypothesis emphasizes the importance of the domestic market size for attracting FDI in terms of economies of scale and efficient utilization of resources. The size of the domestic market is measured by the host country GDP. For the case under study, the market-size hypothesis is not supported. This is not a surprising result as many researchers have provided evidence in favour of this hypothesis and others against it (Agarwal 1980).

Finally, the F-values indicate that the coefficients of determination in all variants are statistically significant. This suggests that a significant proportion of the variation of the inflow of world FDI into Greece is explained by specifications I, II, III, IV and V. The DW statistics denote absence of first-order autocorrelation.

4 Conclusions

The chapter has presented a case study regarding the effects of economic integration on the response of inward FDI for an upper-middle-income newly industrialized economy. The model specification has employed a broad framework of analysis which is consistent with the existing theories of international production. The economic integration of Greece into the EU has provided the ground for the empirical investigation.

The empirical analysis has produced evidence to indicate that the short-run and long-run effects of economic integration for the case of Greece differ substantially. In particular, it was shown that the economic integration has generated only limited short-run effects in terms of inward FDI. However, the long-run impact of the economic integration on inward FDI has been not only favourable but also substantial. Thus, it may safely be concluded that the economic integration of Greece into the EU has increased significantly the ability of the Greek economy to attract world FDI.

References

Agarwal, J.P. (1980), 'Determinants of Foreign Direct Investment: A Survey', *Weltwirtschaftliches Archiv*, **116**, 739–73.

Arge, R. d' (1969), 'Note on Customs Unions and Direct Foreign Investment', *Economic Journal*, **79**, 324–33.

Dunning, J.H. (1980), 'Toward an Eclectic Theory of International Production: Some Empirical Results', *Journal of International Business Studies*, **11**, 9–31.

Dunning, J.H. (1981), 'Explaining the International Direct Investment Position of Countries: Towards a Dynamic or Developmental Approach', *Weltwirtschaftliches Archiv*, **117**, 30–64.

Dunning, J.H. (1986), 'Investment Development Cycle Revisited', *Weltwirtschaftliches Archiv*, **122**, 667–75.

Dunning, J.H. (1988), 'The Eclectic Paradigm of International Production: A Restatement and Some Possible Extensions', *Journal of International Business Studies*, **19**, 1–31.

Goldberg, M.A. (1972), 'Determinants of U.S. Direct Investment in the EEC: Comment', *American Economic Review*, **62**, 692–99.

Horaguchi, H. and B. Toyne (1990), 'Setting the Record Straight: Hymer, Internalization Theory and Transaction Cost Economics', *Journal of International Business Studies*, **21**, 487–94.

Hymer, S.H. (1972), 'The Multinational Corporation and the Law of Uneven Development', in J.N. Bhagwati (ed.), *Economics and World Order*, New York, NY: Macmillan, pp. 113–40.

Hymer, S.H. (1976), *The International Operations of Firms: A Study of Foreign Direct Investment* (PhD Dissertation 1960), Cambridge, MA: MIT Press.

Kindleberger, C.P. (1969), *American Business Abroad: Six Lectures on Direct Investment*, New Haven, NJ: Yale University Press.

Lunn, J. (1980), 'Determinants of US Direct Investment in the EEC: Further Evidence', *European Economic Review*, **13**, 93–101.

Lunn, J. (1983), 'Determinants of US Direct Investment in the EEC: Revisited Again', *European Economic Review*, **21**, 391–3.

Markusen, J.R. (1983), 'Factor Movements and Commodity Trade as Complements', *Journal of International Economics*, **14**, 341–56.

Markusen, J.R. and L.E.O. Svensson (1985), 'Trade in Goods and factors with International Differences in Technology', *International Economic Review*, **26**, 175–92.

Mundell, R. (1957), 'International Trade and Factor Mobility', *American Economic Review*, **47**, 321–35.

Scaperlanda, A. and R.S. Balough (1983), 'Determinants of US Direct Investment in the EEC: Revisited', *European Economic Review*, **21**, 381–90.

Torrisi, C.R. (1985), 'The Determinants of Direct Foreign Investment in a Small LDC', *Journal of Economic Development*, **10**, 19–45.

Tsai, P.L. (1991), 'Determinants of Foreign Direct Investment in Taiwan: An Alternative Approach with Time-series Data', *World Development*, **19**, 275–85.

Wong, K.Y. (1986), 'Are International Trade and Factor Mobility Substitutes?', *Journal of International Economics*, **21**, 25–43.

Yannopoulos, G.N. (1990), 'Foreign Direct Investment and European Integration: The Evidence from the Formative Years of the European Community', *Journal of Common Market Studies*, **28**, 235–59.

10 Japanese manufacturing FDIs in Europe: present idiosyncrasies and future prospects

Mike Pournarakis, Nikos C. Varsakelis and D. Mardas

1 Introduction

The dramatic rise in international production in recent years stands out as a decisive factor in the globalization of economic activity. Foreign direct investment (FDI) stock is approaching 3 trillion dollars and has been growing at a rapid pace, substantially higher than that of world output and world exports.

Global sales of internationally produced goods exceed by far exports in arm's-length trade. It is estimated (UNCTAD 1995) that, if sales are defined broadly to include production by foreign affiliates as well as trade through subcontracting, licensing and franchising, their value for 1992 was 7 trillion dollars, more than twice the value of exports by home-based companies in arm's-length trade.

By far the largest percentage of global sales represents international production by foreign affiliates of transnational corporations (TNCs). For the international economy as a whole these sales for 1992 were estimated at 5.2 trillion dollars. If this is the best proxy for international production, one can see that the recent trend away from arm's-length trade and in favour of local production introduces a new modality in international transactions with important effects on FDI corporate strategies as well as government policies. In this sense, FDI activity in the 1990s presents added interest concerning possible reorientation of FDI strategies to patterns suggested by the new global environment of the 1990s.

Now, most of the FDI activity is concentrated in the Triad (US, EU and Japan). As shown by Tables 10.1, 10.2 and 10A.1, the Triad countries account for more than 80 per cent of total FDI stock and 70 per cent of global outflows. Within the Triad, the European Union (EU hereafter) is the largest FDI recipient over time while Japan's inward FDI stock is extremely small. Flow-wise, the United States resumed its position as the single largest FDI recipient with Japan's share being negligible again.

The outflow of investment presents a different picture in terms of shares by the three members of the Triad. Outside the preponderance of the US as the largest investor abroad, the dramatic increase of Japanese investment in Europe has stimulated a great deal of interest among scholars, policymakers and business people. Despite the slowdown in the inflow of Japanese FDI to Europe in recent years Japan remains the second largest FDI power in the EU. The decline in Japanese FDI outflow to Europe coincides with the recession years of Japan. It should be mentioned, however, that the decline in Japanese FDI flow in Europe continued into 1994 when the FDI recession of 1991–93 ended and Japan moved back up among the top foreign investment countries. Furthermore, in the last years there seems to have been a turn in the interest of Japanese investors towards East Asia.

This turn could be more of a temporary phenomenon that finds its explanation primarily in the adverse economic conditions prevailing in Japan. Japan's economic recession affected negatively the capacity of parent companies to finance new investment projects in countries where their affiliates did not realize large enough profits to accommodate reinvestment activities. Compared to Europe, other areas, such as East Asia and South America, showed larger profitability margins for Japanese subsidiaries. According to Japanese External Trade Organization (JETRO) statistics (JETRO 1995) the sustained growth in Asian markets secured profit rates to subsidiaries five times above the average for all other regions. As a result, reinvestment-based FDI activity by Japanese overseas subsidiaries was convenient during the recession years of the Japanese economy.

Coming back to Japanese investment interests in Europe, then, the massive inflow of Japanese investment in the EU in the 1980s which became known as the 'Japanese Challenge', could be partially explained by the response to the EU 1992 programme by the Japanese FDIs which sought to position themselves strategically in Europe. The prevailing view, however, is that the surge of Japanese FDIs during the mid-to late 1980s was not a temporary phenomenon in response to the 'Fortress Europe' syndrome. Instead, Japan, like the US, had chosen the EU as the appropriate market to implement its long-run global corporate strategy.

The organizational aspects of Japanese FDI in Europe present special interest for researchers. In particular the similarities and differences in structure and performance of US and Japanese FDIs in Europe have become the subject of research by many scholars in recent years (for example, Dunning and Cantwell 1991; Gittleman and Dunning 1992; Dunning 1993; Gittleman and Graham 1994; Encarnation 1993). The central theme of these works is the question whether Japan, as the youngest member of the Triad in massive FDI activity, is following the path of the first foreign investment power, the United States.

In the following we shall attempt to address this question. An attempt is made to examine the Japanese pattern of investment, in the light of the aforementioned tendencies in the 1990s, for increases in international production through the use of foreign subsidiaries. The chapter centres attention on the extent to which the unique pattern of industrial organization domestically, enters as an important factor in explaining the behaviour of Japanese FDIs in Europe.

2 The uniqueness of industrial organization in Japan

It would seem that the common economic and political environment confronted by FDIs in Europe would suggest similar evolutionary paths in structure and behaviour for Japanese and US transnationals in the EU. Of course, the fact that the Japanese FDI surge followed, after a considerable time lag, the FDI expansion by the US may call for some differences in the two groups of transnationals. On the other hand, the existing persistent structural differences of the Japanese FDIs call for a different causality reasoning, which may require more than minor modifications of the existing paradigms that apply in the case of Western FDI. Indeed, in recent years there is a growing predisposition among researchers and business people to view Japanese FDIs from a different perspective on account of the unique institutional environment of the Japanese firm domestically.

There is a growing awareness among policymakers, researchers and business leaders that the institutional characteristics and behaviour of Japanese firms differ substantially from the Western prototypes. To be sure, in the last decades convergence does occur. The change is slow, however. The violent wave of globalization does not seem to have had, so far, substantial effects on the institutional practices of Japanese industrial organization. As we shall see, this resistance to change at home is reflected in the overseas investment traits of Japanese FDIs.

Among the institutional characteristics of Japanese business that resist radical change are the following:

1. The more centralized structure of business administration. Shareholders are virtually powerless when it comes to substantive corporate strategies. Japanese managers have more of a free hand than their Western counterparts in decisionmaking on these matters. On the other hand, employee participation is stronger and reflects the more or less 'permanent' character of employment in Japanese firms.
2. In contrast to their centralized administrative structure, Japanese firms, for the most part, do not compete as independent entities but as members of large groups of interrelated companies known as *keiretsu*

(enterprise group). These companies, as 'stable shareholders' belonging to the same *keiretsu*, hold the majority of shares so that this type of industrial organization implies far more intensive inter-firm relationships.

3. In addition to these differences in the intra- and inter-firm structural idiosyncrasies, the business institutional environment and behaviour of Japanese firms is characterized by a close government – business relationship. Japanese economic policies and bureaucratic practices differ from those in the West in substantive ways. In general, the cooperation between government and business is substantially closer. This closeness is reflected in the behaviouristic traits of typical large Japanese enterprise in such matters as anti-trust practices, R&D policies and several other efficiency-promoting functions.

The relevant question in the present context is the extent to which these and other institutional characteristics affect the pattern and motivations of Japanese FDIs in Europe. Inevitably, the prototype of inter-firm relationships and the prevailing form of Japanese industrial organization stand out as the most important factors in trying to explain and analyse the morphology and idiosyncrasies of Japanese FDI in Europe. It is in this sense that many researchers and business people centre their attention on the webs in interrelated companies known as *keiretsu*.

Keiretsu is a somewhat elusive concept, vastly misunderstood. This is because *keiretsu* relationships can take on forms that vary according to the specific field of industry. In the final analysis the *keiretsu* could be seen as the appropriate tool used to confer special competitive advantages to the firm-members of the group. For export–import industries, such *keiretsu* advantages may translate into capturing large shares of overseas markets and/or act as an organizational barrier for foreign firms to enter the Japanese market. In the technology-intensive industries, on the other hand, *keiretsu* could get the credit for gaining access for Japanese firms to important techno-manufacturing skills.

A common trait of the *keiretsu* which is of special interest in the present context is that, in the final analysis, it acts to replace arm's-length transactions with inter-firm cooperation in order to internalize technological and managerial advantages. It is in this sense that, in view of the heightened attention to Japanese FDI, the implications of the *keiretsu* for international trade and investment surface as an important factor. In plain terms the question is to what extent *keiretsu* organizations characterize Japanese investment in the EU.

In analysing Japan's outward FDI, it is the vertical *keiretsu* which matters, not the horizontal. The latter is more easily defined and identified than the former. It refers to a number of large diversified families of companies (Fuyo, Mitsubishi, Sumitomo, Mitsui, Sonwa and DKB – Dai-Ichi Kangyo) which are interlinked in their economic activity. Cross-ownership of equity among these groups runs high so that the collective interests of these groups guarantee close cooperation which may take the form of an organizational barrier concerning FDI inflow in Japan. In a sense, then, horizontal *keiretsu* could be viewed as an advanced form of *inter-industry* conglomerate.

Now, *intra-industry* or vertical *keiretsu* refers to groups of firms in the same industry which participate in the production process. Production linkages, therefore, stand out as the main element in this vertical web of groups of firms. Cross-holding of equity may be present but it is not a prerequisite for the participation of firms in the vertical *keiretsu.* As long as these firms provide part of the value added in the production process they are part of the vertical interlinkage. It should be stressed that such production linkages are remarkably stable over time. It is also remarkable that these production schemes cover all aspects of the production process, starting from the supply of first materials to parts of the product, to the assembly lines and distribution process. Thus, in assembly-intensive industries such as automobile manufacturers, outside suppliers usually provide a very high percentage of the value added. These suppliers are, for the most part, members of the manufacturer's *keiretsu.* In effect, we have a pyramid-like formation of inter-firm linkage in the production process which is at the heart of the competitiveness of Japanese manufacturing. The loyalty and dedication of the firm-members of the *keiretsu* secures the cost-saving function of internalization which replaces, to a large extent, the arm's-length transactions.

It would seem, then, that the competitive advantage of Japanese manufacturing lies, to a large extent, with this manufacturer–supplier relationship which differs from that practised in other countries. To the extent that this unique competitive advantage may be transferred abroad through FDI activity, one can see the possibility that Japanese investment in Europe could differ markedly from that of other countries.

3 A brief look at the recent history of Japanese FDIs

The most striking features of the Japanese FDI flows in the 1980s are the high rates of growth and its sectoral distribution in favour of services, especially finance, insurance and commerce. Equally important are two other facts, that is (i) the timing of the investment surge which coincides with the single market programme and (ii) the large balance of payments surpluses of the Japanese economy during this period. In relation to this last fact, it has been argued (for example, Balasubramanyam and

Greenway 1992) that, since by far the largest portion of FDI flows during these years is of the portfolio capital variety, this is a balance of payments-related phenomenon which does not guarantee sustained growth in FDI activity.

It could be argued that the above thesis might gain support from the evidence we have so far about the considerable slowdown of Japanese FDI during 1991–93. However, even at this rather superficial level of analysis one could point out the possibility that the developments in Japanese FDI during the mid-1980s could be consistent with long-run corporate strategies. To begin with, the fast growth of Japanese FDI in services could be viewed as an integral part of such globalization strategies. Its preceding chronologically a comparable growth in the manufacturing sector could be the result of a deliberate choice of timing given the competitive potential of the Japanese economy and the developments in the greater economic space in the EU region. Concerning the first factor, it could be argued that investment in banking and finance was an easier way to penetrate foreign markets and thus gain a foothold in the EU. The 'location advantage', therefore, materializes in a non-technology-intensive area where no specific inter-firm relations, for example of the *keiretsu* type, are present. As we shall see in more detail below, one of the structural and organizational characteristics of Japanese manufacturing FDIs is their dependence on Japanese firms as sources of supply. This implies the need for 'bandwagon' type of investment by part and component suppliers to facilitate intra-firm trade. In this sense, banking and finance could be assigned a similar role in supporting the operation of manufacturing, and one could view this pattern of Japanese FDI growth in the EU in the context of a deliberate global strategy which accommodates its structural peculiarities.

We turn now to the manufacturing sector of Japanese FDIs. In the more distant past, a striking feature of the Japanese manufacturing investment in the EU was its shallowness in terms of products supplied by the Europe-based affiliates. Compared to their US counterparts, the contribution of FDIs to total sales of Japanese industrial products was very small. Exports were the main form of Japanese involvement in Europe. Japan relied very heavily on exports for the availability of its products in Europe, despite some progress made in the production component of sales.

The locational advantage of producing in Europe came about as a result of several changes that have occurred in recent years. In the more distant past the Japanese production pattern was characterized by very low mobility of capital abroad for direct investment purposes. In fact, most of Japan's early foreign investment activity aimed at strengthening its export competitiveness through easier access to resources and other inputs for the Japanese industry. Interestingly enough, this resistance to internationalization of Japanese production is carried into the more recent past when cost conditions in the domestic market gradually deteriorated primarily due to rising unit labour costs. It was not until the late 1970s, when the yen started appreciating against the other currencies, that the locational advantage of Japan ceased being as important a factor for certain industrial sectors. By the mid-1980s, the yen had appreciated to levels past those justified by increases in productivity. At the same time, unit labour costs were comparable to those of the United States. As a result, the location advantages of producing abroad rather than in Japan had improved. The US economy became the main pole of attraction for FDIs in certain manufacturing sectors such as electrical machinery, transport equipment, and steel and metals.

Many researchers (for example, Gittleman and Dunning (1992); Ozawa 1991) agree that the driving force behind the increasing FDI outflow of Japan up to the mid-1980s was the need to protect the existing share of the country's export markets. There was no radical change in Japan's industrial landscape towards an outward-looking investment (OLI) policy. Instead, Japan's economic development was still relying on home production-based exporting activity. In terms of Dunning's OLI theory, both the O-advantage and the L-advantage remained very 'domestic' for a long time.

According to Dunning and Cantwell (1991) although there were differences in the locational advantage of the United States and Europe, the Japanese FDIs viewed both areas as targets of export-substituting investment activity. In many ways this was done in reaction to the non-tariff protective measures which had been in effect since the mid-1970s. With the exception of some foreign investment activity by Japanese firms in the low-cost Asian countries, until 1984, the underlying motives of the Japanese FDIs was export upgrading at home as well as export substituting in foreign markets.

In the mid-1980s, the Japanese FDI policy underwent a substantial transformation away from its trade-replacing character. A new phase of a more outward policy with upgrading overseas investment got under way. A series of developments in that period provided the incentive for this change from a defensive, export-substituting policy, to a more offensive policy pursuing rationalization and internalization goals. The revaluation of the yen in 1985 and the decision of the EU to create the single market are usually listed among the main factors that account for this change in Japanese FDI strategy. With respect to the EU 1992 programme, as mentioned above, the 'Fortress Europe' syndrome, combined with the potential gains from market unification, were decisive factors for Japan to pursue more of an 'insider' status in the European Union.

In the years that followed, Japan continued to increasingly 'externalize' its competitive advantage away from its secure national environment. Breaking away from their insistence for greenfield foreign investment, Japanese firms engaged in a variety of strategic alliances, acquisitions and joint ventures. This type of investment activity was directed primarily to the new single market in the context of implementing a policy of 'Europeanization' of Japanese firms. It was estimated (Gittleman, Dunning, 1992) that in 1988–90, 40 per cent of the value of new Japanese investment in the EU took place in the form of acquisitions and mergers.

4 Japanese FDIs in Europe: the decade of the 1990s

In the 1990s the picture of Japanese FDIs differs markedly from the one described above. Most researchers recognize convergence of the Japanese foreign investment in Europe to the pattern established already by the US FDI. Indeed, in the second half of the 1980s there had been a new orientation of the Japanese FDIs, with a reliance on subsidiaries for foreign sales and an increase in local production. These overseas subsidiaries are affiliates of Japanese firms which own the majority of the equity shareholdings. Through their subsidiaries, parent firms acquire a higher degree of managerial control. This enables a more skilful management of their competitive advantage in the areas of technology marketing and organization. In effect, the parent company transfers tangible and intangible assets *internally* to its subsidiaries instead of making use of arm's-length transactions which incur higher costs.

The scheme of intra-company upstream–downstream trade and production, as illustrated in Figure 10.1, provides the basic framework for the implementation by the FDIs of their corporate strategies. It would seem that in recent years FDI activity by all members of Triad converges to this prototype. Within this framework now, there emerge patterns with major and minor differences in the degree of internalization and management control.

As show in Figure 10.1, the transfer from the parent company to subsidiaries could be supplemented by investment in distribution channels which could take the form of sales and service networks. These distribution agents may consist of minority-owned affiliates which are in close cooperation with the parents, so that dedicated sales service can be guaranteed.

The locally produced products by the foreign subsidiaries and the shipments by the home parent company to the distribution networks move on to their final destinations. These are the markets of the host country and the rest of the world but also the home country. This reverse

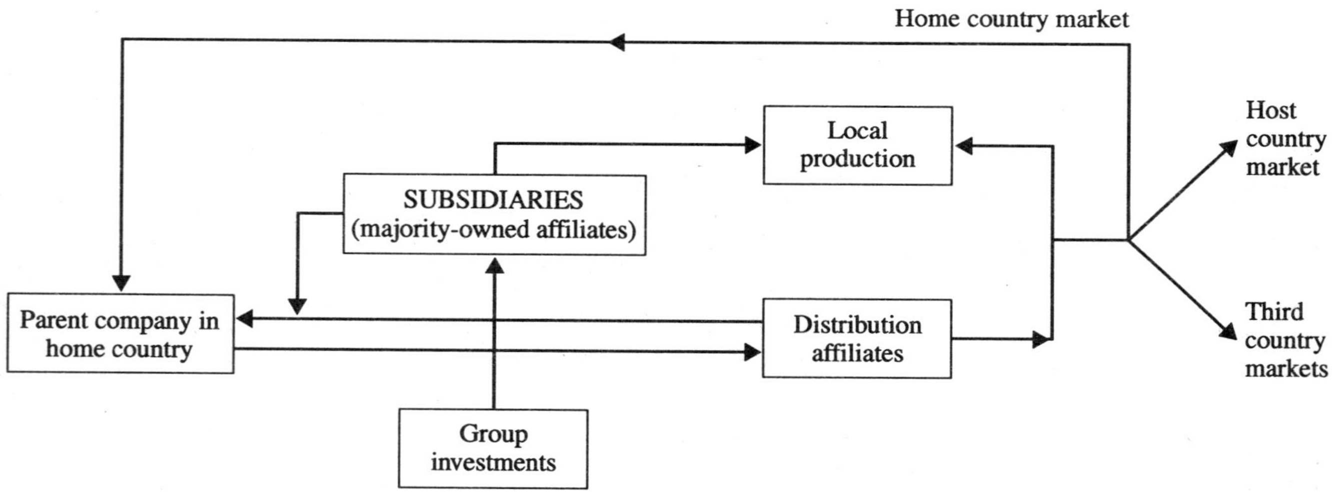

Figure 10.1 Foreign direct investment and intra-company trade

transfer with shipments of goods and services by the foreign affiliates back to their parent firms is supplemented with upstream sourcing of materials by the foreign subsidiary and the minority-owned affiliates.

The above flow of goods and services upstream and downstream gives rise to intra-company trade and ensures greater control and lower costs compared to arm's-length transactions. Obviously, the less the parent companies make use of market transactions and the more managerial control they exercise in the scheme illustrated in Figure 10.1, the greater the degree of internalization of the production and distribution process.

As mentioned earlier, Japan in the last decade has been a more 'mature' foreign investor. The question is to what extent Japanese FDIs have given in to the corporate globalization process described above. Is the basic pattern of FDI in manufacturing markedly different in the case of Japan on account of idiosyncrasies in industrial organization domestically? In answering this question the following points can be made.

1. To begin with, Japanese FDIs, although with some time lag, have followed in the steps of US transnationals in Europe as far as the preference for subsidiaries affiliated with the parent companies via majority ownership of equity. According to Japan's MITI (Ministry of International Trade and Investment) statistics, foreign subsidiaries accounted for the largest percentage of the country's sales to foreigners (about 85 per cent) in 1990. This percentage is slightly higher than the share of the subsidiaries of US transnationals.

   How big are foreign sales of Japanese FDIs compared to exports in arm's-length trade? Surprising as it may sound, the convergence of Japanese FDI to the US prototype was remarkable in this area, too. In the late 1980s, the ratio of foreign sales to exports was 2:1 – double what it was a decade ago (Encarnation 1993). For Japanese sales to the EU in particular, this ratio was twice as high as the average, that is, 4:1, and higher than the ratio that applies for the United States.
2. We come now to the point in the chart flow where Japanese FDI strategies differ markedly from those of the US. It is the persistent resistance of Japanese multinationals to engage, via their foreign subsidiaries, in offshore production in percentages comparable to those of US and EU transnationals. Offshore production has increased substantially in absolute numbers during the last decade. However, this change is behind changes in other areas where convergence to the 'standard' prototype of FDI strategies is obvious. There seems to exist a distinct preference by Japanese FDIs for manufactured exports rather than for foreign production. More emphasis is placed on the establishment of distribution networks via

wholesaling affiliates. These subsidiaries are established by Japanese multinationals for the express purpose of providing dedicated sales services to home-based multinationals.

This is a distinct contrast to US multinationals' sales strategy which places emphasis on local production abroad by majority subsidiaries for sale in the host country's market and other markets including the one back home. This strategy by US multinationals finds its application primarily in advanced markets. According to UNCTAD estimates (UNCTAD 1995), subsidiaries of US majority ownership account for sales of locally produced goods close to five times the exports of US-based companies (Table 10.1).

In the case of manufactured goods the ratio of sales to export is even higher. Table 10.2 shows the importance of local production of manufactural goods by FDIs in the Triad countries for the year 1990. As mentioned above, the US transnationals account for the largest percentage of US goods penetration in the EU. A similar strategy is followed by EU multinationals that operate in the US. The ratio of sales (of manufactured goods by EU majority-owned subsidiaries in the US) to exports was higher than 2:1 in 1990.

In the case of Japan, for the year 1990 sales of locally manufactured goods in 1990 were slightly less in value than that of export trade. Instead, sales by Japanese affiliates of distribution networks in the EU

Table 10.1 United States: forms of international transactions, 1986–1993 (billions of dollars)

Year	Sales of foreign affiliates*	Intra-firm merchandise exports	Merchandise exports	Merchandise exports excluding intra-firm exports
1986	929	83	227	144
1987	1053	89	254	165
1988	1195	112	322	211
1989	1285	130	364	234
1990	1493	135	394	258
1991	1542	148	422	274
1992	1579	163	448	285
1993	1574	169	465	296

Note: * All industries of all foreign affiliates.

Source: UNCTAD (1996).

Table 10.2 *Forms of international transactions in the Triad: FDI manufacturing sales, exports and distribution by affiliates (percentages)*

	Sales by subsidiaries	Exports	Sales by affiliates
US to EU	62.5	12.5	25.0
Japan to EU	16.5	28.5	55.0
Japan to US	16.2	21.6	62.2
EU to US	47.1	17.6	35.3

Sources: UNCTAD (1995), Encarnation (1994).

were three times the value of exports by Japan-based firms. The low ratio of local production to foreign trade applies also in the case of US imports of Japanese manufactures.

3. Despite some convergence of Japanese FDIs to the strategy pioneered by US transnationals of foreign sales growth via local production in the advanced markets, more central to Japanese foreign investment strategies is to secure control in their trade with the EU via intra-company shipments between the parents and affiliated subsidiaries in Europe. Japanese affiliates engaged in wholesaling activities account for the largest percentage of Japanese production penetrating the EU market. Gittleman and Graham (1994) find that a large number of these subsidiaries have the *keiretsu*-type relationships with the Japanese manufacturers.

A possible explanation of the low level of linkage directly with indigenous suppliers in the host countries of Europe is that it takes time to localize satisfactory sourcing of inputs. Since Japanese transnationals in Europe are the products of recent FDI growth, the insistence to apply national market organization practices abroad is to be expected. However, to the extent that these practices are persistent, some researchers (for example Gittleman and Graham 1994; Encarnation 1994) examine the possibility that intra-company trade with wholesaling subsidiaries could be viewed as an extension abroad of the unique industrial organizational structure in Japan which enables trade controls.

Heavy reliance on intra-company export trade could be viewed as the mirror image of the situation prevailing in import trade where Japanese multinationals, through tight control of their proprietary distribution networks, account for the largest percentage of imports. Encarnation (1993) has estimated that Japanese transnationals account for about three-quarters of all Japanese imports. This trade materializes either through intra-company shipments from Japanese equity-owned subsidiaries to their home parents or from other foreign suppliers, mostly affiliates of home firms. This affiliation often takes the form of vertical *keiretsu* relationships.

4. The above scheme of trade through intra-company shipments between international parents and overseas subsidiaries is obviously of pivotal importance for the foreign investment strategies of Japanese multinationals at this point. Japan's dependence on foreign investment for intra-company trade in the early 1990s could be viewed as an integral part of the FDI strategy by Japan which still relies to a large extent on export substitutional practices.

Our discussion above suggests that the novel part of this policy is that intra-company trade between parents and their subsidiaries has become more of an extension of the national industrial organization prototype. Just as in the case of trade with the US, Japan's bilateral relations with the EU are characterized by *keiretsu*-type relations which exert unparallel control and influence on trade. In this sense, this scheme of controlled trade flows in and out of Japan through domestic and foreign affiliates could be viewed as a 'distribution *keiretsu*' that can be traced back to the idiosyncrasies of Japanese industrial organization.

Unlike the 'distribution *keiretsu*', the case cannot be made as easily for 'production *keiretsu*' as a foreign extension of the Japanese industrial organization. In the recent literature, the work of Gittleman and Graham (1994) is one of the few attempts to search for the extent to which (production) *keiretsu* characterizes Japanese FDI in Europe. The authors attempt to examine the extent to which a build-up of vertical *keiretsu* in Europe is discernible at this time. As expected, definitional obstacles as well as lack of availability of statistics stand in the way of reaching definite conclusions. The findings of the paper confirm the hypothesis that 'a significant proportion of Japanese investment in the EU can be characterized by groups of *keiretsu*-related companies. In certain industries, notably automobiles and electrics/electronics there are clear indications that there is a tendency for a build-up of *keiretsu*-type structures. For other areas, the evidence is more inconclusive but large-scale *keiretsu* formation in Europe in the future is a possibility.

5 Conclusions

In conclusion, Japanese FDIs in the 1990s for the most part resemble the US–EU prototype of multinationals. In the last decade, Japanese multinationals did away with many of the characteristics that made

Japan's foreign investment uniquely different. In the 1980s Japan's FDIs entered a new phase of more outward-looking policies, away from its strictly trade-replacing character. Japan started externalizing its competitive advantage away from its secure national environment while rationalization and internationalization entered the picture as primary targets.

In the mid-to-late 1980s, this transformation process entered a phase of acceleration. The EU 1992 programme was obviously of pivotal importance for the new outlook of Japanese FDI. In pursuing more of an 'insider' status in the European Union, Japan's massive foreign investment in Europe was inevitably influenced by the globalization of FDI activity. It is in this sense that Japanese investment in Europe during this period is of crucial importance for the reorientation of Japanese FDIs in terms of global corporate strategy goals.

Japan's foreign investment in Europe followed in the steps of the US FDI prototype as far as giving priority to sales over arm's-length trade. However, this was not done via drastic transformation measures that emphasize local production in Europe by Japanese majority subsidiaries. The choice for investment in distribution networks is a distinct contrast to the 'standard' global FDI prototype which promotes sales of foreign-produced goods. Japan's heavy reliance on intra-company shipments in trade flow which bear a resemblance to the domestic transactions prototype has led to the creation of 'distribution *keiretsu*' in the big markets of Europe. Is 'production *keiretsu*' also at work at this time? Although current research shows movement in this direction for certain areas, in manufacturing, there are serious reservations as to how effectively Japanese FDIs in the manufacturing sector could internalize their competitive advantage in overseas areas on account of the unique structure of the domestic production process. As mentioned earlier, 'total quality control' from the top to the bottom of the production pyramid is based on a relationship between buyer and supplier which is derived from locational factors specific to the Japanese production model. It is a unique supplier–manufacturer relationship which goes beyond the marker mechanism and reflects close cooperation and mutual trust in inter-firm relationships.

It is in this sense that internationalization of Japanese production is not easy. The challenge faced by the Japanese FDIs is to cope with the problem of having to transplant the Japanese organizational structure into Europe. Many researchers (for example, Dunning and Cantwell 1991; Gittleman and Dunning 1992; Ozawa 1992) hold the view that the answer to the question 'what will be the future of Japanese investment growth in Europe?' lies primarily in the handling of this issue by the Japanese FDIs.

References

Balasubramanyam, V. and D. Greenway (1992), 'Economic Integration and Foreign Direct Investment: Japanese Investment in the EU', *Journal of Common Market Studies*, June.

Dunning, J. (1993), *Multinational Enterprises and the Global Economy*, Reading, Mass: Addison-Wesley.

Dunning, J. and J. Cantwell (1991), 'Japanese Direct Investment in Europe', in B. Burgenmeier (ed.), *Multinational Firms and European Integration, 1992*, London: Routledge.

Encarnation, D. (1993), 'A Common Evolution? A Comparison of United States and Japanese Transnational Corporation', *Transnational Corporations*, **2**, February.

Encarnation, D. (1994), 'Investment and Trade by American, European and Japanese Multinationals Across the Triad', in M. Mason and D. Encarnation (eds), *Does Ownership Matter?*, Oxford: Clarendon Press.

Gittleman, M. and J. Dunning (1992), 'Japanese Multinationals in Europe and the United States', in M. Klein and P. Welfens (eds), *Multinationals in New Europe and Global Trade*, London: Springer-Verlag.

Gittleman, M. and E. Graham (1994), 'The Performance and Structure of Japanese Affiliates in the European Community', in M. Mason and D. Encarnation (eds), *Does Ownership Matter?*, Oxford: Clarendon Press.

Japanese External Trade Organization (JETRO) (1995), *White Paper on Foreign Direct Investment*, March.

Ozawa, T. (1991), 'Japanese Multinationals and 1992', in B. Burgenmeier (ed.), *Multinational Firms and European Integration 1992*, London: Routledge.

Ozawa, T. (1992), 'Cross Investment between Japan and the EU', in J. Cantwell (ed.), *Multinational Investment in Modern Europe*, Cheltenham: Edward Elgar.

UNCTAD (1994, 1995), *World Investment Report*.

Appendix 10A

Table 10A.1 *Outflows of foreign direct investment from the five major home countries, 1981–1994 (billions of dollars)*

	Annual average								
Country	1981–85	1986–90	1988	1989	1990	1991	1992	1993	1994
France	3	17	14	19	35	24	31	21	22
Germany	4	16	13	18	29	22	16	15	20
Japan	5	32	34	44	48	31	17	14	18
United Kingdom	9	28	37	35	19	16	16	26	25
United States	11	22	14	34	24	33	33	68	45
Total	32	115	113	151	155	126	113	126	130
All countries	48	168	168	218	243	199	190	222	222

Source: UNCTAD (1995).

11 Tendencies and idiosyncrasies of European trading partners

Evrard Claessens and Annemie Cools

1 Introduction

On the eve of a new world trading system (Zorgbibe 1993; Ohmae 1995), the post-Cold War debate includes the search for Europe's position in the new wave of worldwide regionalism. This debate is sandwiched between the trends towards a global economy and various approaches to regionalism (Kreinin and Plummer 1994), that is, the search for geographical identity of certain regions within the whole.

2 Beyond economics

The dynamics of international relations can be identified by three major components – security (the military and beyond); the economy; and the search for cultural, linguistic and religious identity. These three components are portrayed in Figure 11.1, with explicit reference to the spatial coverage and the time span.

Cultural identities may be confined to a small geographical area, but they feature long-term survival. Examples span the preservation of Thai culture without colonial rule and the Inca culture preserved at Machu

Figure 11.1 Culture, security and economy in time and space

Pichu long after the disappearance of its inhabitants. Ancient Greeks (Sophocles, *Antigone*, verse 456) knew that certain things 'are not of todays or yesterdays, but of all times'. In contrast, the economy adjusts quickly and worldwide. Its long-term options are actually the short term. In between these extremes, Figure 11.1 situates the 'alliances', covering security, the military and related issues.

This approach supports the assumption that socioeconomic grouping can be executed on a cross-sectional basis, because of the (almost) instant adaptation of economic processes.

3 Organization of socioeconomic clusters

Briefly, this contribution questions to what extent nations feature similar socioeconomic characteristics, and whether they cluster together in homogeneous regions. This hypothesis is tested by a hierarchical cluster analysis, using the complete linkage method, following the graph of Figure 11.2. The World Bank's data contain bottom-line statistics of about two hundred nations in 1993, of which 90 provide twelve key variables, including foreign trade. This appears to be a sufficiently large sample for this explorative exercise.

The socioeconomic variables are population, GDP, urban population,

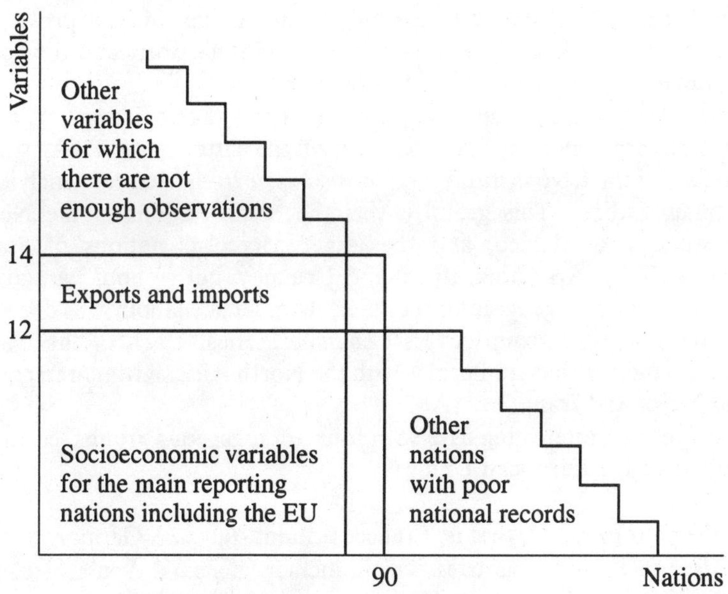

Figure 11.2 Organization of the cluster analysis

Table 11.1 Overview of the four exercises

	With EU	Without EU
Without trade	First	Second
With trade	Fourth	Third

the importance of agriculture, industry and services to the economy, access to communication (for example, telephones), female labour (namely, emancipation), age dependency rate, population growth, energy consumption, gross domestic investment and the export and import value of trade. The trade variables measure the openness of an economy and are used only in the third and the fourth exercises, as shown in Table 11.1.

3.1 The basic first cluster analysis

The first basic exercise (Table 11.2) looks at the European Union within the world economy without trade being a variable.

This cross-section contains 16 clusters of which the African, Caribbean and Pacific (ACP) countries (here only Africa) occupy two (5a and 5b). When taking only 15 clusters, these two groups are joined. This provides a small but clear difference between the poor ACP members and the better off (which are similar to the Himalayan nations).

Some nations are grouped into existing regional associations, whereas others remain separated. An example of the latter is NAFTA, where Canada and the US constitute a separate cluster from Mexico, which joins the 'main Latins'. This group covers the petrol nations of the North (Venezuela and Mexico, and the larger Mercosur nations of South America (Chile, Argentina, Brazil and Uruguay, but without Paraguay). Lebanon joins as a geographical outlier; here, female labour was decisive. The 'small Latins' group covers Central America, much of the 'Pacto Andino', and also has similarities with the North African Maghreb region up to Egypt and Iran.

Europe is an interesting case with four homogeneous groups, covering members of the European Union:

- the European G7, that is, France, Britain, Italy and Germany;
- the small rich countries which include Benelux, Spain, Ireland, Switzerland, Greece and Cyprus. Singapore joins this group because of the city state's similarities;

Table 11.2 Basic clusters of the first exercise

Cluster 1 small Latin and Maghreb-type countries
Algeria, Egypt, Iran, Morocco, Tunisia
Bolivia, Colombia, Dominican Republic, Ecuador, El Salvador, Guatemala, Honduras, Nicaragua, Panama, Paraguay, Peru

Cluster 2 main Latin countries
Argentina, Brazil, Chile, Mexico, Uruguay, Venezuela
Outlier: Lebanon

Cluster 3 richer European countries
Austria, Belgium, Cyprus, Greece, Ireland, the Netherlands, Spain, Switzerland
Outlier: Singapore

Cluster 4 main poor (Asia and Africa) countries
Bangladesh, Pakistan, Mali, Mauritania, Chad

Cluster 5a poor African ACP countries
Benin, Burkina Faso, Burundi, Central African Republic, Congo, Ethiopia, Gabon, Gambia, Ghana, Guinea Bissau, Madagascar, Malawi, Mozambique, Niger, Nigeria, Rwanda, Senegal, Sierra Leone, Tanzania, Uganda

Cluster 5b other ACP and Himalayan countries
Cameroon, Ivory Coast, Kenya, Togo, Zimbabwe, Myanmar (Burma), Nepal, Butan

Cluster 6 Canada

Cluster 7 Scandinavian countries
Denmark, Finland, Iceland, Norway, Sweden

Cluster 8 European G7 countries
France, Germany, Italy, Great Britain

Cluster 9 newly industrialized countries
(this 'others' group is separate in the third exercise)
ASEAN: Indonesia, Malaysia, Philippines, Thailand, Vietnam
others: Mauritius, Sri Lanka, Turkey, Guyana, South Africa

Cluster 10 retarded European periphery
Hungary, Poland, Romania, Portugal

Cluster 11 India

Cluster 12 Japan

Cluster 13 Jordan

Cluster 14 Kuwait

Cluster 15 United States

- the retarded periphery, being mainly the central European 'Visegrad', the Balkans and Portugal.
- the rich North, that is, Scandinavia, later joined by Canada.

The newly industrialized countries (NICs) are best identified in Asia. The Association of South-East Nations (ASEAN) economies are joined by Sri Lanka, Turkey, South Africa, Mauritius and Guyana.

This first exercise shows that 'natural regionalism' exists with clear groups emerging such as ASEAN, the Mercosur, the Pacto Andino, the Maghreb and Central America.

Six countries remain 'single'; their association in intergovernmental agreements thus features strategic items, such as the Triad (with Japan, the US and the EU) or NAFTA (with the US, Canada and Mexico).

The European Union is 'united' but in four natural parts: the bigger G7 members and three groups of smaller nations (Scandinavia, the central rich and the retarded periphery). Here, the strategic item apparently consists in keeping these different groups together.

3.2 The second exercise (the basic cluster without the EU)

When the 1992 EU countries are taken out of the sample, the clustering of the rest changes. The remaining 'small rich' of cluster 3 join the periphery of cluster 10. Scandinavia remains united and is even joined by Canada in a kind of 'Nordic club'. The NICs consolidate their South-East Asian base with Myanmar. Sri Lanka and Guyana now constitute a separate group. Singapore stands alone, and will later join Benelux.

3.3 The third exercise (with trade)

These clusters show only one change, compared to previous examples: Mauritius leaves the ASEAN-dominated NIC group, and joins Sri Lanka and Guyana. The stability of the second and the third group shows that trade is so related to economic development, that it does not change the actual clusters very much, except for very open economies, such as the island state of Mauritius.

3.4 The fourth exercise (with trade and including the EU)

Finally, the analysis repeats the first basic cluster (with the EU) but now with foreign trade (Table 11.3). The argument of open economies now applies to the European Union itself. There, the main changes apply on this basic indication.

Benelux (Belgium or BLEU and the Netherlands) leaves the club of the small rich and joins Singapore; the 'openness' of those economies is without doubt, with a trade dependency factor of more than 3:4. Within

Table 11.3 Clusters with trade

Clusters 1 and 2 unchanged	
Cluster 3a	richer European niche and the periphery
	Austria, Greece, Cyprus, Ireland, Spain, Portugal, Switzerland, Hungary, Poland and Romania
Clusters 3	trading economies (separate cluster)
	Belgium and Luxembourg (BLEU), the Netherlands and Singapore
Cluster 4	unchanged
Cluster 5	5 joins 5/bis in ACP and Himalayan countries
Cluster 7	6 joins 7 in the northern periphery
Cluster 8a	the European G7
	France, Italy, Great Britain
Cluster 8b	Germany leaves cluster 8
Clusters 9 to 15	unchanged

the European G7 club, Germany leaves the others (UK/Great Britain, France and Italy) and plays solitaire. The latter move is not clearly associated with a stable feature of imports or exports, since the observation period synchronizes with the German reunification process; a matter to be followed when things get 'normal' again.

4 Evaluation

The cluster exercise was finally tested by applying iterative clustering instead of the hierarchical clustering. Here, only clusters 3 and 7 of the fourth exercise changed again with:

- a group of the former EFTA (Scandinavia and Alpine states);
- an enlarged Mediterranean club (Greece and Cyprus with Lebanon) joining the South American (major) Latins; and
- a remarkable splitting of Benelux with the Netherlands joining Spain and even Canada joining Belgium.

Apart from these nations, the clusters themselves are quite stable with Euclidean distances smaller than one within the clusters and scoring between 4 and 16 between the clusters. The method proves a stable complement to historical studies on trade partners and their regions (Claessens and Cools 1996). Above all, it can be used effectively for tracing economic integration in transition.

References

Aldenderfer, M.S. and R.K. Blasfield (1984), *Cluster Analysis*, London: Sage Publications.

Andenberg, M.R. (1973), *Cluster Analysis for Applications*, New York: Academic Press.

Berlage, L. and D. Terweduwe (1985), *The Classification of Countries by Cluster and by Factor Analysis*, K.U. Leuven.

Claessens, E. (1984), 'Traffic and Trade Projections on the Eastbound Suez Shipping Route', *Maritime Policy and Management*, **11** (1), 45–55.

Claessens, E. and A. Cools (1996), 'Turning Tides on the North Atlantic', in C. Paraskevopoulos, R. Grinspun and G. Eaton (eds), *Economic Integration in the Americas*, Cheltenham: Edward Elgar; pp. 156–65.

Huizingh, E. (1989), *SPSS/PC and Data Entry*, Amsterdam: Addison Wesley, Amsterdam.

Kreinin, M. and M. Plummer (1994), ' "Natural" Economic Blocs; An Alternative Formulation', *International Trade Journal*, **8** (2), pp. 193–205.

Norusis, M.J. (1990), *SPSS/PC+, Statistics 4.0 for the IBM PC/XT/AT and PS/2*, Chicago: SPSS Inc.

Ohmae, K. (1995a), *The End of the Nation State*, London: Harper.

Ohmae, K. (1995b), *The Evolving Global Economy*, Harvard Business Review series.

Romesburg, H.C. (1984), *Cluster Analysis for Researchers*, Belmont: Lifetime Learning Publications.

World Bank (1995), *World Tables of 1993*, Baltimore and London: Johns Hopkins University Press.

Zorgbibe, (1993), *L'après-guerre froide en Europe* (After the Cold War in Europe), Paris: PUF.

PART III

LESSONS FROM THE CASE OF MEXICO

12 The growing anti-immigrant debate in the North American region and its impact on Mexico

Mónica Verea

1 Introduction

The United States and Canada have traditionally had relatively open approaches to immigration, which has been viewed more as an asset than as a burden. After several years of tight restrictions favouring North-western Europe, both countries liberalized their immigration policies at the end of the Second World War, increasing the numbers admitted in comparison to the lean years of the 1930s and those of the war. Growing racial and ethnic toleration played an important role during the 1960s in shaping the ways in which both North American countries became more liberal in their immigration policies. Today's open acceptance of immigrants and refugees is tempered with caution.

Even though Canada and the United States think of themselves as nations of immigrants, immigration has always been a controversial issue within their societies. While they have been proud of their immigrant heritage and have pointed to its success in integrating various ethnic groups into a cultural mosaic, the growing ethnic pluralism is facing some problems and challenges. Demographic needs to settle and develop societies, economic needs for skilled labourers and political ideologies favouring immigrants from non-communist regimes have all played important roles in the history of opening and closing doors to immigrants. Therefore, Canada and the United States have had different historical experiences on immigration which have affected their policies in several ways. However, one of the main differences is that the United States shares a 1900-mile border with Mexico. The tensions created by Mexican migration to the US is perhaps one of the most sensitive issues in the relationship between the two neighbours, where friction has been at times modest and at others volatile, but it has always been present. This phenomenon does not have the same importance along the US–Canadian border.

During the last years this trend has been changing radically, because immigrants to both countries, who had formerly been mainly European in origin, now come primarily from the Third World countries of Asia and

Latin America. Particularly in the United States, a significant number of undocumented aliens have arrived and many refugee claimants have been demanding asylum. This situation has changed the ethnic composition of communities, with the result that tolerance and humanitarianism have been severely tested. This has led – in the mid-1990s – to a situation in which the topic of migration arouses very strong feelings, and policy and legislation are vulnerable to criticism.

2 The heightened anti-immigrant debate in the United States

Perception of immigrants in the United States has become increasingly negative during the 1990s, and a new anti-immigrant attitude has emerged. Immigrants have been labelled as problematic, and well-known arguments from the past have been raised: immigrants are criticized by labour unions for taking workers' jobs and lowering the earnings and labour market opportunities of native workers, and by xenophobes for not learning English and for introducing unacceptable foreign customs into American society. Undoubtedly, ideas on immigration began to change with the most recent economic recession, especially in California where it lasted longer. This has led to a new verbal offensive and a harsh political debate against immigrants in general and against illegal Mexican immigrants in particular.

This situation provided fertile ground for the birth of the initiative known as Proposition 187 in California, prohibiting the use of public education and free medical services (except in emergencies) to illegal immigrants.[1] Those who orchestrated the 187 were helped by the anti-immigration climate and by the strong support of the Republican candidate for state governor, Pete Wilson, who obtained an overwhelming majority for his reelection.[2]

In general terms, Proposition 187 and similar initiatives[3] have created a hostile environment against immigrants, altering the tone of the political debate and radically changing expectations for future migration policy. The theme of immigration control now has an important role both in US foreign policy and also in the domestic policy context. Since the Republicans gained control of the House of Representatives for the first time in forty years and of the Senate since 1986, immigration has been a frequent issue for discussion in both chambers. It was also introduced into the presidential campaign for 1996.

President Bill Clinton has responded energetically on the subject of immigration within the new domestic debate. His objectives appear to be to find a middle ground between the extremes of American political opinion on immigration, and at the same time to be reelected as president. Although he has recognized the important contribution of legal immigrants to American society, his latest declarations express intolerance towards illegal immigration, while stating the need to establish limits.

During his administration, fences have been erected at critical points, and border patrol operations (such as *Blockade* in El Paso, Texas; *Guardián* in San Diego, California; and *Safeguard* in Nogales, Arizona) at the commonest crossing places on the Mexican–US border have tried to make illegal entrance as difficult as possible. Although apprehensions are less frequent in these areas, it is difficult to measure the efficiency of these methods by the numbers of those caught. Aliens have attempted to enter through other more remote areas, for example, the Arizona desert, where the US Border Patrol launched a 'Stay Out, Stay Alive' programme, to dissuade potential illegal aliens. Because of this situation, smugglers are raising their rates for a guaranteed safe passage to Los Angeles which would mainly bring aliens across the 2013-mile US–Mexican border.

It is important to mention that more than 90 per cent of the apprehensions made by the border patrol are of persons who 'enter without inspection' (EWIs), which in most cases occur at the US–Mexican border. Nevertheless, it has been calculated that, since 1992, about 50 per cent of illegals enter the country on temporary visas and overstay their permits.[4] Half the illegal immigrants who have overstayed their visa limits come from a wide spectrum of countries, not exclusively from Mexico. The debate on migratory control has been distorted, since most of the human and economic resources for the control of illegal immigration have been concentrated on the southern border. Therefore, discussion has centred on stopping the entry of undocumented immigrants through mechanisms such as: an increase in border security with the deportation of the undocumented immigrants; a struggle against smugglers of undocumented immigrants; promotion of a national identification register; and the reduction of public benefits for non-citizens.

Although Clinton is trying to appear firm on illegal immigration, his position should not be seen as straightforwardly anti-immigration. His opposition to Proposition 187 was emphatic and was backed by the ruling of the United States High Court that since 1982 children without papers have had right of access to public schools.[5] His proposals for a cutback on public services for illegals were not made with the intention of preventing access to public schools or public medical services. He also proposed a two hundred and fifty million dollar fund for the support of those states affected by medical or health expenses incurred by illegal immigrants.[6]

Unfortunately, Clinton's lukewarm attempts to contain the upsurging of anti-immigration politics have not restrained politicians either in

Congress or in the states. So, the immigration issue, in a highly emotionally charged atmosphere, divides along partisan lines or viewpoints. It has more impact with the new Republican majority in Congress. It is important to stress that both houses, led by Republicans Alan Simpson in the Senate and Lamar Smith in the House of Representatives, have pushed for drastic measures to control immigration, above all along the southern border.

On 30 September 1996, President Clinton signed the Illegal Immigration Reform and Immigrant Responsibility Act of 1996 (IIRIRA). During his recent official visit to Mexico City, he supported the law, stating that 'if I would have to sign it tomorrow, I would do it ... we are a nation of immigrants but also of laws. Those who obey our laws are welcome, those who break them must suffer the consequences'. He thinks that the new law provides a better opportunity to control the borders, removing illegals from the labour market.[7]

The IIRIRA is complex and far-reaching, and represents a radical change in US Immigration law, including increases in criminal penalties for immigration-related offences, authorization for increases in enforcement personnel and new enforcement powers. It also undertakes a comprehensive reorganization of the process of removal for inadmissible and deportable aliens arriving at any port of entry. The act requires the implementation of three specific types of employment authorization and verification programmes. Finally it includes restrictions on the eligibility for public benefits and imposes new requirements for sponsors of immigrants in 1996.[8] There was also another very important law, approved in August 1996, which significantly affected legal and illegal immigrant rights; this was the Personal Responsibility and Work Opportunity Act (PRWORA).[9]

The result of both laws is more rigidity in order to promote safe, legal and orderly migration. At the same time, both acts try to restrict immigrants' natural welfare rights, which legal American immigrants have been paying for for years with their taxes. The supporters of the restrictions on immigrant access to federal benefits believe that this will have positive consequences in balancing the budget. On the other hand, opponents argue that public health minimizes the spread of communicable diseases and improves the health of US citizens, especially babies. Another 'hot initiative' was the one related to the new provision for sponsors, which could lead to unfair deportations. Now only those who earn a salary 125 per cent above the poverty level would be permitted to sponsor immigrants, but they might not necessarily be willing to do so. The result, if immigrants cannot be sponsored, is that they become a 'public charge', thus making deportation possible. Both measures would have very important consequences in Mexico and, of course, in bilateral relations.

Most of the research that has been done in recent years suggests that the main cause of immigration is to seek jobs and not for welfare or other benefits. Nowadays lawmakers are seeking a range of restrictions on immigrants, since they consider that, overall, immigrants cost the nation much more than they contribute. The theory behind these proposals is that fewer benefits will discourage illegals from migrating or staying in the United States. Perhaps this will become the new trend that will be used to control immigration flows.

3 Implications for Mexican immigrants

Mexican migration to the United States has traditionally been a difficult and thorny issue in bilateral relations. The United States has unilaterally opened and closed the door on legal and undocumented immigration many times during this century. There is a long history of inviting foreign workers to the United States to meet employer's labour needs and rejecting them during times of economic downturn. At the end of the bilateral 'Bracero Program' agreement in 1964, there was a significant increase in undocumented immigration as well as a rise in tension in bilateral relations. We could say that the substantial increase in Mexican migration to the United States is a direct response to the natural economic forces which have always existed, with a high demand for cheap labour on one side and a large supply on the other. In most cases people who emigrate do it for various reasons, including a wage differential of about one to ten times for similar work and strong links among members of the communities on either side, making emigration easier and more attractive. Thus an illegal but natural bilateral labour market is produced.

Traditionally, the government of Mexico has adopted a passive position towards the migration issue – mainly of undocumented workers – officially declaring that its highest obligation is to protect the physical integrity and dignity of its nationals who emigrate abroad, regardless of their migration status in the country where they are. Mexicans have considered that migration bows to the fundamental forces of supply and demand. Although this has not been recognized in the US, it meets a legitimate need in the US and it does so without damage to American workers.[10]

The presence of illegal and even of legal immigrants has acted as a kind of political lightning rod, on which many Americans have vented their frustrations in times of economic difficulties. This presence was shown up by the number of undocumented Mexican immigrants who applied for legalization in 1987 and 1988 under the provisions of the Immigration

Reform and Control Act of 1986 (IRCA). There is evidence from a wide variety of research studies that IRCA brought about a reduction in illegal Mexican immigration to the United States during the three years immediately after the legislation was passed. Since that period, INS statistics suggest that undocumented immigration is on the rise again.

Through IRCA, two types of immigrants were legalized. Under the first programme,[11] those who could prove that they had resided in the US continually since 1982 (1 757 957 people) were legalized. The second category consisted of 1 480 971 'special agricultural workers' (SAW), who could prove that they served as temporary workers in the agricultural sector for a minimum of 90 days between May 1985 and May 1986.[12] Both programmes benefited 2 270 725 Mexicans by regularizing their immigration status and therefore making them eligible for citizenship at the beginning of 1994.

Mexicans also benefited – although to a much lesser degree – from the Immigration Act of 1990 which, starting in 1992, allowed an increase in the legal immigration quota of Mexicans through three provisions: an increase of approximately 40 per cent over and above the 500 000 immigrants who had previously been admitted annually; an increase in the limit per country, which in Mexico's case rose from 20 000 to 26 000; and an independent number (55 000) of three-year visas – which expired in 1995 – for immediate family members of those recently legalized through IRCA and/or who were legally residing in the United States in May 1988. These measures were designed to reunite the families of newly legal immigrants because these other members were, in some cases, already in the US illegally. The law also made it easier to become employed in professional and highly skilled jobs, raising the limit from 58 000 to 140 000.[13]

Even though NAFTA negotiations did not include immigration issues, they did lead to a number of provisions similar to those agreed upon in the Free Trade Agreement (FTA) between Canada and the United States. The treaty permits the entry of four categories of 'business people' into the United States, Canada and Mexico, on a reciprocal basis. The limit set for Mexican professionals who may work temporarily in the United States is 5500 a year – a figure which has not yet been reached.

It is fair to recognize that the data mentioned earlier show that Mexicans have been favoured by a special treatment or a kind of concession over the past eight years – mainly through the IRCA's amnesty programmes and some legal measures included in the Immigration Act of 1990. Both acts have fostered legalization of illegals and permitted more legal entrants. They have probably contributed to an increase in immigration by dependants who have come to the US illegally, while waiting to be granted entry visas. In spite of the legalization implemented by the two laws, the presence of the total number of Mexicans in the US – legalized or not – has become more visible in this new age of ethnic transformation of the Southwest which, at the same time, has triggered an important political resistance against former liberal admission policies for new immigrants.

Moreover, IIRIRA, the new law, was approved without any amnesty programme like IRCA's. Therefore Mexican undocumented immigrants, who have been working for many years and have not applied for the legalization of their status, are now liable to be deported if they do not leave the country voluntarily during the next six months of its application. Undoubtedly, this negative provision is going to lead to a very unfortunate situation for Mexican nationals living in the US without any protection.

4 New debate of the reforms needed to Canadian immigration legislation

In general terms, Canada's outlook on migration has been positive, since immigrants have been perceived as important human capital contributing to Canadian growth, a source of investment feeding foreign trade links, rejuvenating its population and encouraging consumption. Nevertheless, during recent years, Canadians, aware of the problems arising from uncontrolled immigration, have been concerned to formulate a new migration policy which would answer demographic and labour needs on a federal and regional level. This situation has led to an attempt to determine the level, categories and kinds of immigrants Canada needs to accept each year.

The years under the conservative Canadian government between 1984 and 1993 witnessed a heightened debate on the inadequacy of immigration legislation, particularly in its treatment of the growing numbers of refugee claimants arriving at the Canadian borders. Concern during that period was that if significant measures were not taken to ensure management of the flow of people into the country, and to administer the programme fairly, then immigration policy might become a major grassroots political issue. This continued warning has contributed to the recent backlash against immigration.

The government has recently dealt with the refugee question and tightened up on the entry of 'illegal immigrants'. Now they are turning their attention to an overhaul of the whole immigration legislation, particularly in its treatment of the increasing numbers of refugee claimants, as well as the growing number of illegal immigrants arriving at Canadian borders or trying to enter the country, for example, by hiding on ships. The new restrictionist movement worries not only about the quantity but mainly the quality of immigrants.

The Liberal Party now in power, which has traditionally been sympathetic towards immigrants, announced its intentions of setting immigration levels at one per cent of Canada's population, an intake of 270 000 a year. Nevertheless, the economic recession and the anti-immigrant climate, expressed through public opinion, has made this more difficult. It is important to note that, between 1983 and 1994, Canada's newcomers have increased significantly from 89 157 in 1983 to 152 098 in 1987 and to 252 137 in 1993.[14] During 1996, the number was drastically reduced to 225 313 immigrants, a trend that will continue.

There has also been an important change with respect to the source countries, that is to say, in the ethno-demographic composition, even much more than is commonly perceived: 48 per cent of immigrants in Canada come from Asia and the Pacific Basin, 18 per cent from Europe, 15 per cent from Latin America and 16 per cent from Africa and the Middle East. Only 3 per cent come from the United States. In 1993, the top ten countries of immigration to Canada for all classes were Hong Kong, India, the Philippines, Taiwan, China, Sri Lanka, Vietnam, the United States, the United Kingdom and Poland. On the other hand, the top ten countries for refugee claimants seeking asylum in the same year were Sri Lanka, Somalia, Iran, Israel, India, Russia, Yugoslavia, Romania, Pakistan and Bangladesh.[15] As can be seen, immigrants as well as refugees are arriving from non-white cultures and they enter a mixed race society dominated by whites. Nevertheless, Canadians have always expressed pride in their cultural diversity, encouraging pluralism and ethnic identity which has been the main premise of their multicultural policy, enshrined in the Multiculturalism Act of 1988.[16]

A central theme running through the new policy is a reform of the selection process in order to produce more immediate benefits to Canada, by reducing integration costs and concentrating on people who have the language and other skills to adapt quickly to Canadian conditions. There are three main categories of newcomers to Canada: independent immigrants (those who are approved because they are considered worthy of bringing economic or social benefits to Canada); those being reunited with their families already in Canada; and refugees. Just as in the US, in order to reduce the proportion represented by the family category, the government plans a tougher enforcement of sponsorship obligations of Canadian residents who wish to bring in their family members. The government's ten-year plan seeks to change the emphasis on the relative proportions in each category – to raise the independent category from 43 to 53 per cent by the year 2000, while the family category will drop from 51 to 44 per cent. In the family class, spouses and dependent children will continue to get almost automatic approval, but grandparents and siblings will be relegated to a separate category that could be capped if numbers become excessive.[17] The government is definitely shifting its focus from a strong commitment to family reunification to economic immigrants, a shift that some criticize as creating the opportunity for immigrants with financial resources to buy their way into Canada.[18]

With respect to the acquisition of permanent resident status, there is also a strategy which emphasizes that immigration is a right that should be paid for by those who benefit. It was announced that all adult immigrants applying for permanent resident status are required to pay $975 Canadian dollars right-of-landing fee, in addition to a $500 dollar processing fee already in place. Fees for other immigration services were also increased.[19] Obviously some immigrants and especially refugees will have a hard time finding the amount required for a family of two adults and two children to apply to emigrate to Canada. The fee has been widely opposed by the groups representing immigrants.

The strategy for future immigration has changed. It is now trying to ensure that a greater share of immigrants will be selected on the basis of their ability to contribute to the Canadian economy, which in turn will reduce demand for services such as language training, which is necessary for their integration into Canadian society. It also emphasizes that immigrants should be more entrepreneurial, literate and able to adjust rapidly to the labour market and contribute more to the current technology-driven global economy.

It has been recognized that contributions by immigrants have been very important in the past; but the benefits to the economy have currently been declining. According to a study carried out by the Howe Institute, 'Immigrants still represent a net gain to the country, paying on average far more in taxes than they receive in benefits. But the net gain is dropping and the study suggests that immigration may begin to be a drain on government coffers'.[20] For some Canadians, the new migration policy reforms are not a direct consequence of an anti-immigrant sentiment, but a confirmation of the real problem of high levels of immigration. There are unquestionably more traces of racism than before in Canada and some Canadians hold anti-immigration views that are rooted in xenophobic reactions to the changing ethnic, cultural, linguistic and racial composition of the immigrant and refugee arrivals. Nowadays some of the population object to the current immigration policy and are more intolerant.

It is important to mention that, in spite of the fact that Canada accepts more immigrants per capita than any other Western country, it has now become more selective, allowing itself the luxury of choosing among the world's best and brightest. Therefore, the new prototype is geared to produce immigrants who will immediately be compatible with Canadian society and its predicted economic priorities: instant consumers and taxpayers with education and training conveniently prepaid by foreigners.[21] The same contradictions that exist in the reforms of American immigration policy persist in Canadian policy, in terms of the low-tech jobs which have traditionally been taken by a high percentage of immigrants. Who will take them in the near future, given the new trends reshaping Canadian immigration policy?

5 Mexican migration to Canada

Mexican migration to Canada has been insignificant in comparison to Mexican migration to the United States. Mexican legal migrants to Canada have accounted for a total of 10 215 between 1978 and 1992. They emigrate as landed immigrants (permanent residents), temporary workers and students, mainly to the provinces of Ontario (48 per cent), Quebec (22 per cent) and British Columbia (16 per cent). Toronto and Montreal are the main cities of attraction. During the last twenty years, however, the governments of Mexico and Canada have had an arrangement to provide Mexican labour to the Canadian agricultural sector. In 1974 an intergovernmental agreement known as the 'Program for Temporary Mexican Agricultural Workers in Canada' (*Programa de Trabajadores Agrícolas Temporales Mexicanos con Canada*) was signed, to facilitate the movement of Mexican temporary agricultural workers to provinces selected by the Canadian government, and thus satisfy the needs of the agricultural labour market.[22] It was recently extended until the year 2,000.[23] A forerunner to this programme was the Bracero Program between the United States and Mexico, which was in force from 1942 to 1964. The Canadian programme is much more modest than the Bracero agreements, not only in respect to quantitative terms but also in the way it is formulated, so that in the case of a conflict it would not be strong enough to mediate in a dispute.

This programme has been very successful and has increased geometrically. It began in 1974 with 203 workers and this figure doubled in the following ten years to 550 workers a year. But from 1985 there was a far greater increase: to 874 in 1985, 1004 in 1986, 1538 in 1987, 2623 in 1988, 4369 in 1989 and by 1990 there were 5143 workers.[24] The flow has remained more or less constant since then: 5148 Mexican agricultural workers were admitted in 1991, 4778 in 1992, 4872 in 1993, 4910 in 1994 and 4970 in 1995, for an average of about six months each.[25]

There is an apparent preference for Mexican labour in agriculture. Nowadays Mexicans make up about 40 per cent of the total number of foreign workers in Canada on similar programmes. In Mexico this represents an employment alternative for a sector that has been at a disadvantage in the labour market. The resources generated are extremely useful for the migrant workers, who complement their family income and obviously contribute to the regional economy, given the difference in wages earned by the worker in Mexico and Canada or the United States which is as much as 1:10, for the same kind of work.

The programme has worked well and can be seen as an example of the understanding and communication that the two countries have maintained to date. It should be noted that when the Bracero Program began between Mexico and the United States, it was dealing with small numbers so it worked perfectly well. It was only when it involved from 200 000 to 400 000 workers a year that it caused difficult problems for Mexican–US bilateral relations.

Given the geographical distance between Mexico and Canada, the fear of a harsh winter and the lack of contacts and networks between labour markets, there is little likelihood of massive illegal migration of workers – a situation that will not damage the Mexican–Canadian relationship, which is radically different from, and which (mainly since the NAFTA negotiations) has been closer and more productive than, the relationship with the United States.

6 Implications for Mexico in a regional context

There is no doubt that US and Canadian perspectives and views on immigration have changed in significant ways, which has led to a debate, that is quantitatively and qualitatively different from the one heard only a few years ago. This new situation of an anti-immigrant atmosphere prevails in both nations but is much more dense in the United States.

The migration of Mexicans to the United States, particularly illegal immigration, has always been a difficult and sensitive problem within Mexican–US relations. It is true that through NAFTA negotiations there has been a much closer and cooperative interaction between both countries on different issues and it has created a positive atmosphere for bilateral collaboration. As has been described above, the issue of immigration has also come to the fore in domestic politics, and has had an important impact on Congress and in some southern states, especially California, where various sectors have been pushing for drastic changes in the structure towards a new reform of American immigration policy, as in the case of the new act (IIRIRA), which was approved in 1996.

Increasing border operations have given rise to a series of Mexican protests by the public and the government at the violations of the human rights of illegals apprehended close to the border.[26] It is also important to mention that hate crimes have increased substantially since Proposition

187 was approved, for example, the dramatic videotape of the recent beatings of undocumented Mexican immigrants in Riverside[27] and the tragic deaths of several of them in a police chase. Mexican society and its government have at last been obliged to respond to what is seen as American aggression towards Mexican nationals in US territory, and have also raised concerns about the vulnerability of undocumented workers in a very harsh environment without the minimum protection.

Within this context, two phenomena arise in parallel which are analytically different: an increasingly active style in Mexican foreign policy and an increasingly intense series of bilateral discussions. Examples of this new attitude can be seen in the recent establishment of a binational study on migration – which should be completed at the end of 1997 – and which has the purpose of analysing bilaterally most of the facets of the migration issue, with the objective of not only reaching some joint conclusions but also diminishing the perceptions gap. It is interesting to point out that just after Proposition 187 was approved in California, Mexican officials proposed to Congress an initiative of double nationality for Mexicans who are naturalized abroad. This became law in November 1996. This law (*Ley de la Doble Nacionalidad*) would allow Mexicans living legally in other countries to opt for naturalization without losing their Mexican nationality. While remaining Mexicans, it will permit them to have some influence on political life in the United States, and also allows for the possibility that they might eventually return to Mexico. This proposal represents a clear indication of the change of attitude, part of this new era of more activism in Mexican foreign policy.

The recent approach of cooperation is surprising, precisely because it is occurring in the context of a new anti-immigrant atmosphere, which, at the same time, is a crucial source of conflict and tension in current Mexican–US relations. It is important to understand that bilateral relations have advanced along the road of dialogue, from being scarcely cordial in the 1970s to being characterized by the spirit of bilateral collaboration in the 1990s. In other words, there has been a transition from a unilateral to a more bilateral approach.[28]

Nevertheless, it should be recognized that there is an enormous contradiction between the intrinsic purposes of NAFTA and the new anti-immigrant debate. Every year about 300 million people cross the border, which is a reflection of the linkages that unite both countries. The construction of fences in an effort to close one of the busiest borders in the world does not convey a positive spirit. We are confronting an ambivalent situation where there is a policy of opening the door for trade goods, services and flows of investment and, at the same time, a policy of closing it with respect to movement of people.

Is a freer movement of labour within the three countries of the North American region possible where one is relatively poorer than the other two, and where the gap in living standards and wage differential (1:10) is so large? Is the European Union system a model for the North American region? Are the differences in ethnicity, language and culture among Mexico, US and Canada so profound that they represent an obstacle to an agreement involving the freer movement of labour?

These are some of the questions that governments should be discussing. But if discussions on freer and liberalized movements of people were not included during the negotiations preceding NAFTA, perhaps it is time to consider and negotiate a way to manage migration in this new era of economic integration. In this context it might be necessary to establish specific concessions for Mexico, which would include joint action and/or new programmes.

Even though migration policies are domestic issues, the Mexican government should make it clear to its North American partners that all kinds of migrants, including those undocumented, have been essential to the economic prosperity of the region, including the United States. It should also be recognized that, even though the question of migration was not addressed during the NAFTA negotiations, there has been an increasing interdependency between the US–Mexican labour markets. Finally it should be stressed emphatically that if both countries have engaged in a 'migration system' for different reasons, they should not forget that migrants have basic human, labour, social and economic rights that should not be withdrawn unilaterally.

Notes

1. Proposition 187 soon became entangled in a complex litigation so the Supreme Court blocked its implementation because it might be unconstitutional, in 'For them Proposition 187 is just Beginning', *Los Angeles Times*, 28 January 1995, p. 1A.
2. Although most of the small electorate of Latin origin opposed it, and there was an active campaign organized by human rights workers, the law was approved by a devastating majority of 59 per cent of the total California electorate.
3. Movements in favour of similar measures soon appeared in other states, such as Florida and Arizona.
4. The Immigration and Naturalization Service (INS) estimates that in 1994 illegal foreigners in the United States were made up of 48 per cent (1 909 000) who entered via illegal border crossings and 52 per cent (2 070 000) visitors who prolonged their stay without permission. Only 357 000 of the latter are apparently Mexicans while 1 199 000 more Mexicans crossed the border without papers, in Ashley Dunn, 'Greeted at Nation's Front Door: Many Visitors Stop on Illegally', *The New York Times*, New York, 2 January 1995, p. 1A.
5. The case of Pyler vs. Doe established that states must provide public education (grades 1 to 12) for all children regardless of their migratory status.
6. Holly Idelson, 'Proposals would Crack Down on Ilegals and Tighten Rules for Legal Immigrants', *Congressional Quarterly*, **53** (15), Washington, DC, 15 April 1995, p. 1068.

7. President Clinton's speech during his official visit to Mexico City, Auditorio Nacional de México, México DF, Wednesday 7 May 1997.
8. For more information: Manuel Garcia y Griego y Mónica Verea, 'La nueva ley de Inmigración 1996', *Voices of México*, CISAN, UNAM, México DF, in press.
9. 'House Passes Sweeping Welfare Reform, Measure with Grim Immigration Consequences', *Interpreter Releases*, **72** (13), Washington, DC: Federal Publications Inc., 31 March 1995, 453.
10. Sidney Weintraub, 'US Foreign Policy and Mexican Immigration', paper presented at the Conference on Immigration and US Policy, CSIS, Washington, DC, 13–15 June 1996 (mimeo), p. 6.
11. Seventy per cent, that is 1 230 457, of them were Mexicans, of whom 54.4 per cent were legalized in California and 17.7 per cent in Texas, Carlos González, 'The Mexican Diaspora in California: Limits and Possibilities for the Mexican Government', in Abraham Lowenthal and Katrina Burgess, *The California–Mexico Connection*, Stanford: Stanford University Press, 1993, pp. 224–5.
12. Of the applicants, 1 040 268 (81.5 per cent) were Mexican; the majority (53 per cent) of applications were made in California., ibid., p. 225.
13. George Vernez, 'Mexican Labor in California's Economy', in Abraham Lowenthal and Katrina Burgess, *op. cit.*, p. 162.
14. Hugh Winsor, 'Canada to Cut Immigration in 1995', *The Globe and Mail*, Ottawa, 29 October 1994, p. A4.
15. Citizen and Immigration, 'Facts and Figures: Overview of Immigration', Ottawa, 1994.
16. Hellen Szewello Allen 'Immigration and Ethnic Communities in Quebec', in Beach, Kissner and M. Verea (eds), *Quebec and Ontario*, CISAN–UNAM, CESCA–SUNY Plattsburgh, in press.
17. In terms of where family class immigrants come from, during 1993, of the 110 000 admitted, India ranked first place with 17 081 Hong Kong with 9307, the Philippines with 8080 and China with 7208. The United States ranked 8th place with 4811, from 'Family Immigration Faces Change', *The Globe and Mail*, 24 October 1994, p. A2.
18. Hellen Szewello Allen, op. cit.
19. 'Increase in Fees for Immigrants Called "New Chinese Head Tax" ', *The Globe and Mail*, 1 March 1995, p. 6a.
20. 'Why We Need Skilled Immigrants', *The Globe and Mail*, 6 February 1995, p. 18A.
21. 'Designer Immigrant v. Immigrant Classic', *The Globe and Mail*, 20 April 1995, p. 29a.
22. The work conditions established in this agreement are: (a) normal working hours of a maximum of 8 hours a day, 40 hours a week; (b) wages must be paid weekly at the work place and at the same rate as for a Canadian worker for the same work (on average $5.50 Canadian dollars per hour); (c) adequate free food and lodging; (d) return transport paid by the employer; (e) payment of compensation to workers for personal injuries or sickness contracted as a result of the work; (f) workers to be insured for medical expenses, hospitalization and death benefits; (g) the minimum contract should be six weeks, the maximum six months. (For further information on the operation of this programme see Monica Verea, 'La Política Migratoria Canadiense', in Maria Teresa Gutierrez Haces and Monica Verea C. *Canada en Transición*, CISAN–UNAM, Mexico DF, 1994, pp. 535–7.
23. 'Exitoso pacto laboral migratorio con Canada', *La Jornada*, Mexico, 8 July 1996, pg. 64.
24. Secretaria de trabajo y previsión social, 'Programa de Trabajadores Agrícolas Temporales Mexicanos con Canadá', México, February 1991 (mimeo).
25. Secretaria de Relaciones Exteriores, 'Desarrollo Anual del envio de Trabajadores Agrícolas a Canada', Mexico, 1995, (mimeo).
26. Human Rights Watch denounced numerous cases of beating, shooting, rape and death, apparently at the hands of members of the border patrol, in 'Denuncia Human Rights a la patrulla fronteriza', *La Reforma*, Mexico, 12 April 1995, p. 4a.
27. On 1 April, two white Riverside County Sheriff's deputies were videotaped beating two unauthorized Mexican aliens who had led them on an 80-mile high-speed chase after

trying to evade an INS checkpoint in southern California. The aliens who were beaten were in the cab of a pick-up truck that had 18 aliens crammed under a camper shell. Immigrant rights groups protested about the beatings, calling them the 'Rodney King' incident that may wake up the nation to violence against illegal immigrants, in the same way that the 1991 tape of the police beating of King illustrated police violence against African Americans.

28. In a recent article we defend the hypothesis that there has been a transition in the US–Mexican relationship towards a more positive one, in Manuel Garcia y Griego y Mónica Verea, 'Colaboración sin concordancia: la migración en la nueva agenda bilateral México-Estados Unidos', paper presented during the international seminar on The New Bilateral Agenda, FCE–CISAN–ITAM, in press.

13 NAFTA and Mexico: the future of democracy and economic development

José Luis Valdés-Ugalde

World history is a house that has more staircases than rooms (Börne)
Quoted in Robin Blackburn (ed). After the Fall. The Failure of Commission and the Future of Socialism. Verso, London, 1991.

1 Introduction: the new needs of globalism: modernity at any cost

From the historical dispute taking place during the years of the Cold War in which the ideological controversy was basically solved in the East–West corridor, and after the fall of Communism there was one dominant argument in the West which referred to the need for reaching modernity – a modernity meant to reach the economies of the underdeveloped countries in order to assure the success of the economic project of capitalism at the end of the century.

Issues such as fine trade, continental integration, economic development and democracy were important in defining the nature of 'the new world order'. For this reason, trade agreements, among other things, became the means to achieve such a purpose. To a great extent, NAFTA responded to the needs of the incipient new global order which resulted from the end of the Cold War. As a trade agreement, NAFTA represents one instrument to enter, in regional bases, into this new order. The fact that Mexico has been included as a new actor within this framework – the weakest one to conventional wisdom – makes it important to discuss in an extra new dimension in this country within the present political and economic development, both at the domestic and at the international level.

It is for such reasons that it is pertinent to understand the relationship between Mexico, the United States and the new world order, in particular, the impact that NAFTA and the attempts to reach modernity have had upon Mexico. The objective in this chapter is to explore the impacts of NAFTA and economic liberalization on Mexico with respect to the democratic process and some of the consequences of this on the economy of the country. One of the arguments concerns to what extent trade agreements in general can ensure economic growth without sacrificing democratic political stability. In this respect, it will be examined to what extent Mexico has been vulnerable to this. This is relevant because it could present the case of an incompatibility between a democratic project and a liberalizing economic project. That is, has the economy kidnapped the polity to the extent that not only is the latter, given its backwardness, unable to survive as it is (I refer to the integrity of the political system), but also it makes it impossible for the system to remain stable and to allow the economy to go forward?

Thus the argument of this chapter is that Mexico, by attempting to reach modernity through NAFTA and liberalization (two variables that come together) has on the contrary retreated on some basic aspects of the economic and political development of the nation. Following this argument, development, as one of the instruments of modernization and within the context of the economic and political process, has so far been playing a dubious game which eventually will provoke (or is already provoking) conditions which militate against political and economic stability. Behind this view there is a more profound theoretical dilemma which has been present since the very beginning of the negotiations and which demonstrates exactly where the arguments for, and especially against, the treaty stem from, namely: an open market economy cannot exist and survive, let alone endure, within a closed political system and a closed political system will eventually not survive the new dynamics of an active society for which the likelihood of economic prosperity and political progress was put forward as a definitive promise towards the achieving of modernity. Within this dynamic, the relationship with the United States is preponderant.

2 Mexico, modernity and the United States: some comparative history

In trying to reconcile with modernity, progress and prosperity, Mexico has finally turned its eyes to the North. Taking into consideration the oscillation of Mexican history, especially in the US–Mexican bilateral dimension, this is, to say the least, paradoxical. As Octavio Paz, the Mexican Nobel prize winner once stated,

> before becoming a reality, the US was an image to (us). That is not surprising: we Mexicans begin as children to see that country as the *other, an other that is inseparable from us and that at the same time is radically and essentially alien*. In the north of Mexico the expression 'the other side' is used to mean the United States. The other side is geographical: the frontier; cultural: another civilization; linguistic: another language; historical: another time (the United States is running after the future while we are still tied to our past); metaphorical: it is the image of everything that we are not. It is foreignness itself. Yet we are condemned to live with this foreignness: the other side is right next to us. The United States is always present among us, even when it ignores us or turns its back on us: its shadow covers the entire continent. It is the shadow of a giant.

> To us this giant is the same one that appears in fairy tales and legends – a big overgrown fellow and something of a simpleton, an ingenious sort who does not know his own strength and who can be fooled, though his wrath can destroy us. The image of the goodhearted, doltish giant is juxtaposed with that of the shrewd and bloodthirsty cyclops. A childish image and a licentious one: the ogre that eats children up alive in Perrault, and the ogre of Sade ... and Prometheus as well – the fire of industry and of war. The two faces of progress: the automobile and the bomb.[1]

The United States enters our history during this second moment, making its appearance not as a foreign power that must be fought, but as a model that must be imitated. This was the beginning of a fascination that, despite having changed form during the last 150 years, is still as intense as ever. The history of that fascination goes hand in hand with the history of the groups of intellectuals who since Independence, have drawn up all those programmes of social and political reform aimed at transforming the country into a modern nation. Since early in the nineteenth century this project of modernization has always been defined *vis-à-vis* – whether for or against – the United States. The passion of our intellectuals for US civilization ranges from love to bitter rancour, from adoration to horror.

As our dreams of modernization faded, the fascination exerted on us by the United States grew. The war of aggression of 1847 turned it into an obsession. An ambivalent fascination: at one and the same time, the titan was the enemy of our identity and the unacknowledged model for what we would most like to be. In addition to being a political and social idea, the United States was an interventionist power, an aggressor. This double image, which corresponded then, and stills corresponds today, to a reality – the United States is both a democracy and an empire – lingered throughout the nineteenth century. The United States was the immediate example of this universality: in its presence we could see a vision of our future – a telltale mirror: like the stepmother's mirror in the fairy tale; each time we asked it to show us our image, it showed us that of the *other*.

The adoption of the US model contributed somehow to the disintegration of traditional values; the political and economic action of US imperialism shored up the archaic social and political structure. This contradiction revealed that the ambivalence of the giant was not imaginary but real: the country of Henry David Thoreau was also the country of the first Theodore Roosevelt. This is the question we ask ourselves endlessly, without having yet arrived at any definite answer. We may not have found a way to accept our past, but neither have we found a way to criticize it.

The conquest of the future is the US tradition, therefore a tradition of change, whereas the Hispanic tradition is one of resistance to change. For example, Mexican workers who emigrate to the United States have shown a remarkable capacity for *not* adapting to American society, a capacity that has its roots in an insensitivity to the future. In them the past is alive. It is the same past that has preserved the Chicanos, the minority group in the United States that seems to have been able to keep its identity. 'In Mexico it has not been the professionals of anti-imperialism who have put up the strongest resistance, but the humble folk who make pilgrimages to the Sanctuary of the Virgin of Guadalupe. [In some way] our country survives thanks to its traditionalism'.[2]

3 NAFTA, the reforms, and the choice of the people

If there is something important to stress in Mexican history, it is the fact that Mexico is a country as diverse as it is complex. Moreover this picture is even more intricate when it comes to establishing new bases of negotiation with the United States, being far more difficult when these bases settle the conditions towards accomplishing steps in the process of modernization of the country which were not contemplated in the recent past. Sometimes this complexity overcomes some rational approaches which have attempted to understand the polity and the economic system. The latter involves the way that history is made and the evolution that the polity has had as a result of this. It also involves a notion of progress. Apparently Salinas's[3] NAFTA plays a very important role in hastening some changes in the economy that now are proving to be relatively unsuccessful, and/or also the demonstration of a blindness of the political class that did not accept that the country needed to enter into a process of pre-modernization before trying to enter into a race towards an empty future.

In the light of the brief history of modernity Mexico has produced *vis-à-vis* its contiguity with the US, let us illustrate the very process of modernity taking place between 1982 and 1994 when President Salinas gained ground within the political arena of the country and started designing the series of economic and political strategies that would eventually change the face of the nation for a long time, and consequently established the bases on which NAFTA would exist. The central factors that we should consider in this process of change are: (i) the changing size, organization and operation of the productive and administrative structure of the government: (ii) budgetary, fiscal and taxation measures; (iii) privatization policies; and (iv) changes in economic legislation and social policy, as well as reduction in inflation and interest rates, and the gradual increase of salaries.

> Clearly the purpose of the reforms was to establish a difference between public and private responsibilities, in response to the demands of the business community. The state was to restrict economic intervention to 'guidance' of the economic process and to intervene only in those 'strategic areas' which were specified in the constitutional reform. This constitutional reform laid the foundation for policies of adjustment and privatization.[4]

That is to say, an institutional shift was the main purpose in order to make possible the changes and reforms of the system.

Mexico, to the surprise of financial analysts, has deviated from the proposed economic development embraced both in the agreement and in the reform process launched by the regime. The plummeting of the peso (the series of devaluations since December 1994 account for more than 50 per cent of losses for the peso so far), the fall of GDP (between the end of December 1995 and June 1996) by 6.4 per cent, high interest rates (almost reaching 30–29.18 per cent in July 1996) the high level of unemployment (about 26 per cent including the underemployed population), a level of inflation between July 1995 and July 1996 of 30.03 per cent (16.94 per cent accumulated in 1996), extended poverty (almost forty million), and the fall of real salaries by 33 per cent in the last 18 months, among other things, are indicators which demonstrate so far the serious limitations of the economic project within NAFTA.[5] Moreover a short-run recovery is unfortunately not foreseen: the predictions of Mexican and US economists for enhancing the current conditions of the economy are the return to the conditions experienced in the 1980s if something is not accomplished before, namely: high levels of inflation, close to those of 1987; an NGP inferior to that existing fourteen years ago; because the country has been far from a constant and permanent growth in the last thirteen years, the economy will require a 3 per cent per year growth in order to make it possible for the GDP to recover within a 70-year period; and last but not least, according to reports of the Mexican Ministry of Finance, the InterAmerican Bank for Development, the World Bank and the International Monetary Fund, the external debt in 1996, providing that the economy will make it possible to reach an estimated growth of 3 per cent, is going to represent more than 50 per cent of the whole GNP.[6]

Since 1993, according to the Mexican analyst, Jorge G. Castañeda, NAFTA

> was to provide Mexico's ailing economy with the foreign capital injections it has long required for sustainable growth. Politically, an expanding Mexican economy – one linked to the United States – would help lay the foundations for an eventual and controlled democratic transition. Overlooked, however has

been the fact that NAFTA entails great risks. No country has ever attempted to develop an export manufacturing base by opening its borders so quickly and indiscriminately to more efficient and lower-cost producers. No nation today, not even the United States, has so willingly sacrificed an industrial policy or an equivalent form of managed trade. By unilaterally renouncing these advantages, Mexico will lose far more jobs in the next few years than it will create. Old industries and agricultural producers will die, be swallowed up or join with foreign ventures, long before the new jobs arrive. ... Much of the problem has been Mexico's inability to hurdle an apparently immovable obstacle to its economic growth: the need for substantial foreign capital injections.[7]

Further on Castañeda develops his argument and provides us with figures from 1993 which easily foreshadow today's reality:

> Mexico's lacerating social and economic inequality stems partly from the antidemocratic nature of its politics. High levels of postwar economic growth, progress in education and health, and the emergence of a significant middle class have not remedied Mexico's atrociously lopsided income distribution. If 40 years of growth did not help, then a decade of economic stagnation in the 1980s only made matters worse. A recently published survey found that the richest ten percent of Mexicans, those who earned 32.8 percent of national income in 1984, saw their share jump to 37.9 percent by 1989. Conversely, the share of the poorest 40 percent shrank from 14.3 percent to 12.9 percent. The 1990 census, moreover, revealed that 63.2 percent of the nation's inhabitants made no more than twice the minimum wage – US$200 per month at that year's exchange rate, 3.00 new pesos per dollar – while price levels approached those in the United States [something that is actually happening right now]. The long absence of free elections, of an emancipated labour movement and of the rule of law has helped keep the fruits of any economic expansion in the hands of a minority.[8]

Thus, the institutional shift was not only decided from above but was brought about by a very few members of the economic and the political system at the expense of the majority's prosperity, and for this reason imposed on the whole of the country. What took place was what has been called an 'élites' transition'. Adam Przeworski in his book *Democracy and the Market* has stated when establishing the relationship between democracy and the market that 'as soon as these institutions (the reformist institutions) are in place, the question arises whether they will evoke spontaneous compliance; that is, whether, willing to subject their interests to the uncertainty of competition and to comply with its outcomes, they will absorb the relevant political forces as participants'.[9] This is to say, accomplishing a basic consensus is necessary to reach such a transformation of a country. This brings us to the theoretical discussion of the critical relationship there has always been between politics and the economy, and the identification existing in recent debates between democracy and capitalism, especially in the case of the weakest actor, Mexico. It has to be stressed that the polemic about democracy and NAFTA began at the very moment when Salinas's government decided on 27 March 1990 to launch the initiative without taking into account the general feeling of the Mexican people. Indeed, because of a press leak in the *Wall Street Journal*, it was learned in Mexico that a 'private' meeting took place between officials of both countries: 'officials of both the United States and Mexico gathered together in Washington at the end of February in order to negotiate a free trade agreement'.[10] Neither the Mexican Congress nor the general public were in any real sense involved in the decisionmaking process.[11] Because this happened in Canada and the United States, the lack of debate in Mexico was interpreted in some academic and political circles of the country as the logical result of being part of a closed society and an authoritarian political system, and also of the accommodation process followed by Washington: instead of pressing the Salinas government to obtain the necessary consensus within the country, the United States did not hesitate to support the authoritarian nature of the Mexican system (or simply ignore it) in order to implement the 'fast track' in the US Congress.

4 Implications

Is it true that far from accomplishing the economic development it planned, and far from being the engine of the South of the continent, Mexico turned into the tail of the North? Did NAFTA change Mexico? Did NAFTA make Mexico more democratic or more open? Whether this is true or not, it is certain, however, that the most recent evidence shows that Mexico has failed in its endeavour to meet the future before reconciling itself with the past.

> As the Europeans have learned, bringing together advanced and backward economies is an expensive proposition. Since the disparities between Mexico and its neighbours are greater than any comparable differences in Western Europe, odds are that the North American experience will be [or is already] more costly. The three governments hope whatever must be done will be accomplished with private investment ... But private money is unlikely to prove sufficient; nor will it flow to Mexico as freely as expected [as already seen]. For now NAFTA incorporates no contingency provision – no special funds and no special taxes.

Moreover, Mexico's regulatory situation was largely excluded from NAFTA, with the exception of those areas where strong American interests are involved: foreign investment, intellectual property[12] and the textile industry. But if Mexico differs profoundly from its neighbours in any way besides overall wealth, it is in the absence of the rule of law and the regulatory framework that characterize developed market economies. The Mexican judicial branch is totally subservient to the executive; regulatory agencies have no independence whatsoever; corruption is egregious. By omitting both supranational mechanisms for enforcement of norms and rights – on the environment, labour, consumer protection, and due process – and any demand for the overhaul of Mexico's political and legal system, NAFTA's signatories ignored a fundamental facet of the Mexican reality.

NAFTA does not address the issue of whether Mexico has – or should have – the same type of market economy as that espoused by the United States. Is Mexico more like the United States, where nearly everything is left to the private sector and the relatively free workings of the market? Or are Mexican traditions closer to those of the European social market economy model, with greater emphasis on state involvement and more stringent regulations and constraints on the market?[13] Has Mexico understood all there is and was involved in order to make NAFTA work? Does Mexico have a real and compromised economic class and a private sector willing to take the necessary risks that are imperative within the liberalizing framework? We have to say: no.

On the other hand, there is a contradictory and paradoxical evidence of decadence in the very inside of the political system, an example of this being the fact (it is important to say it) that President Zedillo[14] is in power as a result of the fragility of the political and economic system within the limits of NAFTA and a fragile market economy strategy promoted from above: he is the replacement for a murdered candidate who was a victim of the tension provoked from within the system as a result of the struggle existing between different political cliques of the dominant party, the Revolutionary Institutional Party (PRI), and the strong polarity between a closed political system and the need for an open economy and an open society.

In this view, it seems as though the achievement of progress for the majority of the people within the framework of NAFTA has been elusive. The permanent instability of the economy,[15] the assassination of presidential candidate Luis Donaldo Colosio, the tensions produced within the polity, the fear for change, Chiapas and the Zapatista uprising on 1 January 1994 – the same date of the launching of NAFTA – in short, the gradual rigidity and more profound inflexibility and intolerance among some important, although sometimes hidden, sectors of the political class, offer some – among many – of the reasons of the incompatibility of a modernity programme within a closed political system which has not offered to the people anything other than more of the same.

> Economic adjustment has been achieved partly through the reform process. But the foundations for a new and balanced development have not been yet laid. This reveals a twofold problem: (1) a market economy cannot be created solely by reducing of state economy intervention; and (2) state reform cannot be limited to economic matters; it has to address democratization of the political system. Privatization measures and the reduction of state economic intervention do not automatically constitute either the adequate entrepreneurial function or the appropriate governmental regulation. Efficient resource allocation does not spring only from these policies. It needs proper economic, social, and political equilibria which bring actors – both collective and individual – into a virtuous economic game. State and economic modernization in Mexico have not even come close to accomplishing their objectives. Mexico does not have a market economy in the modern sense of the word. Neither has it found an adequate way to focus on social justice. If the economy cannot meet the social needs, and the state cannot make it possible, the only thing we can expect is the polarity of a minimally modem Mexico – one that is made up of a handful of giant enterprises and a few dozen technocrats on the one hand, and the vast impoverished majority of the backward Mexico on the other.[16]

5 Conclusions

NAFTA's success has been short and disappointing. This epilogue was also the return from the silence of dreams to the noisy province of nightmares. But above all it showed that progress

> is elusive as a ghost. Progress is brutal and insensitive, has no notion of nuance or of irony, speaks in proclamations and watch words, is forever in a hurry, and is brought up short only if it crashes headlong into a wall. All of which takes us to recognize that societies die not from their contradictions but from their inability to resolve them. When this happens, a sort of paralysis immobilises the social body – the thinking and deliberating centers first, then the executive arms. The paralysis is a society's response to questions to which its tradition and the assumptions of history offer no answer but silence.[17]

Finally, regarding the United States and Mexico it must be said that in the light of the experience of the United States during the last forty years, it is worthwhile asking to what degree Washington – in the context of the extensive process of pronounced globalization that envelops the world today, where order, stability and justice are at best precarious realities, and one in which NAFTA is a living–dying component – considers the movement towards democracy as an imperative linked to the achievement of development and, ultimately, to the problem of ever-expanding modernity that impels the formation of relationships among nations and among blocs of nations.

In other words, is it possible to say – that – Washington is as seriously interested in democracy in Latin America today as it is in the region's economic development – given that it is clear that the US historical macroeconomic project has been intrinsically associated with forces and actors that have sought to restrain, and in some cases, nullify, social movements that aspire to the perfection of democratic political systems in the region and regards it as an objective of the highest priority?

This question is highly relevant, because it may reveal the incompatibility between the democratic political project and the liberalizing economic project: more democratic forms may appear, but a democracy that really means *something* depends on the elaboration of concrete policies that activate an authentic globalizing modernity in the political as well as in the economic sphere.[18]

The risk is to avoid turning modern times into precarious antiquity (social polarization and concentration of power and wealth). Today there is a modern language of progress which

> takes on in its apparent dispersion, an ominously unipolar cast [both at the domestic and at the international level], urgently posing the question of whether history will be forced to become a process without a subject. If so, we are speaking of a history that Walter Benjamin saw as an angel impelled from behind toward the future; but the angel who strives to return in order to repair the damage of the past is halted by a storm that drives him from Paradise, the storm of progress.
>
> Led by this Benjaminian metaphor, we are drawn to reconsider the long history of opposition between two concepts of progress and two ways of exercising power – each supposedly modernizing in its prospective symbolic rationalizations – in the light of realities and epochs in which the two great actors vied to establish historical reason.... Indeed, the alignment of forces and the arrangement of the actors and the scenes of which they were a part were defined as real only insofar as they were components of what I would call a symbolic dichotomy: the two great powers act[ed] in terms of opposing and superimposed realities that were in essence no more than the contradictory manipulation of *images* that they attempted to impose on a reality cast in a form of a thesis defense, debated as to whether it participated in history as 'irony in motion' or as a phenomenon subject to permanent secular change.
>
> Today, in Washington the movement to end the Cold War [which is also the time for regional treaties such as NAFTA], has taken on [at least for Mexicans] fundamental importance and monopolises the unipolar discourse that accompanies the reordering of the world. The direction of this movement, as well as the benefits yielded by global reordering, belong essentially to the United States, the country that still unilaterally defines the worldwide system of inclusions and exclusions. Now, hegemony acquires its most definitive form in a globalization whose essence is to impose uniformity [the dogmatic uniformity of an open market that cancels the free language of the polity] on every discourse, scene, and actor. Ultimately (and this is the risk of an asymmetric opening of the polity and the economy), this process of uniformalization brings to an end multiplicity – and perhaps, we must anticipate, the end of that pluralism – which, because of its very civilising tendencies is also the bearer of democracy.[19]

Notes

1. O. Paz (1985), *One Earth, Four or Five Worlds. Reflections on Contemporary History*, London: Carcanet Press Limited, pp. 137–8.
2. See ibid., pp. 141, 154.
3. Carlos Salinas de Gortiari, President of Mexico (1988–1994).
4. See Francisco Valdés-Ugalde, 'The Changing Relationship Between the State and the Economy in Mexico', *Challenge*. May–June 1995, 32–6.
5. See most of the financial and political newspapers of Mexico, such as *El Financiero, La Jornada, Reforma, El Universal* of 12 August 1996, front page, and *Economía Informa*, Nos 237, 238, 239, 240 and 241, Facultad de Economía, UNAM, Mexico, April, May, June, July and September 1995. Data also obtained from the official figures of the Central Bank.
6. 'Mexico will remain as the main capital exporter in Latin America, despite the fact that its debt – at least until 1994 – was below that of Brazil . . . just as capital payments of the public debt Mexico will have to pay in 1996, US$8078.00 million [according to the World Bank Debtors Register System (DRS)]; between 1989 and 1994 [precisely the time when NAFTA was consolidated] the Mexican economy transferred abroad Mexican resources as part of the total external debt service compromises for $106,959.00 million. This amount represents 33.92 per cent of the total external debt payments of the whole Latin American countries during that period, which was US$315,297.00 million. In short, and according to figures of the World Bank, at the end of 1994 the total debt compromised by Mexico reached US$124,192.00 million, representing 24.22 per cent of the total external debt of Latin America (this was US$512,757.00 million). In 1989 the proportion of this payment was 22.21 per cent'. On the other hand, and according to financial reports of the FED, Mexico exported both private and public resources amounting to US$24 582 million to the American financial system at the end of 1995. This corresponds to 10.26 per cent of the NGP that year. According to this data, in twelve months Mexican savings increased by US$12 333 million, growing from US$12 250 million to the aforementioned US$24 582 million altogether representing 100.66 per cent during the period. In short at the end of 1995 the total amount of Latin American capital allocated in the American banking system was US$89 303 million, corresponding to 27.52 per cent (US$24 582 million) to Mexico. The list of capital exporters that year was as follows: Mexico: US$24 582 million; Brazil: US$23 816 million; Argentina.: US$17 203 million; Venezuela: US$11 812 million; Colombia: US$3666 million; Chile: US$2825 million; Uruguay: US$1835 million; Ecuador US$1325 million; Guatemala: US$1275 million; Peru: US$974 million. See *La Jornada*, 12 November 1995, pp. 1 and 57 and 19 June 1996, pp. 1 and 43–4, Mexico, DF.
7. Jorge G. Castañeda, Can NAFTA Change Mexico?, *Foreign Affairs*, September–October 1993, 66 and 71.
8. Ibid., p. 71.
9. Adam Przeworski (1993), *Democracy and the Market. Political and Economic Reforms in Eastern Europe and Latin America*, Cambridge: Cambridge University Press, p. 66.
10. *Wall Street Journal*, 27 March 1990.
11. The official party controlled 60 out of 65 seats in the Senate. Because the Senate was the last constitutional stage for any reform, it was this body that was responsible for allowing the President to continue the NAFTA negotiations to the end. Between 18 and 21 May 1990 and within a controlled atmosphere, the Senate finally decided that 'given the geographic allocation of Mexico, the history of its commercial relations and of the complementary potential of its economy *vis-à-vis* the United States, Mexico would negotiate with the US a trade agreement'. See Foro Nacional de Consulta, *Las Relaciones comerciales de Mexico con el Mundo (Commercial Relations between Mexico and the World Memory), Memoria*, Tomo II, Senado de la República, Mexico, DF, 1990, p. 293. Although there is a significant difference in the decisionmaking process in the US, recent reports inform us that the union-based Labour Advisory Committee (LAC), established by the Trade Act of 1974 to advise the executive branch

on any trade agreement, 'was informed that its report on NAFTA was due on September 9'. The text of this intricate treaty was provided just one day earlier. In its report, the LAC notes, 'the Administration refused to permit any outside advice on the development of this document and refused to make a draft available for comment'.

12. As an example of the considerable asymmetry between the three NAFTA partners it is important to note first that such agreements have only a limited relation to free trade. In regard to intellectual property there is one primary concern for the US: 'to increase protection [of for example] software, patents for seeds and drugs, and so on. The US International Trade Commission estimates that American companies stand to gain $61 billion a year from the Third World if US protectionist demands are satisfied at GATT (as they are in NAFTA), at a cost to the South that will dwarf the current huge flow of debt-service capital from South to North. Such measures are designed to insure that US-based corporations control the technology of the future, including biotechnology, which, it is hoped, will allow protected private enterprise to control health, agriculture and the means of life generally, locking the poor into dependence and hopelessness'. See Noam Chomsky, 'Notes on NAFTA, Masters of Mankind', 10 April 1996, 17:21:21–0700. Internet draft, pp. 3 and 4.N.
13. Castañeda. op. cit., pp. 74–5.
14. Ernesto Zedillo Ponce de León, President of Mexico (1994–2000).
15. The role of the state was not transformed: privatization meant the monopolic control of the economy; changes in the legislation could not avoid going in line with the strong subordination of the Congress to the Executive power, the high interest rates cannot compete with the international ones; wages have decreased by more than 40 per cent; the national currency, was, in December 1994 of 3 pesos per US dollar, today it has reached almost 8 pesos per dollar. Even though NAFTA could have beneficial consequences for the country, Mexico 'is only of secondary concern to the masters, who are playing a different game. Its rules are revealed by what the *New York Times* called "Paradox of '92: Weak Economy, Strong Profits". As a geographical entity "the country" may decline. But the interests of the "principal architects" of policy will be "most peculiarly attended to"'. Chomsky, op. cit., p. 5.
16. See F. Valdés-Ugalde, op. cit., p. 36. In some ways it can be seen how the economy has taken the polity as a hostage. Furthermore, if we follow the classical principles of economic liberalism from Adam Smith we must say that in Mexico these principles are far from being applied, namely, the principle of turning a selfish society into one able to satisfy the general interest without resorting to authoritarianism; the criterion of perfect competition in which the economic actors will have a symmetric relationship and in the event that this is not respected those responsible for breaking the agreement would be punished; that the actors will have access to all the information there is on the market; that as result of this the actors will carry out rational decisions including those concerned with priorities and preferences. None of these features work in the 'liberalized' Mexican economy of today and this country is the empirical demonstration of the relative failure of economic liberalism, and the fact that there are no signs (or systemic potentiality) of any political determination to establish them also reflects the general failure of the Mexican system and the political class to prove reliable as a means to carry out these changes. Moreover, the market as an alleged substitute of the state as a regulator mechanism between private and collective ends, has been overcome by a government, the other political institutions and a small group of investors committed exclusively to maximize, without any rationality (except that of making profits at any cost), their particular interests.
17. Paz, op. cit., p. 157.
18. See José Luis Valdés-Ugalde, 'The Mirror of the Hemispheric Past: The United States and Latin America', *International Journal of Politics, Culture and Society*, New York: Human Sciences Press, Inc., **9** (1), Fall 1995, 113–22.
19. See ibid., pp. 114, 115–16. One of the most interesting aspects of the appearance of NAFTA within the context of 'Globalization, market civilization and disciplinary

neoliberalism' as Stephen Gill calls it, is that it shows, as the other regional treaties also do, that there is, according to *Financial Times* journalist James Morgan, a 'de facto world government' that is taking shape in the 'new imperial age': the IMF, the World Bank, the Group of 7 industrialized countries, the General Agreement on Tariffs and Trade (GATT) and other institutions. In fact the US as the dominant actor within NAFTA, and the other industrialized countries, have resorted to protectionist measures in order to protect themselves from market forces. As a result of this a real transfer of resources from South to North has taken place which has helped to double the gap between rich and poor countries. For example, these resource transfers amounted to more than $400 billion from 1982 to 1990, 'the equivalent in today's dollars of some six Marshall plans provided by the South to the North', observes Susan George of the Transnational Institute in Amsterdam; she notes also that commercial banks were protected by transfer of their bad debts to the public sector. See Stephen Gill, 'Globalization, Market Civilization and Disciplinary Neoliberalism', *Millennium: Journal of International Studies*, **24** (3), 1995, 399–423; and Chomsky, op. cit., p. 2.

14 Successful integration and economic distress: the case of Mexico in NAFTA*

Sima Motamen-Samadian and
Etelberto Ortiz Cruz

1 Introduction

The year 1994 was the first year of Mexican integration into the North American Free Trade Agreement (NAFTA), and the beginning of a period when Mexico was supposed to benefit from further opening of its economy. It turned out, however, to be one of the most turbulent years in Mexico's recent history. The question which was frequently raised, was what went wrong with the Mexican economy? After all, it appeared that the stabilization and liberalization programmes which were implemented by the Mexican authorities since the mid-1980s were rather successful in reducing the rate of inflation and improving the efficiency of Mexican producers.

The core of the policies for 'structural change' rested essentially on two programmes; a reorientation of trade policies; and a complete turnaround of government subsidies and direct intervention. The first steps, in early 1984, were to start a continuous process of trade liberalization. By 1985, Mexico joined GATT and started a unilateral process of reduction of tariffs. The economy went from an average tariff rate of more than 100 per cent and a long list of direct controls in 1982, to a common tariff with a maximum of 20 per cent in early 1988. The main results of this period were the achievement of a relatively homogeneous tariff structure, and the elimination of direct controls, except for a few branches, such as the automobile industry.

The process of change from 1988 up to the beginning of NAFTA, was also a process of reduction of protection, and a reduction of the real exchange rate, which led to an appreciation of the peso *vis-à-vis* the US dollar. By the time the negotiations on NAFTA started in 1989, the Mexican economy was almost completely open to foreign trade. The sole exceptions were the automobile industry, telecommunications and a few

* This chapter was presented at the International Conference on Economic Integration In Transition in Athens on 20–24 August 1996. It is one of the research outcomes of the Academic Link Project on 'NAFTA and Structural Change in Mexico' sponsored by the British Council in Mexico.

other industries, where direct controls continued to prevail. Nevertheless, the purpose of economic integration within NAFTA was the most ambitious gamble for the development of the Mexican economy. It was thought that a grand entrance to the 'biggest market in the world', would provide a powerful impulse for investment and trade. To such a degree was this believed to be the case that advocates of these policies claimed that Mexico was on the verge of becoming part of the 'first world'. There were also other important aims in joining NAFTA, which included the need to form a legal framework on trade with the US economy. It was thought that this would help to eliminate the vast degree of discretionary powers that American enterprises were exercising prior to NAFTA on the basis of their own internal legal system.

The idea that the whole model of structural change should rest on trade policies, particularly on economic integration into NAFTA, is questionable. As pointed out by Bairoch and Kozul-Wright (1996), the idea that free trade and integration should lead to growth in exports and a faster improvement in income and employment is not necessarily a valid argument.

The objective of this chapter is twofold. First, it intends to show that the experience of trade liberalization, which was observed during the 1980s and early 1990s, reflects the actual capabilities of response of the Mexican economy to trade conditions. Second, it will show that the crisis which emerged in 1994, although appearing to have been instigated by the sudden outflow of portfolio capital, had its roots in problems which were related to the pattern of structural change that took place.

To address the above issues, this chapter is organized as follows: Section 2 discusses the pattern of trade liberalization policy which was implemented in Mexico. Section 3 analyses the relationship between the trade conditions and actual changes in the structure of production. This includes an assessment of the effects of trade liberalization programmes on patterns of trade. Section 4 discusses the effects of financial liberalization on the mobilization of domestic and international capital in Mexico. Section 5 offers some policy recommendations and a conclusion.

2 Trade liberalization, objective and process of implementation

In the early 1980s, the Mexican economy was a highly protected economy. Tariffs were very high and direct controls were widely exercised. In some important sectors, direct control covered up to 100 per cent of the activities of the sector. The 1982 crisis revealed the need for a dramatic reduction of tariffs and elimination of direct controls.

The initial moves were made in 1983, in the direction of attaining a more efficient structure of protection, and a more homogeneous tariff.

Nevertheless, high protection continued to prevail in selected sectors such as automobiles, electronic appliances, plastics, rubber, textiles, and so on. Direct controls, too, continued to prevail in few sectors such as automobiles, oil, sugar, tobacco and telecommunications. By 1988, tariff rates dropped to a more homogeneous level well below what it used to be. The new rates were not much higher than the tariff rates in the US and other OECD countries.

The next step was a move towards NAFTA. By 1994, tariffs and direct controls on about 43 per cent of import items from the US were almost eliminated. In this respect, it is important to note that about 70 per cent of Mexico's total imports come from the United States (Lusting 1992). The above list includes mostly capital goods. The schedule for full reduction of tariffs within NAFTA allows for a five-year period of adjustment for 18 per cent of industries such as textiles, and ten years for about 38 per cent of other industries. The latter group includes industries such as the automobile industry, for which adjustment may be more difficult. Thus, the scheme enables the above industries to benefit from a positive rate of effective protection for the next five to ten years. That is because while they continue to benefit from a tariff on their output, their imported capital inputs are not subject to any tariff. It is important to point out that between 1993 and 1994, the exchange rate, based on 1988 prices, was estimated to be about 30 per cent overvalued. This implies that by the time NAFTA started in 1994, the combination of tariff reduction and overvaluation of the peso made the Mexican economy extremely unprotected *vis-à-vis* imports.

3 Structural change in Mexico

The first growth boom period after the crisis of the 1980s, and after the process of structural change, was between 1988 and 1991. The next three years, between 1992 and 1994, were years when the economy was affected by the negotiations on NAFTA, and the first year of NAFTA. The economic growth rate that was experienced during 1992–94, was considerably lower than the previous years and characterized by an uneven rate of growth across various sectors. That is, while some sectors, such as automobiles, chemicals, electronics, cement and beer, showed an increased rate of growth during 1988–94 compared with 1982–87, other sectors such as primary, light industries, textiles and food,[1] exhibited either a reduction or a very small rate of growth after the opening of the economy. (See Table 14.1.)

Table 14.1 shows that the automobile and chemical sectors can be considered to be the leading growth sectors. These were in fact the only sectors which continued to benefit from protection, and the primary

Table 14.1 Rate of growth and net exports, 1982–1994 (sectoral indexes)

	Rate of growth[1]		Rate of net exports[2]	
Sector	1982–87	1988–94	1982–87	1988–94
Primary	1.4	1.02	−4.78	−15.67
Extractive	0.43	1.01	149.43	199.1
Food industry	0.85	3.97	12.49	0.063
Light industry	−1.29	0.34	−6.04	−42.52
Chemical and petrochemical	2.54	3.45	−10.63	−54.61
Iron ore industry	1.62	3.42	−2.38	−4.811
Automobiles and others	−0.97	6.88	−38.07	−204.2
Services	0.79	2.67	−0.02	−0.43

Notes:
1. Average rate of growth, per year, GDP.
2. Average share of the trade balance (exports–imports), to the total balance (NIPA).

Sources: National Income and Product Accounts (NIPA), 1970–1994, INEGI.

recipients of foreign investments from big concerns, as far back as the early 1980s. Therefore, the advance of their exports cannot be attributed to an improvement in their comparative advantage in the international markets, or to technological advantages. They can only be explained by a particular linkage of transnational corporations with the Mexican economy that rests primarily on intra-firm trade.

It is also important to point out that the above growth sectors were the main recipients of imported intermediate and capital goods. Nevertheless, a sectoral analysis of net exports reveals that the only sectors which showed any surplus were the old food industry and the extractive sector which is dominated by the oil industry. In other words, all the leading growth sectors showed a growing deficit. In particular, as can be seen from Table 14.1, both the automobile and petrochemical sectors experienced a growing trade deficit after the opening of the economy, and contributed to the rise in trade deficits between 1990 and 1994.

Table 14.1 also shows that the net exports should be assessed more carefully, as the contribution of various sectors to the total net exports varied significantly. Considering that the manufacturing sectors in Mexico are highly dependent on imported intermediate and capital goods, any assessment of the effects of trade liberalization should take into account the changes in both exports and import requirements of each sector. A closer examination of data reveals that while between 1988 and 1994, exports of the leading sectors appeared to have grown by 20 per cent in nominal terms, in real terms they grew by an average of only 8 per cent per annum. This is at a time when their imports grew at the considerably faster rate of 17 per cent per annum in real terms.

The structure of imports shows that the share of intermediate goods of total imports stayed very much the same throughout the transition period between 1981 and 1987, and afterwards when the economy was more open to trade. This is more evident from Table 14.2, which shows that the sum of imports of intermediates and maquila[2] temporary imports (rows 11 + 13), adds up to 71.2 per cent in 1994, and 80.5 per cent in 1995. Thus, it is apparent that despite all the criticisms which were attached to the import substitution industrialization (ISI) strategy for its role in increasing the dependency of the manufacturing sector on imported intermediate goods, the new export-led growth strategy did not do much to change this pattern of production dependency.

In this respect, the data on the leading tradable sectors (automobiles, communications and chemical industries) reveals that they have managed to grow mostly on the basis of a massive inflow of imports whose rate of growth far exceeded the growth of their exports. Moreover, their growth did not contribute much to the growth of real GDP. This is particularly so

Table 14.2 Trade structure, exports and imports (percentage shares)

Year	1976	1981	1988	1994	1995
Total exports	100	100	100	100	100
Oil	15.4	72.5	32.5	12.2	10.6
Primary sector	32.1	7.4	8.1	4.4	5.0
Extractive	5.7	3.4	3.2	0.6	0.7
Manufacturing	46.7	16.7	56.2	39.6	44.6
Net of maquila	10.0	4.9	11.3	9.5	6.2
Maquila (gross)				43.1	39.1
Total imports	100	100	100	100	100
Consumption	8.9	11.7	10.2	12.0	7.4
Intermediate	60.4	56.6	68.5	45.4	44.5
Capital	30.6	32.5	21.3	16.8	12.0
Maquila				25.8	36.0

Note: Figures are rounded.

Source: Bank of Mexico (1996).

between 1990 and 1993, when real exports were growing at an average rate of 8 per cent per annum, but real GDP grew at a much slower pace of 2.27 per cent per annum. More importantly, despite the growth of exports, according to the data provided by the Instituto Nacional De Estadistica Geografia E Informatica (INEGI), the rate of growth of real GDP slowed down steadily, and dropped from 4.5 per cent in 1990 to 0.4 per cent in 1993. A study of GDP composition reveals that while between 1982 and 1987, when the economy was relatively closed, the total export share of real GDP increased from 13.5 per cent to 17.9 per cent, the opening of trade did not help much in raising this share, and by 1994, it had gone up to only 19.5 per cent. Overall, while between 1988 and 1994 the total exports of goods increased by 98.3 per cent, imports of goods increased by 182.2 per cent, forcing the trade balance into a deficit. Thus, between 1988 and 1994, the trade deficit increased from −2.4 billion dollars to −28.8 billion dollars.

Despite the above-mentioned deterioration of trade balance, it is fair to say that trade liberalization has led to some gain in efficiency and rise in productivity. However, the rise in productivity has been achieved mostly at the expense of employment. This is evident from Table 14.3.

The question which may be posed now is whether NAFTA, so far, has made any difference to the pattern of trade? This is not very evident yet, partly because some of the changes which were implemented from 1992 onwards, were made in the expectation of joining NAFTA. The size of the

Table 14.3 Productivity and employment, 1982–1994 (sectoral indexes)

	Productivity[1]		Employment[2]	
Sector	1982–87	1988–94	1982–87	1988–94
Primary	104.31	104.72	104.44	105.01
Extractive	103.96	101.0	120.25	130.1
Food industry	102.25	113.52	108.46	114.1
Light industry	104.01	109.6	94.44	92.87
Chemical and petrochemical	104.57	124.65	113.79	119.25
Iron ore industry	99.33	126.1	99.62	95.03
Automobiles and others	102.76	136.85	90.99	97.52

Notes:
1. GDP per worker index, 1980 = 100.
2. Employment index 1980 = 100.

Source: National Income and Product Accounts. (NIPA) 1970–1994.

increase of the external sector, in terms of either exports or imports, is threefold compared to 1988, or fourfold if compared to 1987, the latter being a year of contraction of the external sector in Mexico. But the amazing increase of trade did make a difference in terms of growth. From 1989 to 1993, the Mexican economy saw a systematic drop in its rate of growth from 4.2 per cent in 1989 to 0.4 per cent in 1993. The growth of imports and the trade deficit occurred in the middle of a basically stagnated economy.

One may ask to what extent was this result attributable to exchange rate policies or to what extent was it a consequence of the very conditions under which economic integration was undertaken? To approach these questions it is necessary to discuss the behaviour of imports. The current hypothesis is that imports grew without limit because of the overvaluation of the domestic currency. The alternative hypothesis is that imports would have grown to such an extent anyway, either as a result of the opening of the economy with NAFTA, or even because of the mere anticipation of joining NAFTA. There is evidence to support both hypotheses. On the one hand, we have the real exchange rate estimates made by the Bank of Mexico, the Central Bank, which show that, based on the 1988 level, the exchange rate was 38 per cent overvalued by 1993. The exchange rates during 1987 or 1988 could be considered as the equilibrium rates, given the fact that they were derived from the situation when the external trade was in balance. Under the same index the extent of overvaluation for 1994 is calculated to be 39.49 per cent.[3] On the other hand, the officials argued that the pressures for obtaining imported intermediate inputs were very high at any price of the dollar. Consequently, they preferred to stick to the pegged exchange rate under the pretext of controlling inflation.

Nevertheless, the real impact of that policy was to introduce a violent distortion in prices which created a particularly profitable condition for sectors whose productive conditions rested heavily on imports. This is the case of the leading export and growth sectors mentioned earlier.

Now, let us see to what extent the distortion could have transformed the conditions of profitability. If we reevaluate imports at the real exchange rate of 1988, and subtract them from the nominal value of imports, the difference indicates the extra amount of imports which was made possible because of overvaluation of the exchange rate. As can be seen from Table 14.4, in some sectors such as the automobile industry, this accounted for up to 4 per cent of their share of GDP between 1988 and 1993.

This poses the question of would those sectors have been able to grow as fast as they did, under a non-overvalued exchange rate? Or, would they have undertaken a different pattern of integration with domestic producers and international suppliers? To answer this question, we have

Table 14.4 Difference between the nominal value of imports and the real value of imports measured in 1988 real exchange rate (share of sectoral GDP)

Sector/ Year	Primary	Extractive	Food	Textile	Light industry	Chemical	Iron ore	Machinery, Automobiles
1977–81	−0.082	−0.261	−0.339	−0.078	−0.398	−1.602	−0.497	−2.905
1982–87	−0.026	−0.070	−0.088	−0.024	−0.105	−0.550	−0.101	−0.748
1988–93	−0.064	−0.207	−0.703	−1.279	−0.646	−1.457	−0.412	−3.960

Source: Elaboration on National Income and Product Accounts (NIPA) 1970–1993.

to take into account two considerations. The first is that throughout the period of exchange rate overvaluation, the economy suffered a loss in terms of extra costs of imports. This can also be observed by the fact that import prices were increasing a lot faster than export prices. For certain industries such as automobile parts, this was a rather strange situation, because they were continually cutting their links with domestic Mexican producers of their inputs, and increasing their imports from their own suppliers. The argument for this was that the quality of goods produced by domestic producers was not good enough. Another argument is that they might have been overinvoicing their intra-firm trade. Integration in this field might imply that producers stick to their own pattern of integration.

4 Financial liberalization and its impact on the economy

In 1988, in order to improve the availability of funds for investment purposes, a programme of financial liberalization was introduced. This was implemented mostly through privatization of the banking sector, elimination of selective credit controls, and bank reserve requirements. In addition, the government authorized the formation of financial groups whose members included large private business corporations, banks, insurance companies, stock exchange agencies and other intermediaries.

The sale of public banks at a price higher than the market value of banks not only increased the government's revenue, but also reduced its expenditures, and helped to reduce the budget deficit. As can be seen from Table 14.5, between 1988 and 1992, the ratio of the public sector deficit to GDP declined steadily and in 1992, the deficit turned into a surplus. Over

Table 14.5 Public finances

End of period	Public sector balance (% of GDP)[1]	Total net debt of the public sector (% of GDP)[2]	Domestic debt (% of GDP)	External debt (% of GDP)
1988	−9.3	66.0	17.0	48.9
1993	0.7	24.4	5.5	18.9
1994	−0.3	24.8	4.3	20.5

Notes:
1. Data exclude revenues from privatization in years 1991–94.
2. Includes the Federal government, public enterprises and entities, development banks and official trust funds.

Source: Bank of Mexico (1995).

the same period, the ratio of both domestic and external debt of the public sector to GDP declined, and the ratio of total net debt of the public sector to GDP declined. Financial liberalization led to some rise in domestic bank savings, and an improvement in the bank savings ratio. The rise in bank deposits, however, was not sufficient to meet the growing domestic demand for investments.

Another approach to savings, however, provides a different view of the actual savings behaviour. The overall savings of the economy can be calculated using the national account items and decomposed to give various sources of savings. These are reported in Table 14.6, which includes external savings, public savings and private savings. As can be seen from Table 14.6, despite the financial liberalization, the ratio of gross national savings to GDP in real terms declined from 19.26 per cent in 1988 to 15.72 per cent in 1994. The same trend can be observed in the case of the private savings ratio which declined from 30.13 per cent in 1988 to 14.85 per cent in 1994. The comparison of the investment ratio and external savings ratio reveals that even though the investment ratio did increase, this was not in the same proportion as the rise in external savings ratio.

Table 14.6 Gross national savings, external, public and external, gross rate of investment, ratios to GDP, 1980–1995

Year	Gross fixed investment	GNS saving[1]	External saving, functional[2]	External saving net[2]	Public saving[3]	Private saving[4]
1988	19.26	22.27	−3.01	−8.2	−7.86	30.13
1989	18.17	19.25	−1.09	−6.3	−4.72	23.97
1990	18.61	18.54	0.07	−0.28	−1.19	25.33
1991	19.47	17.27	2.2	3.6	0.48	16.79
1992	20.8	15.89	4.9	2.77	2.28	13.62
1993	20.04	16.42	3.62	6.74	1.25	15.18
1994	23.4	15.72	4.61	−3.19	0.87	14.85
1995*	14.12	17.81	−3.7	−9.16	0.69	17.12

Notes and sources:

* Preliminary estimates.

1. Source: National Income and Product Accounts (NIPA) 1980–1994.
2. Functional rate: trade deficit + net non-factorial income + interest received by domestic residents. Net rate: net debt + foreign investment – foreign debt service. Balance of payments, 1980–1995, Bank of Mexico.
3. Estimated as public balance + inflation tax, Secretoria de Hacienda y Crédito Publico, The Ministry of the Treasury (SHCP) and Bank of Mexico.
4. Is obtained as a residual.

Here again, one can argue that the overvaluation of the peso played an important role in encouraging both the spending behaviour of the private sector and the borrowing behaviour of the bank and non-bank private institutions.

The reduction of inflation which allowed the real interest rate to become positive again, though, did not help much in raising savings, and contributed in increasing the cost of borrowing for domestic producers. In this respect, economic openness was considered instrumental in attracting foreign savings, and increasing domestic borrowers' access to cheaper international funds. Accordingly, in November 1991 exchange controls were abolished. But, to keep a control over inflation, the exchange rate was used as an anchor and, from November 1991, a regime of flotation band for the exchange rate was adopted.

In the early 1990s, economic recession in the US and other industrialized countries, forced the US and other international interest rates below the Mexican market interest rate. The relaxation of capital controls in 1991 thus opened a window of opportunity for private banks to borrow at a cheaper rate from international markets and use the funds for lending at a higher rate in the domestic market. Thus, between 1991 and 1994, the external debt of both commercial banks and the private non-financial sector increased by 42.1 and 131.4 per cent, respectively. Overall, as mentioned earlier, while between 1988 and 1994 the external debt of the public sector increased by 5.4 per cent, and that of the commercial banks and private non-bank sector increased by 246.6 and 221.8 per cent, respectively (see Table 14.7).

Between 1988 and 1994, while the interest payments on external debt by the Bank of Mexico declined from 0.4 to 0.2 billion dollars, that of the non-financial private sector increased from 0.9 to 2.2 billion dollars, which was an increase of 144 per cent. The rate of increase in interest payment on external debt of commercial banks was even higher. It increased from 0.5 billion dollars in 1988 to 1.6 billion dollars in 1994, which amounts to a rise of 220 per cent. The above figures clearly indicate that the financial liberalization programme did not exactly reduce the pressures of the external debt burden of the country as a whole. Rather, it resulted mostly in a transfer of debt burden from the public to the private sector.

The relaxation of capital control also led to a significant rise in portfolio investment. As reported by the Bank of Mexico, between 1990 and 1993, while direct investment increased from 2.6 to 4.4 billion dollars, portfolio investment increased from 3.4 to 28.9 billion dollars. The rise in portfolio investment also contributed to the significant rise in the total amount of funds traded in the stock market which increased from 5.2 billion dollars in 1991 to 14.4 billion dollars in 1993.

Table 14.7 Total external debt (billions of US dollars)

Year	1988	1989	1990	1991	1992	1993	1994	Rate of growth (%) 1988–1994
Total external debt	101.8	95.3	104.3	116.6	117.6	131.9	142.6	240
Public sector	81.0	76.1	77.8	80.0	75.8	78.7	85.4	5.4
Commercial banks	7.3	7.8	12.2	17.8	18.7	23.8	25.3	246.6
Bank of Mexico	4.8	5.1	6.5	6.8	6.0	4.8	3.9	–18.75
Private non-bank sector	8.7	6.4	7.9	12.1	17.1	24.6	28.0	221.8

Sources: Bank of Mexico (1995); International Financial Statistics (1995); and authors' calculations.

The above increase in portfolio investments appeared to signify an increase in confidence of foreign investors in the Mexican economy, but it was not exactly related to the fundamentals of the economy. In effect, the significant rise in portfolio investments exposed the Mexican economy and the peso to the adverse effects of sudden outflows of capital, as illustrated most dramatically in late 1994.

In 1993, as reported by the Bank of Mexico (1995), the total amount of portfolio investments in Mexico was 28.9 billion dollars, of which 10.8 billion dollars was invested in securities denominated in foreign currencies, 10.7 billion dollars in the stock markets, and 7.4 billion dollars in securities denominated in new pesos. The last two items were the type of portfolio investments which were most susceptible to fluctuations in the exchange rate, and comprised the most likely form of capital which could flow out of the country with the slightest possibility or a hint of currency devaluation.

All that was at a time when the economic growth in Mexico had come to a halt, and the trade deficit was growing. In 1993, while the trade deficit amounted to −13.5 billion dollars, the interest payment on foreign debt was 7.9 billion dollars, and portfolio investment denominated in pesos amounted to 18.1 billion dollars. Yet the total amount of international reserves was merely 24.5 billion dollars, which was clearly insufficient to withstand any sudden desire for a capital outflow. Significantly, 1994 was an election year, and despite all the above factors which indicated the difficulty in maintaining the value of the peso, the outgoing regime of Carlos Salinas refused to abandon the pegged exchange regime and devalue the peso.

The above critical position further deteriorated in late 1994, when on the one hand, the uncertainty about the political climate increased the risks of investments in Mexico, and on the other hand, the rise in the US interest rate provided the international investors with a new investment opportunity at a lower risk. The rise in US interest rates not only increased the cost of debt repayments for Mexican commercial banks and the private sector, it also reduced the price of Brady bonds which was inversely related to yields on very long-term bonds in the United States. These bonds were mostly bought by US investment funds which had invested in Mexico. As reported by the Bank of Mexico, the fall in the price of Brady bonds compelled the investment funds to sell their most liquid assets which were in the form of *Cetes*.[4] The above factors increased the expectation of a forthcoming devaluation, and led to the growing capital outflow which took place throughout 1994. From the beginning of January 1994 to 20 December 1994, international reserves dropped by 19.124 billion US dollars, and about 80 per cent nominal percentage depreciation of the peso.

Overall, it can be said that financial liberalization did not help much to raise the overall savings and investment ratios. Instead, it mostly led to an increase in the private sector's foreign borrowing, and erratic short term capital flow.

5 Conclusion

The basic conclusion of this chapter is that the whole package of policies that was adopted, though leading to some advances on different grounds, not only did not achieve its main targets, in some respects worked against them. Structural constraints were at the root of the problems, and the appeal of the new strategy was that it was supposed to confront those structural restrictions. The key difficulties that are associated with the adopted strategy are the following:

1. The process of integration rested primarily on trade policies, with no consideration for improvement of overall economic condition, or the domestic response to the new economic environment.
2. The fixing of the exchange rate, though, might have been adopted to control inflation and accelerate the process of financial integration, in practice undermined the effectiveness of the trade liberalization process in reallocation of resources. The overvaluation of the peso, implicitly increased the relative price of home made goods, and encouraged both consumers and producers to opt for imported goods. This in turn, while contributing to a rise in the trade deficit, discouraged investors from investing in domestic industries. It also disguised the profitability of the leading export sectors, and undervalued that of other sectors which could have otherwise attracted investment and possibly developed a competitive edge in the international markets. Finally, it encouraged the private sector to increase its borrowing from the international markets and thus acted as a conduit in raising the debt burden on the economy.
3. The relaxation of capital control soon after the financial liberalization which opened the doors to capital flows, created a stock market boom which was unrelated to economic fundamentals. The capital flows were taking place at a time when the economy was still struggling with the process of transformation, and the adherence to the policy of a fixed exchange rate was feeding the growing trade deficit. The financial sector and the economy as a whole thus became totally exposed to fluctuations of interest rates in international markets, and were therefore unable to cope with any change in expectation of exchange rate devaluation.
4. The absence of a welfare system was another shortcoming of the

structural programme. The presence of a welfare system is particularly important in view of the significant rise in the level of labour displacement which took place after the trade liberalization, and the fact that the population increased by 20 million over the period 1980–94.

5. Finally, the successful integration into NAFTA depends crucially on the economy's ability to address the above difficulties. If NAFTA leads to further growth of intra-firm industries with few linkages with the rest of the economy, then the duality within the Mexican economy may widen, and the economy may move away from full integration rather than approach it. The above considerations clearly indicate the need for a more comprehensive integration package capable of addressing all the above shortcomings and structural constraints.

Notes

1. The growth of the food sector in Table 14.1, corresponds mostly to the growth in beer production.
2. Maquila or maquiladora plants are allowed to import intermediate inputs duty free so long as they export their output to the country supplying the inputs.
3. Different government officials, even within the Bank of Mexico, have argued that there was no overvaluation, considering peculiar indexes built about the cost of labour (Gil-Díaz and Cartens 1995) or other money baskets built on different international price indexes. Nevertheless, all of them seem to ignore the extent of the balance of payments, which by 1994 was more than 28 billion dollars.
4. *Cetes* is the Mexican Treasury bill which is denominated in pesos, and its maturity varies between 28 and 91 days.

References

Bairoch, P. and R. Kozul-Wright (1996), 'Globalization Myth: Some Historical Reflections on Integration, Industrialization and Growth in the World Economy', United Nations Conference on Trade and Development, Discussion Paper No. 113.

Bank of Mexico (1995), *The Mexican Economy 1995*. Mexico.

Gil Díaz, F. and A. Carstens (1995), 'Some hypotheses related to Mexican 1994–95 crisis', Research document No. 9601, El Banco de Mexico (Bank of Mexico), Mexico.

Bank of Mexico (1996), *Indicadores Economicos*, June 1994.

Lusting, N. (1992), *Mexico, The Remaking of an Economy*, Washington, DC: Brookings Institute.

Mexican Bulletin of Statistical Information (1994), No. 13, July–September.

15 Economic integration, exchange rate and competitiveness: Mexico and the US

Pablo Ruiz-Nápoles

1 Introduction

The United States is Mexico's major trading partner; exports to and imports from the US account for 80 per cent of Mexico's total foreign trade. This close economic relationship has turned into economic integration since the opening of the Mexican economy in the 1980s and the signing and operation of the North American Free Trade Agreement in the 1990s.

A very important issue for the Mexican economy is the current account balance, in the balance of payments, which has almost always been negative; the main determinant of the current account deficit is the trade deficit. With the opening of the economy, the government relied entirely on monetary and exchange rate policies to achieve a balanced current account.

However, the real issue for the situation of the Mexican economy in the world economy is *competitiveness*. This has usually been associated, on the one hand, with the exchange rate, its regime and policies and, on the other, with comparative costs as determinants of relative advantages and trade specialization. In this chapter we analyse the measurement and the determining factors of *competitiveness* for the Mexican economy, *vis-à-vis* the US.

2 Mexico's exchange rate and commercial policies

For twenty-two years, from 1954 to 1976, Mexico maintained a fixed exchange rate. During that time a very complex protectionist system was the instrument of commercial policy, utilized to deal with the trade deficit.

In the early 1970s, domestic inflation caused the Mexican peso to be overvalued to a significant degree. So the government had to depreciate the peso in the last quarter of 1976, bringing about the first foreign exchange crisis in many years (Ortiz and Solís 1979). After this, there were two other crises of the same kind, one in 1982 and the most recent are in 1994, both of which have been worse than the one in 1976.

A common element in these crises has been the foreign exchange shortage brought about by a current account deficit, large amounts of capital flights and an overvalued currency. The adjusting programmes, implemented in turn by the administration, have all followed the IMF prescription: a strong depreciation of the currency, a severe reduction of government expenditures, a credit contraction and a real wage reduction.

As a way out of the 1982 crisis and with the purpose of establishing a new model for the economy, the government started a series of economic and legal reforms in 1983. Free market orientated they were deepened and accelerated in the period 1988–94. Among them, a new commercial policy opened the economy at a speed not experienced by any other economy. As a corollary of this policy in 1994 the Mexican government joined the North American Free Trade Agreement (NAFTA).

The purpose of opening the economy, apart from the apparent objective of reducing inflation, was clearly to stimulate foreign investment. However, most of the new foreign investment went either to the stock exchange market or to the money market and only a fraction was direct investment.

From 1982 to 1987, the balance of goods and services changed dramatically from the traditional deficit to a surplus. This improvement in the trade balance was attributed by some economists to the flexibility in the exchange rate market during that period, which allowed the exchange rate to keep up with increasing inflation differentials between the Mexican and the US economy.

In the next seven years (1988–94), however, the trade deficit reappeared and widened. During the same time the nominal exchange rate was maintained, with minor adjustments.

According to a measure of the real exchange rate, the Mexican peso was already overvalued in 1992 (Bank of Mexico, *Annual Report*, 1994), calling for a devaluation. In the context of the liberal policies followed by the government, the reestablishment of a flexible exchange rate regime might have been expected. But policymakers learned that in some cases the impact of a devaluation on the inflation rate is particularly strong, as has been empirically proved, and for the same reason a devaluation policy tends to reverse itself in the short run (Brailovsky 1981; Edwards 1993b). So what followed was a policy of a 'crawling peg' exchange rate, supported by the central bank's reserves, and adjusting balance of payments disequilibria through money flows (Ortiz and Solís, 1979, 1981). It seemed to work, as long as there were capital inflows (mainly from the US) which financed the trade deficit, until the outburst of another foreign exchange crisis at the end of 1994.

The commercial and exchange rate policies proved to be insufficient to make permanent the so-called 'structural' change in Mexico's foreign trade. Even though some export activities in manufacturing were growing with the opening of the economy and the liberal economic reforms, they had no impact on the level of employment in manufacturing; nor did they offset the rising level of manufacturing imports, once the economy started to grow. An analysis of Mexico's foreign trade shows that there are still structural difficulties involved in attaining growth while trying to maintain an external balance (Ruiz-Nápoles 1996).

3 Economic policies and orthodox theories

The liberal commercial policy, the exchange rate policy and the adjusting programmes followed in Mexico are all based on orthodox economic theory. This theory relies on comparative costs as the determinant of trade advantages under free trade, and on the exchange rate as the adjusting mechanism to achieve and maintain some degree of competitiveness. The argument is that in a general equilibrium neoclassical framework, competitiveness between countries would be determined by the comparative costs relative principle; and the real exchange rate would be determined by the purchasing power parity doctrine. Under such principles, a country may be more competitive in some industries than in others, with respect to its trading partners, but it would always find at least one industry in which it is competitive and, if the exchange rate is adequately managed to achieve and maintain such competitiveness, foreign trade will tend to be balanced (Friedman 1953).

A currency is overvalued, according to the purchasing power parity theory, when the inflation rate in the home country is higher than the rate of inflation in its trading partners, and this is presumably what produces a loss of competitiveness and, consequently, a trade deficit in the balance of payments. So, to correct the deficit, the nominal exchange rate should be adjusted to the real exchange rate, either directly by the authorities in a fixed exchange rate regime, or through the market mechanism, in a flexible exchange rate regime (Krueger 1983).

If the theory is correct, then in the long run the nominal exchange rate should move around the real exchange rate as defined by the purchasing power parity theory. Most empirical models test precisely to what extent this is true, that is, they test the market *efficiency* in adjusting one exchange rate to the other, under assumed free market and competition (Levitch 1985).

However, the purchasing power parity theory and the policy based on it, have some important flaws. On the one hand, the theory involves the use of price indexes, which, while expressing the effects of supply and demand conditions in general, do not necessarily show the degree of competitiveness of the economy, but only the general price level. The cost structure would in this case be more revealing (Officer 1975, 1980).

On the other hand, evidence has shown that devaluations did not significantly correct current account deficits in most economies, while they had a very strong impact on domestic inflation rates (Thygesen 1979; De Grauwe et al. 1985).

Trade theories based on comparative costs also have some important restrictions. They usually assume perfect competition and identity of tastes and technology, between countries, ruling out technological differences and increasing returns. In particular, these theories assume identical production functions across countries and the existence of a generalized market-clearing process.

The existence of economies of scale and a continuous technical progress in the world and some degree of unused resources (labour and capital) in many national economies, make it difficult to believe that relative prices are, in fact, determined by relative scarcities and that there are no important differences in technology between countries.

In the case of Mexico, an analysis of the foreign trade pattern in manufacturing, shows that some of the assumptions of comparative costs theory and perfect competition do not apply to the manufacturing sector: inter-industry trade is declining while intra-industry trade is growing and economies of scale are very important in explaining competitive advantages (Casar 1989). Also, a previous study (Boatler 1974) found that, on the one hand, there is a tendency for capital-intensive exports to increase, which does not correspond to what is expected according to the relative factor proportions of the Heckscher–Ohlin theorem and that, on the other hand, the assumption of identical production functions across countries does not hold either. Finally, the relative immobility of capital, the basis of the comparative costs theory, does not apply to Mexico's foreign trade. It has been proved in both studies that foreign corporations in Mexico have become the main determinants of its trade pattern.

Implicitly or explicitly, comparative costs and purchasing power parity theories still prevail, despite all criticisms and empirical evidence against them. They are, none the less, insufficient and inadequate to deal with real economic problems, such as persistent foreign trade deficits, or for the analysis of general competitiveness between countries.

4 Alternative theories

The so-called 'new trade theories', while critical of some of the neoclassical assumptions, are anyway made to fit the general neoclassical framework (Gandolfo 1987). Outside this general framework, however, there have been some theoretical developments. Within these alternative approaches there are, on the one hand, those based on the consideration of absolute advantages as main determinants of competitiveness and trade flows and, on the other hand, exchange rate theories which emphasize the relative unit labour costs as determinants of real exchange rates.

4.1 Absolute advantages and technology gaps

The technology gap argument points out that trade theory has generally focused on the comparative aspects of trade flows and what needs to be explained, in the first place, are the origins and the effects of the absolute advantages based on technological differences, which are sector specific and the main element in explaining trade flows (Dosi et al. 1990; Cimoli 1994).

This line of thinking also argues that according to empirical studies, what appears to be a comparative advantage is not the result of factor endowment, but the outcome of processes of learning which are specific to both sector and country. This type of process, by allowing various sorts of increasing returns, entails forms of market interactions that differ from perfect competition.

Technological asymmetries between countries are related to the capability of some countries to produce innovative commodities (irrespective of relative costs) and to use process innovations more efficiently in the reduction of input coefficients. These technological asymmetries induce international differences in labour productivity, which then express *technology gaps* in relation to techniques that can be ranked independently of input prices. International competitiveness is thus determined by the relationship between sectoral absolute technological advantages and wage rates.

The pattern of absolute advantage in these dominant technologies is an autonomous determinant of international competitiveness, independent of the pattern of comparative advantage. Absolute advantages dominate over comparative advantages as determinants of trade flows. This dominance means that they account for the composition of trade flows by country and by commodity at each point in time, and explain the evolution of such trade flows over time.

The international pattern of sectoral absolute advantages is a fundamental determinant of sectoral competitiveness as expressed by the sectoral market shares of each country. The main adjustment mechanism to changes in the pattern of absolute advantages does not occur through changes in relative quantities and relative prices in each economy; but through changes in world market shares, in the total level of employed resources and in the levels and rates of growth of incomes and wages.

Any absolute measure of the international competitiveness of a country or industry is based primarily on its absolute advantages in terms of product technology and labour productivity (Dosi et al. 1990).

4.2 Real exchange rates and unit labour costs

Unit labour cost theories of real exchange rate determination are essentially of two types: one is to be found within the neoclassical tradition (Officer 1975); the other is based on David Ricardo's theory of relative prices (Aglietta and Oudiz 1984).

In Aglietta's model the real exchange rate, defined as the 'nominal exchange rate adjusted unit labour costs for traded goods',[1] is estimated by econometric techniques, using data of various countries. The estimation shows that this real exchange rate is determined by three structural variables, namely the ratio between the two countries with respect to: income growth, income distribution and national specialization (Aglietta and Oudiz 1984).

5 Unit labour costs and competitiveness in Mexico and the US

Using these theories as a basis, we analysed the exchange rate and the foreign trade of the Mexican economy for the period 1970–94. Our propositions are that relative unit labour costs are the basic determinants of the real exchange rate between Mexico and the US, and that real unit labour costs are an indicator of Mexico's degree of competitiveness and, as such, an important factor determining Mexico's exports and imports.

Unit labour costs can be calculated in different ways. An important one is the *vertically integrated* unit labour costs derived from Pasinetti's model of Ricardo's theory of relative prices (Pasinetti 1977), because they include direct and indirect labour inputs and capture technological changes, through the input–output matrix coefficients.[2]

However, because of a lack of some of the required information, they were calculated as here only as the *direct* unit labour costs of the manufacturing sector.[3] This method is used for the calculation of the 'real effective exchange rates' of the International Monetary Fund's country members. In this calculation, it is assumed that the manufacturing sector represents the majority of tradable goods, which is correct for all industrialized countries and for some of the semi-industrialized ones. In the case of Mexico, manufacturing trade has grown in importance and it currently represents 80 per cent of total exports and 90 per cent of total imports.

Unit labour costs (ULC) of manufacturing for Mexico and for the US appear in Table 15.1 in current and in real terms. It can be observed that in the case of the US, unit labour costs have been declining from 1980 on, while for Mexico, they declined from 1979 to 1987 and then started to rise, up to 1993.

Relative ULC show a downward tendency in the 1980s, which turns back up in 1987; in current terms they went down constantly from 1976 to

Table 15.1 Mexico–US unit labour costs

	Mexico		United States		Relative ULC	
Year	ULC	Real ULC	ULC	Real ULC	Current	Real
1970	0.373	0.373	0.626	0.626	0.596	0.596
1971	0.367	0.378	0.602	0.607	0.610	0.623
1972	0.368	0.378	0.597	0.606	0.617	0.623
1973	0.360	0.365	0.600	0.606	0.599	0.602
1974	0.365	0.371	0.621	0.614	0.587	0.605
1975	0.372	0.373	0.590	0.586	0.630	0.637
1976	0.388	0.398	0.581	0.577	0.668	0.689
1977	0.364	0.391	0.571	0.566	0.637	0.690
1978	0.348	0.362	0.575	0.569	0.606	0.637
1979	0.349	0.360	0.582	0.567	0.598	0.635
1980	0.328	0.349	0.606	0.569	0.542	0.613
1981	0.337	0.352	0.594	0.546	0.568	0.646
1982	0.332	0.344	0.596	0.537	0.557	0.641
1983	0.260	0.269	0.579	0.524	0.449	0.513
1984	0.235	0.245	0.576	0.518	0.408	0.473
1985	0.230	0.239	0.587	0.513	0.391	0.467
1986	0.220	0.228	0.580	0.512	0.379	0.446
1987	0.200	0.222	0.566	0.476	0.354	0.467
1988	0.201	0.214	0.552	0.464	0.364	0.462
1989	0.224	0.219	0.546	0.453	0.410	0.483
1990	0.235	0.215	0.548	0.442	0.429	0.486
1991	0.245	0.217	0.545	0.433	0.450	0.500
1992	0.269	0.225	0.549	0.429	0.489	0.524
1993	0.277	0.224	0.530	0.404	0.521	0.554
1994	0.265	0.214	0.524	0.398	0.505	0.536

1987 and then up from 1988 to 1993; in real terms they declined from 1981 up to 1986, and from thence rose until 1993.

5.1 Real exchange rate and unit labour costs

The real exchange rate of the Mexican peso to the US dollar[4] was calculated according to the following equation:

$$E = 1/e_r = (P/e \div P^*)$$

where: E = real exchange rate of the Mexican peso to the US dollar, in dollars, e_r = real exchange rate, pesos per dollar, e = nominal exchange rate, pesos per dollar, P = Mexico's consumer price index, in pesos, and P^* = US consumer price index, in dollars.

A comparison of relative unit labour costs, and the real exchange rate, between Mexico and the US, is shown in Table 15.2. Based on these data, Figure 15.1 presents the trajectories of the relative unit labour costs index (RULCI) and the real exchange rate index (RERI) for the period 1970–94.

Both the data and the corresponding graph show a very close relation between relative ULC and the real exchange rate. An econometric estimation shows that relative ULC determine the trend for the real

Table 15.2 Real exchange rate and relative unit labour costs (index 1977 = 100)

Years	Relative ULC	Real exchange rate
1970	93.67	106.9
1971	95.77	108.0
1972	96.97	109.9
1973	94.12	115.9
1974	92.23	129.0
1975	98.94	136.3
1976	104.94	120.7
1977	100.00	100.0
1978	95.14	108.4
1979	93.99	114.8
1980	85.14	126.9
1981	89.13	137.9
1982	87.40	89.7
1983	70.56	82.5
1984	64.05	93.6
1985	61.39	93.0
1986	59.53	71.5
1987	55.60	71.5
1988	57.20	89.4
1989	64.46	93.9
1990	67.38	98.5
1991	70.67	108.2
1992	76.83	118.1
1993	81.88	125.1
1994	79.32	116.3

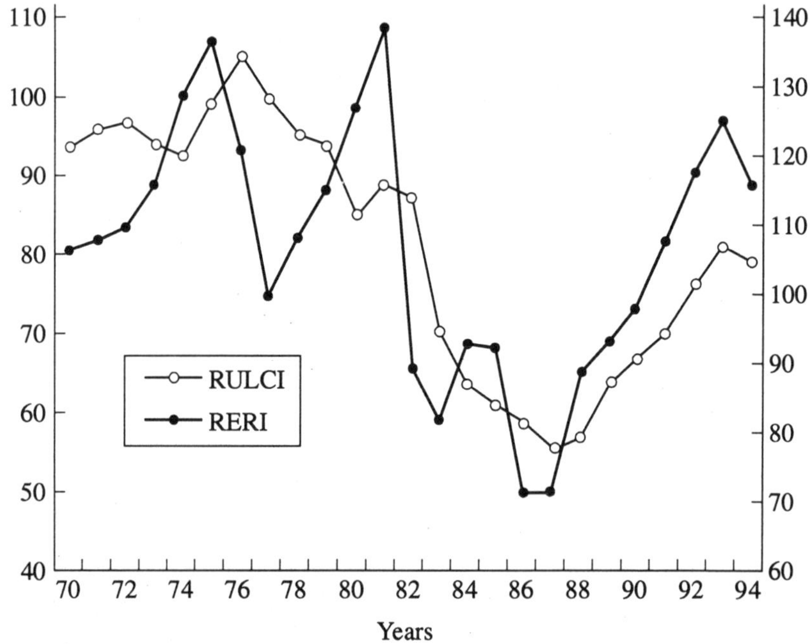

Figure 15.1 Relative unit labour costs and real exchange rate

exchange rate, while two other variables, domestic income and capital flows, determine the fluctuations around it. The way the real exchange rate is measured makes its relation to relative ULC positive. This means that if the relative ULC go down, the currency will depreciate in real terms (competitiveness is improved) and when relative ULC rise, the currency is appreciated in real terms.

To estimate the real exchange rate by econometric techniques, the following dynamic short-run equation was specified:

$$\ln EI_t = \beta_1 \ln EI_{t-2} + \beta_2 \ln RUI_t + \beta_3 \ln Ym_t + \beta_4 K + u_t \qquad (15.1)$$

where $\ln EI_t$ = logarithm of the index of E at time t, $\ln RUI_t$ = logarithm of relative unit labour costs index of manufacturing, Mexico/US, Ym_t = gross domestic product of Mexico, in constant pesos, K_t = net capital movements (other than direct foreign investment) in the balance of payments of Mexico, in dollars.

In this equation, one of the explanatory variables is EI the real exchange rate, the dependent variable, lagged two periods. All variables are expressed in logarithms, except K, and there is no intercept. The results of the estimation by ordinary least squares technique are shown in Appendix Table 15A.1. Then, by making $\ln EI_t = \ln EI_{t-2}$ substituting in equation (15.1), and solving for $\ln EI_t$ we get the solved static long-run equation:

$$\ln EI = +0.71529 \ln RUI + 0.090793 \ln Y + 4.28 - 006K. \qquad (15.1a)$$

In this equation, the real exchange rate index is determined by the unit labour costs index, by the GDP and by capital movements.

5.2 Foreign trade and unit labour costs

Manufacturing imports and exports of Mexico are shown in Table 15.3. The analysis of the real exchange rate necessarily leads us to consider its relation to the trade balance. We did not deal, however, with the trade balance as such, but we analysed imports and exports separately. We assumed that all trade is regulated by manufacturing trade in the sense that it accounts for the greatest part of all foreign trade, and therefore determines its level and its changes. So, we considered only manufacturing imports and exports.

In both, import and export equations, the real ULC play an important role in their determination. There are two other important determining variables in both cases: the level of economic activity, domestically and abroad, which may be called the 'structural' variable; and the terms of trade.

In the case of manufacturing imports, shown in Figure 15.2, there is a close relation with the level of economic activity, measured by the gross domestic product. To evaluate this relationship, an import function was estimated by econometric techniques. It as was used as a typical import function, except that we included as an explanatory variable, the real ULC of manufacturing, and did not include the nominal exchange rate as other models do. The results are highly significant.

For estimation, the econometric specification of the import function is:

$$\ln M_t = \beta_1 \ln Ym_t + \beta_2 \ln Ur_t + \beta_3 \ln T_t + u_t \qquad (15.2)$$

where: M = manufacturing imports, Y_m = gross domestic product of Mexico, Ur = real unit labour costs of manufacturing and T = terms of trade (export/import prices); all variables are measured in logarithms, and there is no intercept. The results are shown in Appendix Table 15A.2.

The estimated income elasticity of imports is 1.4, so imports tend to grow faster than income. This tendency is more acute in the period of opening (1983–94) in which all previous restrictions to imports were withdrawn. Unit labour costs are in this case the real unit labour costs

Table 15.3 Manufacturing trade of Mexico (millions of dollars)

Year	Exports	Imports	Balance
1970	444.4	2 253.3	−1 808.9
1971	545.0	2 174.8	−1 629.8
1972	677.1	2 573.3	−1 896.2
1973	960.2	3 115.7	−2 155.5
1974	1 499.8	4 807.6	−3 307.8
1975	1 524.5	5 561.7	−4 037.2
1976	1 708.2	5 693.0	−3 984.8
1977	2 082.7	4 805.4	−2 722.7
1978	2 485.4	6 791.6	−4 306.2
1979	2 726.2	10 563.5	−7 837.3
1980	2 651.0	16 002.8	−13 351.8
1981	2 688.2	20 259.2	−17 571.0
1982	3 017.6	12 971.4	−9 953.8
1983	4 573.8	6 644.2	−2 070.4
1984	5 438.2	8 192.2	−2 754.0
1985	4 969.9	11 261.1	−6 291.2
1986	7 055.1	10 202.2	−3 147.1
1987	9 745.7	10 771.3	−1 025.6
1988	11 504.0	16 743.9	−5 239.9
1989	12 607.5	20 802.9	−8 195.4
1990	13 955.5	28 523.1	−14 567.6
1991	15 768.8	35 473.1	−19 704.3
1992	16 740.4	44 631.4	−27 891.0
1993	19 832.1	45 710.6	−25 878.5
1994	24 809.7	54 843.0	−30 033.3
1995	36 333.3	42 728.8	−6 395.5

Source: Banco de México *Indicadores de Comercio Exterior*. Foreign trade indicators (monthly) Dec 1970–1995.

of manufacturing, an indicator of the country's competitiveness. Since these ULC are entirely determined within the economy, it can regarded as an absolute measure of competitiveness and not a relative one. The relation is straightforward, if real ULC rise, imports rise.

For manufacturing exports, we take the exports share as an indicator of the country's competitive position. The exports share is measured as the percentage share of manufacturing exports in the world's total exports.[5] The data are shown in Table 15.4. Figure 15.3 illustrates how the exports

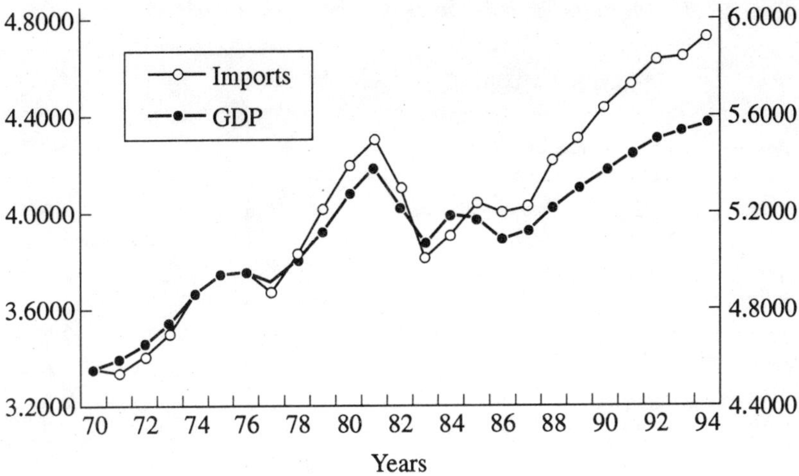

Figure 15.2 Imports and GDP

share of Mexico has moved in the period 1970–93 and shows the close relationship that exists with the evolution of unit labour costs of manufacturing.

One important aspect to be stressed is that the exports share coefficient and the inverse of the real unit labour costs move together. This can be seen by looking at Figure 15.3. Both are indicators of the country's competitiveness.

As a proxy of technological differences between Mexico and the US, we took the absolute difference of their respective levels of income. It is this variable which determines the trend for the exports share coefficient. The export equation was also estimated by econometric techniques. The two other explanatory variables included were the real ULC and the terms of trade. The results show that the real ULC were highly and negatively correlated as expected, and the terms of trade also had a significant parameter, negatively related to the exports share.

The exports share equation (see note 5) was defined as:

$$Xs = X/Xw$$

where Xs = exports share, Xw = total world exports and X = manufacturing exports, both measured in dollars.

The econometric specification for the exports share equation is:

$$\ln Xs_t = \alpha_0 + \beta_1 \Delta \ln Yd_t + \beta_2 \ln Ur_t + \beta_3 \ln T_t + u_t \qquad (15.3)$$

Table 15.4 Manufacturing exports and unit labour costs

Years	World total exports ($ billion)	Manufacturing exports ($ billion)	Exports share (%)	Real ULC	Inverse of RULC
1970	291.8	0.444	0.1523	0.373	2.679
1971	362.8	0.545	0.1502	0.378	2.644
1972	389.0	0.677	0.1741	0.378	2.646
1973	539.5	0.960	0.1780	0.365	2.739
1974	793.3	1.500	0.1891	0.371	2.695
1975	816.7	1.525	0.1867	0.373	2.678
1976	919.6	1.708	0.1858	0.398	2.515
1977	1 043.5	2.083	0.1996	0.391	2.557
1978	1 210.4	2.485	0.2053	0.362	2.759
1979	1 546.4	2.726	0.1763	0.360	2.777
1980	1 896.8	2.651	0.1398	0.349	2.869
1981	1 875.2	2.688	0.1434	0.352	2.838
1982	1 740.6	3.018	0.1734	0.344	2.907
1983	1 697.2	4.574	0.2695	0.269	3.721
1984	1 800.6	5.438	0.3020	0.245	4.077
1985	1 819.4	4.970	0.2732	0.239	4.176
1986	1 998.6	7.055	0.3530	0.228	4.377
1987	2 352.6	9.746	0.4143	0.222	4.504
1988	2 689.7	11.504	0.4277	0.214	4.668
1989	2 914.3	12.608	0.4326	0.219	4.575
1990	3 336.9	13.956	0.4182	0.215	4.654
1991	3 441.9	15.769	0.4581	0.217	4.616
1992	3 687.5	16.740	0.4540	0.225	4.444
1993	3 685.5	19.832	0.5381	0.224	4.470
1994	N.A.	24.810		0.214	4.684

Sources: International Monetary Fund, *International Financial Statistics*; Banco de México, *Indicadores de Comercio Exterior*. Foreign trade indicators Dec 1970–1994.

where, $\ln Xs_t$ = logarithm of the percentage share of manufacturing exports of Mexico to total world exports, $\Delta \ln Yd_t$ = first difference of the logarithm of the GDP difference US–Mexico, $\ln Ur$ = logarithm of the real unit labour costs of manufacturing in Mexico and $\ln T$ = logarithm of the terms of trade. All variables are expressed in logarithms, and in the case of $\ln Yd$ (the GDP difference), it is taken in first differences to estimate the equation. The results are shown in Appendix Table 15A.3.

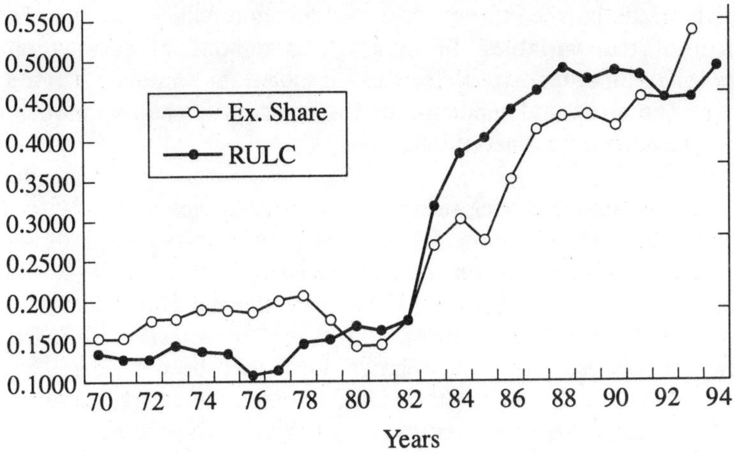

Figure 15.3 Exports share and real unit labour costs

5.3 Some implications for policy

If our proposition is correct, a nominal depreciation of the currency does not imply *ipso facto* a real depreciation, since this can only be produced by reducing the unit labour costs. These, in turn, have two determinants: wages and productivity. Thus, in order to reduce unit labour costs, either the real wage rate is to be reduced or productivity raised, or both. Moreover, this has to be done at a faster rate than the country's main competitor in the world market, so as to improve the country's competitive position.

A nominal depreciation of the currency, together with a recessionary policy, may in fact produce a reduction of real wages and, thereby, a reduction of unit labour costs, in the short run, assuming constant productivity. This can be accomplished either by directly reducing the wage rate or by reducing the level of employment, to a given output level (Corden 1977; Dornbusch 1980).

However, a lasting reduction in unit labour costs can only be produced by the use of more productive techniques of production. If this happens, it will have an effect on the input–output matrix, and on the output–labour ratio. If we assume that wages do not rise as fast as productivity, ULC will decline when productivity increases. This would imply a real depreciation of the currency, even with a constant nominal exchange rate. As an effect of this real depreciation, the trade balance will tend to improve, that is, exports will rise and imports decline, and also the competitive position of the country improves – the exports share goes up.

We may conclude that unlike the pure monetarist view, we must consider the trade balance to be a real phenomenon, which requires the adjustment of real variables. In as much as a nominal devaluation produces inflation, it tends to defeat itself as a means to adjust a trade imbalance. The structural tendency to trade disequilibrium cannot be adjusted by temporary monetary means.

6 ULC and the manufacturing sector of the Mexican economy

As the figures in Table 15.1 show, ULC in the manufacturing sector of the Mexican economy are about one-half of the corresponding ULC in the US, and the relative ULC Mexico–US has gone down almost constantly from the mid-1970s until the second half of the 1980s. Since 1987, the tendency was reversed and the relative ULC has been rising. This increasing tendency of the relative ULC in manufacturing occurred despite the fact that unemployment was also rising in this sector.

The constant decline of relative ULC during the 1980s was the result of one particular policy: the systematic reduction of the real wage rate in Mexico since 1981. The rate of growth of wages has been below the rate of growth of prices in general.

As for the relative Mexico–US wage rate, it is clear that the purpose of such policy was to reduce relative wages below the ratio of prices between Mexico and the US. This policy was successful between 1983 and 1994. Table 15.5 and Figure 15.4 show clearly the results of this policy. The effect of the decline of unit labour costs and its impact on the exports share rise, between 1983 and 1992, can also be seen in Figure 15.3.

The increase in manufacturing exports which has been measured by the export share did not, however, produce a trade surplus in manufacturing, but only a reduction in its traditional trade deficit. This was so because, as a result of the opening of the economy starting in 1983, imports increased very fast despite the economic crisis. Thus, when the economy started to grow between 1989 and 1991, the deficit increased significantly.

There was also an increase in productivity in the manufacturing sector in Mexico, beginning in 1983. However, this increase was slower than the increase in productivity in the US, especially after 1986 as can be observed in Figure 15.5.

To sum up, relative ULC in the manufacturing sector declined between 1982 and 1987 and this meant a real depreciation of the currency, making the Mexican economy more competitive. However, this decline was based essentially on a relative wage decrease.

In the next period, starting in 1988, this tendency was reversed by a higher increase in productivity in the US, so that ULC in Mexico increased, eliminating the undervaluation margin in 1991.

Table 15.5 *Relative wages and relative prices (indices base 1977 = 100)*

Year	Wage rate: Mexico	Wage rate: US	Ratio of wages	Ratio of constant prices
1970	52.6	60.5	86.9	106.9
1971	56.5	64.0	88.2	108.0
1972	62.6	68.3	91.7	109.9
1973	70.8	72.5	97.7	115.9
1974	91.0	78.1	116.5	129.0
1975	110.0	85.5	128.7	136.3
1976	112.2	92.6	121.2	120.7
1977	100.0	100.0	100.0	100.0
1978	114.1	107.8	105.9	108.4
1979	137.7	117.5	117.2	114.8
1980	167.4	129.5	129.3	127.0
1981	206.0	141.7	145.4	137.8
1982	137.9	151.3	91.1	89.7
1983	101.4	160.5	63.1	82.4
1984	112.7	169.7	66.4	93.6
1985	116.5	179.5	64.9	93.0
1986	84.0	187.2	44.9	71.5
1987	86.3	192.8	44.8	71.5
1988	111.7	201.6	55.4	89.4
1989	131.2	208.0	63.1	93.9
1990	150.2	216.2	69.5	98.5
1991	181.1	225.2	80.4	108.2
1992	221.1	238.1	92.8	118.1
1993	250.5	242.1	103.5	125.1
1994	240.9	250.0	96.4	116.3

Under conditions of unrestricted opening of the economy and maintaining the nominal exchange rate within narrow margins, the trade balance showed an unprecedented deficit which by 1994 was out of control.

The modernization of the economy was promoted by the administration which took over in 1988, encouraging foreign investment and accelerating the opening process, but the results were very poor since most of the new foreign investment went into the stock exchange and the

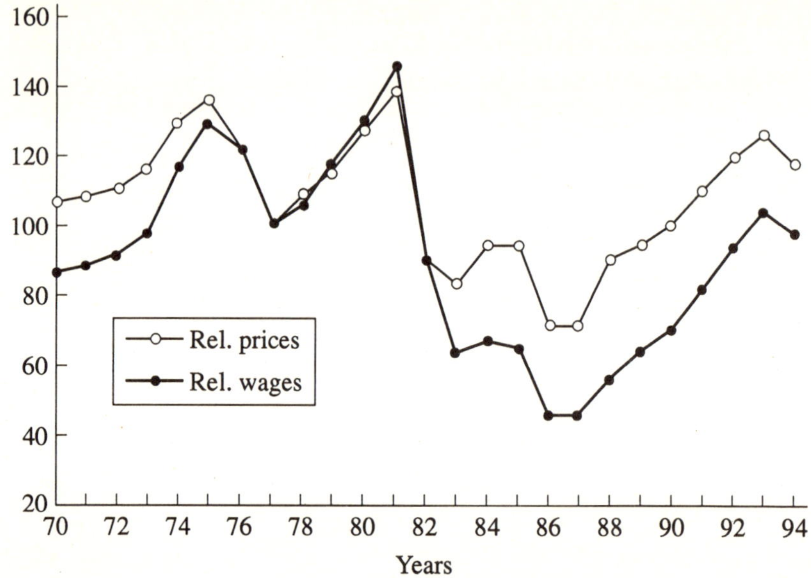

Figure 15.4 Relative wages and relative prices

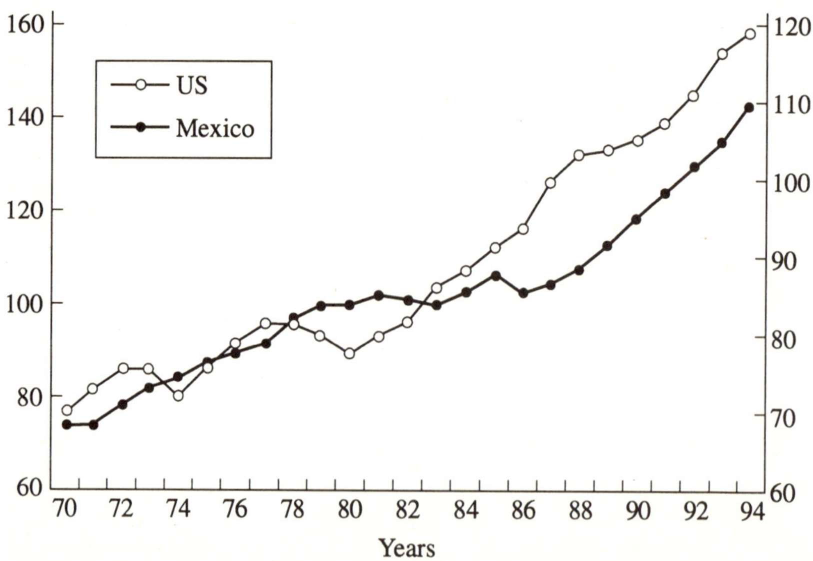

Figure 15.5 Productivity indexes

money investment markets, so it could leave the country when conditions seemed unfavourable, as happened in the last quarter of 1994.

The Mexican government and the private sector tried to improve the competitiveness of the manufacturing sector based mainly on the reduction of real wages. It worked for almost a decade, when the exports share increased at a very high rate, and were favoured by an increasing demand.

From the point of view of the unit labour costs approach, the nominal depreciation of the currency has only a temporary and limited impact on competitiveness. A lasting improvement of competitiveness and therefore of the trade balance requires the use of more productive and cost-reducing techniques.

Notes

1. Aglietta's real exchange rate equation:

$$e_r = T \cdot \frac{wl}{w^* l^*} \tag{1}$$

where e_r = real exchange rate, w = rate wage rate, l = labour–output ratio in the traded good sector and T = terms of trade.

2. The calculation of vertically integrated unit labour costs for each country would be:

$$wv = \mathbf{a}(\mathbf{I} - \mathbf{A})^{-1} w \tag{2}$$

where: $\mathbf{A}$ = matrix of inter-industry input coefficients, $\mathbf{a}$ = row vector of labour inputs w = wage rate (scalar); $(\mathbf{I} - \mathbf{A})^{-1}$ is a non-negative matrix representing total input requirements (direct and indirect) to produce a final product; the product wv is the row vector of vertically integrated labour coefficients multiplied by the wage rate, that is, the unit labour costs. If it is not assumed a uniform wage rate throughout the economy, instead of w, we can have $\mathbf{w}$ = column vector of wages.

$$\mathbf{vw} = \mathbf{a}(\mathbf{I} - \mathbf{A})^{-1}\mathbf{w} \tag{4}$$

$$\mathbf{vw}_a/\mathbf{vw}_b \cdot e = \mathbf{a}_a(\mathbf{I} - \mathbf{A}_a)^{-1}\mathbf{w}_a/\mathbf{a}_b(\mathbf{I} - \mathbf{A}_b)^{-1}\mathbf{w}_b \cdot e \tag{5}$$

where subscripts a and b stand for country a and country b, $a \neq b$.

$$V = \mathbf{vw} = \mathbf{a}(\mathbf{I} - \mathbf{A})^{-1}\mathbf{w} \tag{6}$$

$$\mathbf{a} = (l_1, l_2, \ldots, l_n)$$

$$l_i = L_i/Q_i \qquad i = 1, \ldots, n \tag{7}$$

$$\mathbf{w} = (w_1, w_2, \ldots, w_n)$$

$$w_i = W_i/L_i \tag{8}$$

where: V = vertically integrated unit labour costs, $\mathbf{v}$ = row vector of direct and indirect labour inputs, $\mathbf{w}$ = column vector of wage rates w for each industry, $\mathbf{a}$ = row vector of direct labour inputs l, for each industry, $\mathbf{A}$ = input–output matrix (order n by n),

L_i = total labour of industry i, Q_i = gross output of industry i, W_i = total wages of industry i, n = number of industries in the economy.

3. For the calculation of ULC as direct labour requirements the equation utilized is:

$$U = \frac{L}{Q} \cdot \frac{W}{L} \quad (9)$$

The variables for each country are: L = total number of workers in manufacturing, W = total wages and salaries paid in manufacturing, Q = gross domestic product of manufacturing.

For the calculation of ULC of manufacturing in constant terms, the following formulas were used:

$$Ur = W_r/Q_r \quad (10)$$

$$Q_r = Q/P_p \quad (11)$$

$$W_r = W/P_c \quad (12)$$

$$Ur = (W/Q) \div (P_c/P_p) \quad (13)$$

$$URr_{mu} = Ur_m/Ur_u \quad (14)$$

where, r stands for *real*, that is, measured in constant terms, the subscripts m for Mexico and u for the US; P_p = GDP price deflator index, and P_c = consumer price index; price indexes are both measured in dollars. So, URr_{mu} = real relative unit labour costs of manufacturing, Mexico/US.

4. Starting from the definition:

$$e_r = e \div (P/P^*) \quad (15)$$

where e_r = real exchange rate, pesos per dollar, e = nominal exchange rate, pesos per dollar, P = Mexico's consumer price index, in pesos, and P^* = US consumer price index, in dollars. From this equation we get:

$$E = 1/e_r = (P/e \div P^*) \quad (16)$$

where E is the real exchange rate of the Mexican peso to the US dollar, expressed in dollars.

5. It is defined by the equation:

$$Xs = X/Xw \quad (17)$$

where Xs = exports share, Xw = total world exports and X = manufacturing exports, both measured in dollars.

References

Aglietta, M. and G. Oudiz (1984), 'Real Exchange Rates and Structural Transformations', in P. Malgrange (ed.), *Contemporary Macroeconomic Modelling*, Oxford: Basil Blackwell, pp. 91–127.

Boatler, Robert W. (1974), 'Las predicciones de la teoría del comercio internacional y el crecimiento de las exportaciones manufacturadas de México', (international theory predictions and Mexico's manufactured export growth) *El Trimestre Económico*, No. 164, October–December Fondo de Cultura Economica, Mexico, 811–41.

Brailovsky, Vladimiro (1981), *Exchange Rate Policies, Manufactured Exports and the Rate of Inflation*, Mexico: Institute for Industrial Planning, Ministry of National Resources and Industrial Development.

Capdevielle, Patricia and Alvarez Donato (1981), 'International Comparisons of Trends in Productivity and Labour Costs', *Monthly Labor Review*, December, pp. 14–20.

Casar, José I. (1989), *Transformación en el patrón de especialización y comercio exterior del sector manufacturero mexicano 1978–1987 (The transportation in the pattern of specialization and trade of the Mexican manufacturing sector 1978–1987)*, Mexico: Institute Latinoamerican de Estudios Trasnacionales (ILET).

Cimoli, Mario (1994), 'Technological Gaps, Specialization and Growth: A Structuralist/ Evolutionary View' (unpublished), Universitá degli Studi di Venezia.

Corden, William M. (1977), *Inflation Exchange Rates and the World Economy*, 2nd edn, 1980, Chicago: University of Chicago Press.

Corden, William M. (1993), 'Importa la cuenta corriente? El punto de vista tradicional y el moderno', (Does the current account matter? The traditional and the modern approaches) *Economía Mexicana Nueva Epoca*, **II** (1), January–June, pp. 7–34.

De Grauwe P., M. Janssens and H. Leilaert (1985), 'Real Exchange Rate Variability from 1920 to 1926 and 1973 to 1982', *Princeton Studies in International Finance*, No. 56, Princeton University.

Dornbusch, Rudiger (1975), 'Exchange Rates and Fiscal Policy in a Popular Model of International Trade', *American Economic Review*, **65** (5), December, 859–71.

Dornbush, Rudiger (1980), *Open Economy Macroeconomics*, New York: Basic Books.

Dornbusch, Rudiger (1987), 'Exchange Rate Economics: 1986', *Economic Journal*, **97**, March, 1–18.

Dornbusch, Rudiger (1988), 'Purchasing Power Parity', in *Exchange Rates and Inflation*, Cambridge, MA: MIT Press, pp. 265–292.

Dosi, G., K. Pavitt and L. Soete (1990), *The Economics of Technical Change and International Trade*, New York: New York University Press.

Edwards, Sebastian (1985), 'Are Devaluations Contractionary?', Working Papers Series, No. 1676, National Bureau of Economic Research.

Edwards, Sebastian (1989), 'Exchange Rate Misalignment in Developing Countries', *World Bank Research Observer*, **4** (1), January, pp. 3–21.

Edwards, Sebastian (1993a), 'Openess, Trade Liberalization and Growth in Developing Countries', *Journal of Economic Literature*, **XXXI**, September, 1358–93.

Edwards, Sebastian (1993b), 'Exchange Rates as Nominal Anchors', *Weltwirtschaftliches Archiv*, **129**, 1–32.

Frenkel, Jacob (1981), 'The Collapse of the Purchasing Power Parities during the 1970's', *European Economic Review*, **16**, 146–65.

Friedman, Milton (1953), 'The Case for Flexible Exchange Rates', in American Economics Association, *Readings in International Economics* (1968), pp. 413–17.

Gandolfo, Giancarlo (1987), *International Economics I*, Heidelberg: Springer-Verlag.

International Monetary Fund (1985), *International Financial Statistics*, Supplement on Exchange Rates, Supplement Series No. 9.

Isard, Peter (1978), 'Exchange-Rate Determination: A Survey of Popular Views and Recent Models', *Princeton Studies in International Finance*, No. 42, May, Princeton University.

Katseli-Papaefstratiou, Louka (1979), 'The Reemergence of the Purchasing Power Parity Doctrine in the 1970's', *Special Papers in International Economics*, No. 13, December, Princeton University.

Krueger, Anne (1983), *Exchange Rate Determination*, Cambridge: Cambridge University Press.

Krugman, Paul R. (1978), 'Purchasing Power Parity and Exchange Rates', *Journal of International Economics*, **8**, 397–407.

Krugman, Paul R. (1979), 'Increasing Returns Monopolistic Competition and International Trade', *Journal of International Economics*, **9** (4), November, 469–79.

Krugman, Paul R. (1992), *Currencies and Crises*, Cambridge, MA: MIT Press.

Levitch, Richard M. (1985), 'Empirical Studies of Exchange Rates: Price Behavior, Rate Determination and Market Efficiency', in R.W. Jones and P. Kenen (eds), *Handbook of International Economics*, Vol. II, Ch. 19, Elsevier.

Lustig, Nora (1992), 'Tipo de Cambio, Protección Efectiva y Exportaciones Manufactureras. México 1983–1987', (Exchange rate, effective protection and manufacturing exports 1983–1987), *Investigación Económica*, No. 200, April–June, UNAM, Mexico, pp. 75–109.

Lustig N., B. Borthsworth and R. Lawrence (1992), *North American Free Trade*, Washington, DC: The Brookings Institution.

Officer, Lawrence H. (1975), 'The Purchasing Power Parity Theory of Exchange Rates: A Review Article', *International Monetary Fund Staff Papers*, **XXIII** (1), pp. 1–60.

Officer, Lawrence H. (1980), 'Effective Exchange Rates and Price Ratios Over the Long Run: A Test of the Purchasing-Power-Parity Theory', *Canadian Journal of Economics*, **XIII** (2), May, pp. 206–230.

Ortiz, G. and L. Solís (1979), 'Financial Structure and Exchange Rate Experience: Mexico 1954–1977', *Journal of Development Economics*, **6**, 515–548.

Ortiz, G. and L. Solís (1981), 'Inflation and Growth: Exchange Rate Aternatives for Mexico', in John Williamson (ed.), *Exchange Rate Rules*, New York: St. Martin's Press, 327–46.

Pasinetti, Luigi (1977), *Lectures on the Theory of Production*, Cambridge: Cambridge University Press.

Pasinetti, Luigi (1981), *Structural Change and Economic Growth*, Cambridge: Cambridge University Press.

Ruiz-Nápoles, Pablo (1996), 'Investment, Trade and Employment in Mexico, in the Context of a Liberal Reform and NAFTA', in C. Paraskevopoulos, R. Grinspun and G. Eaton (eds), *Economic Integration in the Americas*, Aldershot, UK: Edward Elgar, pp. 55–69.

Shaikh, Anwar (1991), 'Competition and Exchange Rates: Theory and Empirical Evidence' (unpublished), New School for Social Research.

Shaikh, Anwar (1994), 'Free Trade, Unemployment and Economic Policy' (unpublished), New School for Social Research.

Thygesen, Niels (1979), 'Exchange Rates Experiences and Policies of Small Countries: Some European Examples of the 1970's', *Essays in International Finance*, No. 136, May, Princeton University.

Appendix 15A

Table 15A.1 Ordinary least squares regression equation (15.1)

Dependent variable		ln *EI*	No. obs.	22
Ind. variable	ln *EI*(−2)	ln *RUI*	ln *Y*	*K*
Coefficient	−0.5133527	1.08249	0.137402	6.478E−06
T-stat	(−3.00396)	(7.2652)	(4.92561)	(2.45493)
R squared	0.788476	Durbin–Watson	1.9906	
Adj. *R* sq.	0.753222	*F*-Statistic	22.365	
Equation evaluation tests				*P*-value
Serial correlation LM(1)		*F*(1, 21)	0.00166	(0.9680)
Heteroscedasticity ARCH (1)		*F* (1, 16)	1.24024	(0.2793)
White test		*F* (2, 15)	0.95851	(0.5055)
Normality Jarque–Bera		Chi S.	1.24169	(0.5375)
Ramset reset (1)		*F* (1, 17)	0.32794	(0.5740)
Cusum			Pass	
Cusum Q			Pass	
Coint. test	Dickey–Fuller	*P*-value	ADF(1)	*P*-value
Residuals	−4.3831	(0.0003)	−4.4099	(0.0003)

Sources: For Mexico: GDP and labour data, Instituto Nacional de Geografía, Estadística e Informática (INEGI), *Cuentas Nacionales*; trade, exchange rate and price data, Banco de México, *Indicadores Económicos* and *Informe Anual*. For the US: GDP and labour data from, Bureau of Economic Analysis (BEA), US Department of Commerce, *Survey of Current Business*, and directly from BEA; price data, International Monetary Fund, *International Financial Statistics*.

Table 15A.2 Ordinary least squares regression equation (15.2)

Dependent variable		ln *M*	No. obs.	25
Ind. variable		ln *Ym*	ln *Ur*	ln *T*
Coefficient		1.37303	1.9665	−1.3119
T-stat		(26.913)	(5.1190)	(−14.429)
R squared	0.986677	Durbin–Watson	1.73716	
Adj. *R* sq.	0.985466	*F*-Statistic	814.648	
Equation evaluation tests				*P*-value
Serial correlation LM (1)		*F* (1, 24)	1.74703	(0.2005)
Heteroscedasticity ARCH (1)		*F* (1, 19)	0.53338	(0.4729)
White test		*F* (2, 18)	0.68837	(0.6617)
Normality Jarque–Bera		Chi S.	0.63046	(0.7296)
Ramsey reset (1)		*F* (1, 20)	2.53158	(0.1259)
Cusum			Pass	
Cusum Q			Pass	
Coint. test	Dickey–Fuller	*P*-value	AFD(1)	*P*-value
Residuals	−3.5884	(0.0016)	−2.9438	(0.0078)

Sources: See Table 15A.1.

Table 15A.3 Ordinary least squares regression equation (15.3)

Dependent variable		ln *Xs*	No. obs.	24
Ind. variable	C	D ln *Yd*	ln *Ur*	ln *T*
Coefficient	4.7144	1.38072	−0.8008	−1.1085
T-stat	(3.8833)	(1.1600)	(−3.7175)	(−4.8585)
R squared	0.94385	Durbin–Watson	1.254	
Adj. *R* sq.	0.93499	*F*-Statistic	106.47	
Equation evaluation tests				*P*-value
Serial correlation LM (1)		*F* (1, 23)	1.05274	(0.3185)
Heteroscedasticity ARCH (1)		*F* (1, 20)	0.55825	(0.4637)
White test		*F* (2, 19)	0.69607	(0.6566)
Normality Jarque–Bera		Chi S.	0.77660	(0.6782)
Ramsey reset (1)		*F* (1, 20)	0.09872	(0.7568)
Cusum			Pass	
Cusum Q			Pass	
Coint. test	Dickey–Fuller	*P*-value	ADF(1)	*P*-value
Residuals	−3.2482	(0.0040)	−3.0071	(0.0072)

Sources: See Table 15A.1.

Index

absolute advantage theory, 192–3
Agarwal, J.P., 113, 117
Aglietta, M., 193
agricultural trade, 42–55, 104
  European Union (EU) and, 42, 43–6, 54
  GATT and, 42, 45–6, 49, 52, 54–5
  NAFTA and, 43, 46–53, 54
Ahmad, J., as contributor, 101–11
Amos, O., 69, 75
Anderson, K., 54
Arge, R.d', 114
Arnade, C.A., 51
Auer, L., 75
Australia, agricultural sector, 45
Austria
  economic performance of, 79
  unemployment in, 81
  wages in, 83
  welfare system in, 62

Baily, M., 78
Bairoch, P., 174
balance of payments
  foreign direct investment and, 125
  Mexican, 188, 189, 201–2
Balasubramanyam, V., 125
Balough, R.S., 113, 114
banking sector
  Mexican, 181–6
  transition to market economy and, 94–5, 98–9
Barro, R., 69, 70, 86
Bartik, T.J., 75
Batavia, B., 44
  as contributor, 42–55
Baumol, W.J., 69
Belgium
  economic performance of, 65, 79
  economic policies in, 65
  unemployment in, 81
  wages in, 83
  welfare system in, 61, 62, 63, 64, 65, 67
Benjamin, W., 169
Bergeijk, P. van, 105
Biessen, G., 105
Boatler, R.W., 191
Brailowsky, V., 189
Buchanan, Pat, 48

Canada
  agricultural sector, 45, 46–7, 48, 49, 50, 54
  implications of economic and financial integration for, 3, 71–5, 87
  migration to, 145, 151–5
  NAFTA and, 12–23, 45, 46–7, 48, 49, 50, 54, 71–5, 87
  welfare system in, 4
Canadian-United States Free Trade Agreement (CUSTA), 43, 46–7, 49, 54
Cantwell, J., 121, 126, 133
capital
  economic convergence and, 70
  globalization of capital markets, 6
  Mexican economy and, 183, 186
  transition to market economy and, 94–5
Carayannis, E.G., 69, 76
  as contributor, 69–87
Casar, J.I., 191
Castañeda, J.G., 164–5
Cimoli, M., 192
Claessens, E., 141
  as contributor, 136–41
Clinton, Bill, 48, 146–8
Collins, S., 105
Colosio, L.D., 167
command economies *see* socialist economies
Cools, A., 141
  as contributor, 136–41
Corden, W.M., 201
Coughlin, C.C., 71
Council for Mutual Economic

Assistance (Comecon; CMEA), 101, 102, 103, 110
cultural identity, 136–7
currencies *see* exchange rates
Czech Republic
EU and, 104
transition to market economy in, 97, 102

Davison, C.W., 51
De Grauwe, P., 191
De Long, J.B., 69
debt problems, Mexican, 183, 184, 186
Denmark
economic performance of, 80
unemployment in, 82
wages in, 84
welfare system in, 59, 60, 61, 63, 64, 65
Denny, M., 73
devolution of welfare systems, 63–4
Dixit, A., 27
Dornbusch, R., 201
Dosi, G., 192, 193
Dunning, J.H., 113, 121, 126, 127, 133

Eastern Europe *see* socialist economies
economic growth
economic convergence and, 72–5, 76–9, 80, 87
welfare systems and, 65
economic integration, 5–6
economic convergence and
in EU, 69, 78–86, 87
in NAFTA, 69–78, 86–7, 173–87
foreign direct investment and, 112–18
implications for national public policy of, 3–9
model of, 6–9
transition to market economy and
small business sector and, 91–100
trade liberalization and, 101–11
welfare systems and, 7, 8, 9, 56, 57–8, 66
education and training, transition to market economy and, 95–6, 97–8
Edwards, S., 189
emigration: from Mexico, 145–57
employment
economic convergence and, 70–1, 72, 73, 86
small business sector and, 92–3
welfare systems and, 65
see also unemployment
Encarnation, D., 121, 129, 131, 132
Erickson, R.A., 12
Ethier, W.J., 27
Europe, tendencies and idiosyncracies of trade in, 136–41
European Union (EU), 3
agricultural sector in, 42, 43–6, 54, 104
Eastern Europe and, 101, 104, 110, 111
foreign direct investment and, 112, 120, 121, 125, 126, 127–32, 133
integration of, 5–6, 56, 57–8, 66
case study of impact on Greece of, 26–41
economic convergence and, 69, 78–86, 87
welfare systems (social protection) in, 56–68
evolution of, 58–60
macroeconomic context of, 65–6
organizational changes in, 63–5
performance of, 60–63
exchange rates
Mexican economy and, 179, 181, 183, 185, 186, 188–9, 193–205
model of integration process and, 6–7
purchasing power parity theory and, 190–91
unit labour costs and, 193–205

financial integration, 5–6
implications for national public policy of, 3–9
model of, 6–9
welfare systems and, 7, 8, 9, 56, 57–8, 66
financial system
Mexican, 181–6
transition to market economy and, 94–5, 98–9, 102
Finland
economic performance of, 80
unemployment in, 82

wages in, 84
welfare system in, 60, 65
firms *see* industrial organization
foreign direct investment
economic integration and, 112–18
European Union (EU) and, 112, 120, 121, 125, 126, 127–32, 133
Japanese, 120–33
manufacturing sector, 120, 125–6, 129–32, 133
in Mexico, 183, 185, 189
service sector, 125
France
economic performance of, 65, 79
unemployment in, 81
wages in, 83
welfare system in, 61, 62, 65
Frankel, J., 11
fraud in welfare systems, 62–3
Friedman, M., 190

Gandolfo, G., 191
Gasiorek, M., 26, 40
General Agreement on Tariffs and Trade (GATT), 11, 24, 105, 173
agricultural trade and, 42, 45–6, 49, 52, 54–5
Germany
economic performance of, 79
economic policies in, 65
unemployment in, 81
wages in, 83
welfare system in, 61, 62, 63, 64
Gittleman, M., 121, 126, 127, 131, 132, 133
Goldberg, M.A., 113, 116
government and the state
implications of economic and financial integration for, 3–9
transition to market economy and, 95, 97–100
Graham, E., 121, 131, 132
Greece
economic performance of, 80
foreign direct investment and, 112–18
impact of European single market on, 26–41
unemployment in, 82
wages in, 84
welfare system in, 63
Greenway, D., 125
Grennes, T., 51, 52
Gruber, W.C., 23
Gyourko, J., 76

Havrylyshyn, O., 103
Hayward, D.J., 12
Horaguchi, H., 113
Hubbard, N., 78
human capital, economic convergence and, 70
Hungary
EU and, 104
transition to market economy in, 94, 95, 97, 102, 105
Hymer, S.H., 113

immigration: from Mexico, 145–57
income
economic convergence and, 69–71, 72, 73, 86
inequality of, welfare systems and, 60–61
indexation of welfare benefits, 61–2
industrial organization
Japanese, 122–4
small business sector, 91–100
industrial sector *see* manufacturing sector
inflation, 183
information systems, transition to market economy and, 99–100
interest rates
Mexican economy and, 183
model of integration process and, 6–7
transition to market economy and, 94
international trade
agricultural, 42–55
alternative theories of, 191–3
balance of payments, 125, 188, 189, 201–2
economic integration of former socialist economies and, 101–11
foreign direct investment and, 113–14
free, 11, 24
implications of NAFTA for, 11–25, 43, 46–53, 54, 174–5, 185, 186

labour costs and, 197–200
Mexican, 48–50, 51–3, 54, 174–5, 185, 186, 188, 189
orthodox theories of, 190–91
tendencies and idiosyncracies in, 136–41
welfare effects of European single market programme, 26–41
investment *see* foreign direct investment
Ioannatos, P.E., as contributor, 112–18
Ireland
economic performance of, 80
impact of European single market on, 40
unemployment in, 82
wages in, 84
welfare system in, 61
Italy
economic performance of, 80
impact of European single market on, 40
unemployment in, 82
wages in, 84
welfare system in, 63, 65, 67

Janvry, A.de, 53
Japan
foreign direct investment and, 120–33
industrial organization in, 122–4
Jeffrey, D., 78

Kaminaridies, J.S., as contributor, 11–25
Karemera, D., 47
Kindleberger, C.P., 113
Koo, W.W., 47
Kozul-Wright, R., 174
Kreinin, M., 24, 136
Krissof, B., 51, 52
Krueger, A., 190
Kubik, P.J., 24

labour costs (wages)
economic convergence and, 70–71, 72, 73, 82–6
exchange rates and, 193
Mexico/US study of, 193–205
Lash, N.A., as contributor, 42–55
Levy, S., 52
living standards, indexation of welfare benefits and, 62
Lunn, J., 113, 114, 116
Lusting, N., 175
Luxembourg
economic performance of, 79
economic policies in, 65
unemployment in, 81
wages in, 83

McCalla, A.F., 54
McCallum, J., 25
McCombie, J.S.L., 69
McGuire, T., 76
Mackinnon, K., 7
Malliaris, A.G., 44
as contributor, 42–55
Mallick, R., 69, 70, 76
as contributor, 69–87
Mandelbaum, T.B., 71
manufacturing sector
economic convergence in, 72–3, 75, 76–7, 87
foreign direct investment in, 120, 125–6, 129–32, 133
Mexican, 175–81, 193–205
Mardas, D., as contributor, 120–33
market economies, socialist transition to, small business sector and, 91–100
market growth hypothesis, 113
market imperfections hypothesis, 113
Markusen, J.R., 113, 114
Martin, F., 75
May, J., 73
Mercenier, J., 26, 33
Mexico
agricultural sector, 48–50, 51–3, 54
balance of payments, 188, 189, 201–2
banking sector in, 181–6
debt problems, 183, 184, 186
economy of, 75–8, 87, 160–70, 173–87, 188–205
exchange rates in, 179, 181, 183, 185, 186, 188–9, 193–205
foreign direct investment in, 183, 185, 189
international trade and, 48–50, 51–3, 54, 174–5, 185, 186, 188, 189

labour costs in, 193–205
manufacturing sector in, 175–81, 193–205
migration from, 145–57
modernization in, 160–70
NAFTA and, 12–23, 47–54, 75–8, 87, 160–70, 173–87, 188, 189
US relationship with, 12, 13–18, 19–23, 145–57, 161–3, 188
migration: from Mexico, 145–57
Mill, J.S., 9
Motamen-Samadian, S., as contributor, 173–87
multinational corporations, 120, 122, 129, 130, 131–2, 133
Mundell, R., 113

Netherlands
economic performance of, 79
economic policies in, 65
unemployment in, 81
wages in, 83
welfare system in, 61, 62, 63
new trade theories, 191–3
New Zealand, agricultural sector, 45
Nissan, E., as contributor, 11–25
non-tariff barriers (NTBs), 26–8, 102
Nordhaus, W., 78
North American Free Trade Agreement (NAFTA), 3
agricultural sector and, 43, 46–53, 54
Canada and, 12–23, 45, 46–7, 48, 49, 50, 54, 71–5, 87
democracy and economic development and, 160–70
economic convergence in, 69–78, 86–7, 173–87
implications for US regions of, 11–25
international trade and, 11–25, 43, 46–53, 54, 174–5, 185, 186
Mexico and, 12–23, 47–54, 75–8, 87, 160–70, 173–87, 188, 189
migration and, 150, 155, 156, 157
provisions of, 49–51
USA and, 11–25, 43, 46–53, 54, 69–71, 72, 73, 86

Officer, L.H., 190, 193
Ohmae, K., 136
Oldersma, H., 105
Ortiz, G., 188, 189
Ortiz Cruz, E., as contributor, 173–87
Oudiz, G., 193
Ozawa, T., 126, 133

Pacolet, J., as contributor, 56–68
Papadaki, E., as contributor, 26–41
Paraskevopoulos, C.C., 4
as contributor, 3–9
Pasinetti, L., 193
Paz, Octavio, 161–2
Perot, Ross, 48
Plummer, M., 136
Poland
EU and, 104
transition to market economy in, 97, 102, 105
Portugal
economic performance of, 80
unemployment in, 82
wages in, 84
Pournakis, M., as contributor, 120–33
poverty, welfare systems (social protection) and, 59, 60–61
prices
European single market programme and, 27
indexation of welfare benefits and, 61–2
inflation, 183
socialist economics and, 102
Pritchett, L., 103
privatization
of financial system, 181
in transition to market economy, 92, 93, 97
of welfare systems, 57, 64–5
Przeworski, A., 165
public welfare *see* welfare systems
purchasing power parity theory, 190–91

quota restrictions on trade, 102

regional economic convergence
in EU, 69, 78–86, 87
in NAFTA, 69–78, 86–7
regional impact of NAFTA on USA, 11–25
Ricardo, D., 193

Richardson, D.J., 12
Roderick, R., as contributor, 11–25
Rodrik, D., 102, 103, 105
Romania, transition to market economy in, 105
Ruiz-Nápoles, P., 190
  as contributor, 188–205

Sachs, J., 4, 5
Sadoulet, E., 53
Sala-i-Martin, X., 69, 70, 86
Salinas, Carlos, 48, 163, 166, 185
Scaperlanda, A., 113, 114
service sector
  economic convergence in, 77–8, 87
  foreign direct investment in, 125
Simpson, Alan, 148
small business sector, transition to market–based economies and, 91–100
Smith, D.M., 69
Smith, Lamar, 148
Smithin, J.N., 7
  as contributor, 3–9
social exclusion, welfare systems (social protection) and, 60–61
social protection *see* welfare systems
socialist economies
  EU and, 101, 104, 110, 111
  transition to market-based economies
    small business sector and, 91–100
    trade liberalization and, 101–11
  welfare systems in, 4, 5
socioeconomic characteristics of international trade, 136–41
Solís, L., 188, 189
Sophocles, 137
Spain
  economic performance of, 80
  unemployment in, 82
  wages in, 84
  welfare system in, 61, 64
Sri Lanka, 100
Srinivasan, T.N., 33
state *see* government and the state
Stiglitz, J., 27
subsidiarity principle, 63
Svensson, L.E.O., 114
Sweden
  economic performance of, 65, 80
  unemployment in, 82
  wages in, 84
  welfare system in, 60, 61

taxation, model of integration process and, 7–8
technology gap theory, 192, 199
Testa, W.A., 76
Thygesen, N., 191
Torrisi, C.R., 114, 117
Toyne, B., 113
trade *see* international trade
training, transition to market economy and, 95–6, 97–8
transnational corporations (TNCs), 120, 122, 129, 130, 131–2, 133
Tsai, P.L., 113, 116

unemployment, 65, 67
  economic convergence and, 79, 81–2
  transition to market economy and, 91, 92
unit labour costs *see* labour costs
United Kingdom
  economic growth in, 79
  unemployment in, 81
  wages in, 83
  welfare system in, 4, 59, 61, 62, 64, 65
United States of America
  agricultural sector in, 42, 43, 45, 46–53, 54
  economic convergence and, 69–71, 72, 73, 86
  Far West region, 12, 18, 19–23
  foreign direct investment and, 112, 120, 121, 126, 130
  Great Lakes region, 12, 13–14, 16–17, 19–23, 24
  labour costs in, 193–202
  Mexican relationship with, 12, 13–18, 19–23, 145–57, 161–3, 188
  Mideast region, 12, 13, 16, 19–23
  migration to, 145, 146–51, 155–7
  NAFTA and, 11–25, 43, 46–53, 54, 69–71, 72, 73, 86
  New England region, 13, 16, 19–23, 24
  Plains region, 14, 17, 19–23, 24

Rocky Mountain region, 15, 18, 19–23, 24
small business sector in, 92, 97, 98, 99
Southeast region, 12, 14–15, 17, 19–23
Southwest region, 12, 15, 18, 19–23, 24

Valdés-Ugalde, J.L., as contributor, 160–70
Varsakelis, N.C., as contributor, 120–33
Verea, M., as contributor, 145–57
Versieck, K., as contributor, 56–68

wages *see* labour costs
Waldman, R.J., 24
Wang, Z.K., 105
Wasylenko, M., 76
Welch, O.H., 23
welfare effects of European single market programme
applied general equilibrium model, 28–31
calibration procedure, 33
data set, 31–2
design of experiment, 33, 36
results of, 36–40
case study of Greece, 26–41
welfare systems (social protection)
alternative models of, 4–5
contraction of, 59–60
devolution of, 63–4
European, 56–68
evolution of, 58–60
expansion of, 58
fraud in, 62–3
implications of economic and financial integration for, 7, 8, 9, 56, 57–8, 66
indexation of benefits, 61–2
macroeconomic context of, 57, 65–6
Mexican lack of, 186–7
organizational changes in, 63–5
performance of, 60–63
poverty and, 59, 60–61
privatization of, 57, 64–5
reforms of, 60
selectivity of, 61
Whalley, J., 33
Wijnbergen, S. van, 52
Wilson, Pete, 146
Winters, L.A., 105
Wong, K.Y., 114
World Trade Organization (WTO), Eastern Europe and, 101, 105

Yang, J., as contributor, 101–11
Yannopoulos, G.N., 112
Young, A., as contributor, 91–100

Zedillo Ponce de León, Ernesto, 167
Zestos, G.K., as contributor, 69–87
Zorgbibe, 136